The
COMPLETE

W9-DJI-079

IDIOT'S
GUIDE TO

UNIX

by John McMullen

alpha
books

A Division of Macmillan Computer Publishing
A Prentice Hall Macmillan Company
201 W. 103rd Street, Indianapolis, Indiana, 46290

To Sandi and to our child (who ought to have a name by the time this book comes out).

©1995 Alpha Books

International Standard Book Number:1-56761-511-2
Library of Congress Catalog Card Number: 94-71942

97 96 95   8 7 6 5 4 3 2 1

Interpretation of the printing code: the rightmost number of the first series of numbers is the year of the book's printing; the rightmost number of the second series of numbers is the number of the book's printing. For example, a printing code of 95-1 shows that the first printing of the book occurred in 1995.

Screen reproductions in this book were created by means of the program Collage Complete from Inner Media, Inc., Hollis, NH.

Printed in the United States of America

Publisher
Marie Butler-Knight

Managing Editor
Elizabeth Keaffaber

Acquisitions Editor
Barry Pruett

Product Development Manager
Faithe Wempen

Development Editor
Melanie Palaisa

Production Editor
Mark Enochs

Copy Editor
Audra Gable

Cover Designer
Scott Cook

Designer
Barbara Kordesh

Illustrations
Judd Winick

Indexers
Bront Davis

Production Team
*Gary Adair, Dan Caparo, Brad Chinn, Kim Cofer, Dave Eason,
Jennifer Eberhardt, David Garratt, Erika Millen, Beth Rago,
Bobbi Satterfield, Karen Walsh, Robert Wolf*

*Special thanks to Scott Parker for ensuring
the technical accuracy of this book.*

Contents at a Glance

Contents

Introduction

I don't know anybody who intentionally set out to work with UNIX. I certainly didn't. (I was an unemployed biologist back then.) And when I met UNIX, I felt *so* ignorant, but that feeling (I was sure) would pass. After all, I was smart. (I was sure I was smart.) One hour later, I was sure I was stupid, and by the end of the day, I felt like an idiot. I thought the computer had sucked my brains out through my fingertips.

This book is to save you from that experience—because you're not stupid or an idiot, and you shouldn't have to feel like one.

So, welcome to this book! This is a UNIX book for people who don't want to become gurus, but who just need to get some work done. This is a book that knows:

➤ UNIX is a tool. It's not meant to be as mysterious as the clock on your VCR. UNIX is something you use to get work done.

➤ You don't need to know about every single feature of UNIX. (Although, having bled through the fingers to discover them, I was tempted to tell you all of them.) Instead, I've tried to distill what you need to know into short useful chapters.

➤ Using UNIX isn't brain surgery or rocket science. Lives don't hang in the balance, so hang loose.

What's in This Book?

I'll start with the fundamentals and move on to the more complex items. Your best bet is probably to read it in order, but you don't have to. If you want to read about electronic mail (Chapter 22) before you read about printing files (Chapter 9), that's okay by me.

By the way, I don't assume you have any experience with computers. Because a lot of people have seen PCs, I'll occasionally compare UNIX to PCs (they aren't the same thing). But you don't have to know what a PC is. If you've stayed away from PCs like they carry cooties, you'll still do fine.

Here's how this book is organized:

Part I: UNIX Basix is your basic survival guide. It gives you what you need to stay afloat and navigate UNIX. Besides a little theory (Chapter 2), it covers logging in (Chapter 3), how commands work (Chapter 4), and how to get help (Chapter 5).

Part II: UNIX Tips and Trix is about settling in and getting comfortable. The material here is slightly more sophisticated and assumes you know what's in Part I. Here you'll learn about printing (Chapter 9), disaster recovery (Chapter 10), looking for files (Chapter 11), and looking for words in files (Chapter 12).

Part III: A Textbook on Text covers some of the ways to work with text files in UNIX, including creating them and some of the programs you might find useful. Besides an overview of the editor programs you use to create text files (Chapter 14), this section describes three common editors. You'll need to use either the **vi** or the **emacs** program some day, so you should read either Chapter 16 or Chapter 17.

Part IV: Mastering the Mysteries introduces you to all of that other stuff you hear about in connection with UNIX, including networks (Chapter 21), electronic mail (Chapter 22), and even the Internet (Chapter 23). Just to make it interesting, I also threw in a miscellaneous chapter of neat stuff (Chapter 25) and command summaries of the most important commands (Chapter 26).

How to Use This Book

While you're reading, I hope you'll try typing into your UNIX machine some of the commands I show. (This book, like life, offers bonus points for participation.) To help you follow along, I've marked certain types of text in certain ways.

➤ Anything you see on-screen appears in a special font:

    This is displayed text.

➤ Commands and anything you're supposed to type appear in boldface:

Type this exactly.

➤ Variables, or placeholders, appear in italics; you substitute information for a variable. For instance, in the command **echo *your-name-here***, you'd type your name in place of *your-name-here*.

➤ Key combinations are represented by a key's name, a - symbol, and another key's name. To enter such a command, you hold down the first key and press the second; for example, to enter **Control-Z**, you hold down the Ctrl key and press the Z key.

While you're reading, you'll run across some other items that are not required reading. They offer some extra information that isn't strictly necessary. You don't have to read them; you can save them for a rainy day.

A definition of a nerd-word in everyday terms.

Some extra technical information you don't need but that's relevant to the topic.

A warning about a potential error or a hint on recovering from an error.

A shortcut or hint that could make your life easier.

Acknowledgments (Spreading the Glory)

The people at Alpha Books get a lot of credit for making the book what it is, but I'd like to single out Melanie Palaisa for working with me through much of this and Scott Parker for his help on the regular expression chapter. Without them and Seta Frantz, this book wouldn't be as good as it is.

The people at Mortice Kern Systems get credit for letting me test my understanding of UNIX on their expensive machines.

And last, but not least, my thanks to those who let me ignore other obligations long enough to get this book done: Stephen Walli, David Fiander, and my wife Sandi, who let me sit alone for so long while she was going through so much.

Trademarks

All terms in this book that I even suspected might be trademarks were appropriately capitalized, and all other terms are trademarks of their respective owners. There is no intent nohow of challenging or depriving anyone of ownership or their legal rights, nor any intent of doing anything that might get me sued. There are two things I want to specifically mention:

UNIX is a registered trademark in the United States and other countries, licensed exclusively through X/Open Company, Ltd.

And let me point out that X Windows and **xman** are copyright 1987, 1988 by the Massachusetts Institute of Technology.

In addition:

BSD is a registered trademark of the University of California, Berkeley.

Frame and FrameMaker are registered trademarks of Frame Technology Corporation.

HP PCL is a registered trademark of Hewlett-Packard Corporation.

Motif is a registered trademark of the Open Software Foundation, Inc.

MS-DOS is a registered trademark of Microsoft Corporation.

Part I
UNIX Basix

If you're like most people, you didn't wake up this morning and say, "Gee, I'd like to learn UNIX today." No, you probably said, "What, it's time to get up already?" UNIX didn't even enter into it. But the cold hard truth is that you've got to use UNIX, and you're not even sure what UNIX is—let alone what it's good for.

I'm sure you'd like to go out and kick computer butt right away. But first you've got to get the basics: what UNIX is, what an operating system is, what files are, how you give a command. You remember the first Karate Kid movie? This is the part where you wax the car and paint the fence. Patience. It all has meaning later on. Wax on! Wax off!

OH **THAT**, HE'S BEEN ACTING THAT WAY EVER—
SINCE HE GOT HIS PASSWORD TO FINALLY WORK...

Chapter 1

The Least You Need to Know

Because there are so many different ways to do things in UNIX, this list has to describe the *standard* ways to do things, the ones that are definitely going to be there. So if people have told you a different way to do things, they may be right—but these will definitely work.

What's a UNIX Operating System?

An *operating system* is like an interpreter, and UNIX is a particular kind of operating system for computers. It takes requests from application programs (the kinds of programs you use, such as spreadsheets, word processing programs, and games) and turns them into requests that the computer machinery understands. Any time you put information into the computer (even from the keyboard) or get information out of the computer (even on the screen), the operating system is involved.

UNIX has a number of interesting features, such as its capability to allow more than one person to use the computer at once, or to enable you to run more than one program at a time. I describe the basics of operating systems and of UNIX itself in Chapter 2, "Operating on Systems."

The name UNIX has a specific legal meaning when you talk about operating systems. As of this writing, it means the operating system that was developed by AT&T. I'm not using it that way. I use UNIX to mean any operating system that's modelled after the original UNIX. There are quite a few of these "imitation systems," because software manufacturers didn't want to pay AT&T just to use the UNIX name.

For the most part, what I tell you applies to both real UNIX and UNIX-like operating systems. If it doesn't, I'll let you know. In Chapter 18, "The Shell Game," I'll tell you how to find out what flavor of UNIX you're using.

Captain's Login and Logout

In order to start using UNIX, you have to let UNIX know who you are, and then you have to prove it by giving your password. If you don't login, you can't do anything. (Remember, UNIX has more than one person using it at a time.) If this is your first time logging in, your system administrator should have already told you what your login name and your password are.

When UNIX is ready for you to start up, it displays this message:

```
login:
```

Type your login name (it appears on-screen). Press **Enter**, and UNIX displays the message:

```
password:
```

Type your password. It doesn't appear on-screen (to prevent evil people from reading your password your shoulder). Press **Enter**. Now that you've proven yourself, the computer displays a prompt (usually a $ or a % sign) that looks something like this:

```
$
```

At Your Command Line, Master

No computer can read your mind. UNIX only does something if you tell it to, and you do this by giving it a command. A *command* is just what it sounds like: an instruction to do something. If you don't give UNIX a command, it doesn't do anything.

UNIX is a command line environment, which means you have to enter commands at the prompt instead of using the mouse. (Although there are some mouse-oriented UNIX systems, they are rare. I'll discuss them in Chapter 6, "Surviving Window Pains.") When you see a prompt (usually $ or %), you can enter a command.

A UNIX command is usually short: for example, the **who** command tells you who is currently logged in. Always press **Enter** after you enter a UNIX command to let UNIX know you've finished typing the command.

Rank and File: Working with Files and Directories

On a computer, all information is stored in *files*. Some of the files are text (you could read them if you wanted), and some are in a format that only a particular program understands (these are called binary files).

A file that holds other files is called a *directory*. A directory can hold more directories called *subdirectories*. In fact, all the files on the computer system are held in one big directory, called the *root* directory. The full name of a directory or file always starts with a slash, because / (also called root) is the original directory, the one in which all other directories are created. After the slash, the full name lists every directory the file or directory is a part of, separated by more slashes, such as /recipes/meatloaf. (If you've used DOS, notice that this slash goes in the opposite direction from the ones in DOS.) The slashes separate the names of directories, and the file name is always given last. Therefore, /recipes/meatloaf describes a file named meatloaf in a directory named recipes in the root directory (which is indicated by the first /).

Unlike DOS file names, UNIX files and directories can have long names, and they can include upper- and lowercase letters, dashes, dots, underscores, and even spaces. (Although you can put spaces in the names, I recommend you don't; they're a pain to use.) Names that start with a dot, such as .login, are hidden and won't normally show up when you list the contents of a directory. (You can only see them by using a special command.)

Chapter 7, "The Root of the Matter: Files and Directories" describes files, and Chapter 8, "Branching Out: Working with Files and Directories" tells you how to work with files, directories, and wild cards.

There's No Place Like $HOME

You've got your own personal space on the system where you can store files, make directories, and put your personal programs. This area is called your *home directory*. For more information on moving around directories, see Chapters 7 and 8.

Putting Words on Paper: Printing Files

Printing instructions can be very tricky because your system may be different. In Chapter 9, "Printing Is Pressing," I'll outline standard printing methods; you'll have to check around on your own system to find out how to print. (For example, where I work, the printers expect special files, so we have to use a command that turns regular files into files for the printers.) If you are having difficulty, check with your system administrator.

A Cry for Help

If you need help figuring out how to use a particular command, the manual pages for each command are available electronically. Enter the command **man** followed by the name of the command you want to know about. For instance, if you enter the command man man you'll get information about the man command itself. **man** displays the manual pages one screenful of text at a time; press **Space** to read the next screenful. I describe **man** and other ways of getting help with UNIX in Chapter 5, "Won't You Please Help Me?"

Editors

An *editor* is a program that enables you to create or change the contents of a text file. An editor is a stripped-down word processor: it won't format text, but it enables you to put words and letters into a file. The two most widely used editors are **vi** and **emacs**. Although both editors create the same kinds of files, they are very different to use. I describe **vi** in Chapter 16, "Viva vi!" and **emacs** in Chapter 17, "Circus Emacs-Imus."

Mail Call

All UNIX systems provide ways to send messages to other users. The most often used method is *electronic mail*. It works like regular mail: you write a message using the mail program, and you send the message when you're finished writing it. You also use the mail program to read messages others have sent to you. There are many different mail programs. I describe the standard mail program and the alternatives in Chapter 22, "Send Me a Letter."

An On-Ramp for the Internet Highway

The Internet is a huge network of computers, the basis of the "information highway" that's discussed in the news. Most of the features of the Internet are based on its capability to use a program on a machine that's far away and on its capability to share files easily. In Chapter 23, "Internet Interests," I explain what the Internet is and introduce you to some of the programs and features available.

LET THERE BE UNIX!!

Chapter 2

Operating on Systems

In This Chapter

➤ What an operating system is and does

➤ Where UNIX came from

➤ UNIX's best-selling features

➤ A warning about the UNIX philosophy

Imagine that a lawyer calls you and tells you you're the long-lost second cousin to the king of a little country you've never heard of. Now that the king is dead, you've inherited the throne. You're absolute monarch of the country. You have total control over every inhabitant. You don't want to give individual instructions to each of them; that would be tedious and time-consuming, and a lot of the details are beneath you. Besides, you don't speak the language.

So you take with you a number of chiefs of staff who specialize—army, navy, finance, golf, whatever. (Well, *I'd* have a Golf Chief of Staff.) But you don't expect the chiefs of staff to go out and actually sail the boat or count the money or put the ball on the tee. No, the chiefs of staff just give orders, and somebody turns the orders into instructions that all your willing subjects can carry out.

Congratulations! You've just figured out computers and operating systems.

What's an Operating System?

An *operating system* is a computer program that's like an interpreter for your computer. An *application program* (a program you use, such as a word processor or spreadsheet) asks the operating system to do things, and the operating system tells the computer how to respond to those requests in terms it understands.

To go back to the royal highness example, you are the monarch. The programs you use are the chiefs of staff, the computer represents your loyal subjects, and the operating system is the aide who takes orders from the chiefs of staff and translates them for the people (the computer).

Let's say you tell your application program (your chief of staff) to do something, such as "draw a circle"; the application program turns that into a command for the operating system, such as "draw a line this shape on the screen" (the chief of staff gives the order to the aide); and then the operating system tells the computer (your loyal subjects) to execute the commands necessary to draw a circle. When the job is done—or if the job can't be done—the hardware (your subjects) tells the operating system (the aide), the operating system (the aide) tells the application program (the chief of staff), and the application program (the chief of staff) tells you.

Application program A program you use to accomplish a purpose, such as writing a letter, calculating a spreadsheet, processing words, or killing all the alien space invaders.

Operating system A computer program used by other programs to control the computer's hardware.

Just as the commands go through a series of layers within your "monarchy," computer commands go through a series of layers, and the Law of Computer Layers is, "Every time you go down a layer, the parts get smaller, and the process gets more complicated."

If you remember learning to tie your shoes, you understand this layering. When you say, "Tie your shoes," that's like an instruction to the operating system. The operating system turns that instruction into all of the little steps that you take for granted ("Cross this lace *over* that one and then under…").

Here's a picture of how the layers work. At the very center of the circle is the computer's hardware. Because you don't want to have to deal with all the details of hardware, the operating system is wrapped around the hardware. All the programs deal with the operating system. Well, you don't want to deal with all the details of the operating system either, so you use another program, a *shell* program, to communicate with the operating system. On the outside of the shell is you. (In this book, I will focus on the UNIX operating system and touch on using shell programs. However, I will not cover the use of application programs.)

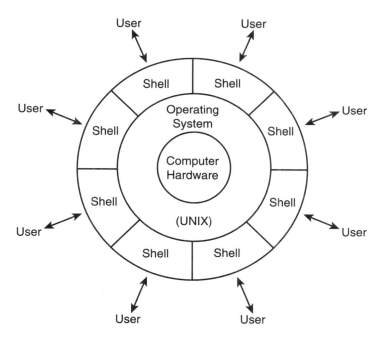

A computer system consists of layers. The operating system connects programs you use to the computer hardware.

In order to use UNIX, you use a program called a shell. The shell is a program that's very good at running other programs; that's what it does for you. When you run another program, the shell "steps aside" for that program; then it comes back when the program is done. I discuss the shell at length in Chapter 18, "The Shell Game."

You might think that it would be simpler to get rid of all these layers, but it isn't. The sort of jobs your operating system handles are all repetitive jobs that are specific to your computer. If every programmer writing an application program had to write all of those instructions every time, there wouldn't be very many applications (fewer word processors, fewer spreadsheets, fewer games), and the applications that were available would be much more expensive.

UNIX isn't the only operating system: there are dozens. In fact, there used to be a different operating system for every brand of computer. UNIX (and the operating systems that imitate it) is available on many different computers, from PCs to mainframes.

Computer geeks have a religious zeal on the topic of their favorite operating systems. A true UNIX fan will spend hours explaining why UNIX is the best and why another operating system (usually DOS or VMS) is worse. However, you and I don't care, because the Law of Operating Systems says that, "All operating systems do basically the same things. Some have a couple of extra bells and whistles. If you don't care about those extra features, what you care about are the application programs."

How UNIX Came to Be

UNIX is a computer operating system that was originally sold by AT&T. AT&T didn't really know what to do with it, but they sold it cheaply to universities where it became very popular. (Eighty percent of American universities and colleges use UNIX operating systems on their computers.)

In the late 1960s, Ken Thompson of Bell Labs in New Jersey wanted to finish writing a space travel game. There was only one catch: he'd just lost his computer. He found an unused one in the basement and (with Dennis Ritchie and a few other Bell Labs people) wrote an operating system for it. (Sure, why not?) One of the things that had a tremendous influence on UNIX was the machinery they used. They had teletypes—*slow* teletypes—to print the computer's responses. Since it took about three seconds to print a message as simple as `Operation successfully completed`, Ken and Dennis opted for short commands and no responses unless something went wrong.

Then they re-wrote it so that it could be made to run on nearly any computer, making it the first operating system that could run on different manufacturers' computers. Bell Labs gave this new operating system inexpensively to anyone who asked for it. A number of universities asked, and they added to it. In particular, the University of California at Berkeley got a copy and added a couple of features that were popular. At that point, there were two versions of UNIX: "standard" UNIX and the Berkeley version (called BSD for Berkeley Software Distribution).

Before long, other people wanted to sell UNIX, too, but they didn't want to pay AT&T money for the privilege. They produced operating systems that were nearly identical to UNIX but had different names. (Usually they put the IX on the end of the name, such as XENIX, ULTRIX, SINIX, and VINIX.) Today, there are even free versions of UNIX.

A few years ago, AT&T formed a separate company to handle UNIX, and that company sold the rights to UNIX. This year (as I write this book), the company that currently owns the rights to UNIX has given the name UNIX to another group, the X/Open Consortium. The X/Open Consortium (a collection of software vendors) will be judging products to see which ones are worthy of being called UNIX. In the near future, there will be a standard checklist of features, and any operating system that can say "yes!" to each feature will be a full-fledged UNIX system.

Throughout its rocky history, UNIX has evolved into a rather complex collection of features and programs—many of which are not-so-user-friendly to us nonprogrammer types. However, it has survived and remained popular because of a number of inherent capabilities. Here's a list of the most popular ones:

➤ The capability to run more than one job at a time. If you've ever had to wait for a computer to finish doing something, you'll appreciate this.

➤ Strong networking support. All UNIX systems come with programs that enable them to hook up to other UNIX systems (by phone or by specialized connectors) or to other computer systems (such as DOS and Windows PCs). One of the major reasons for buying UNIX is because UNIX understands networks, and you can hook up lots of different computers to a UNIX network—including the Internet.

A **network** is a group of connected computers that share information, and UNIX is very good at connecting computers. In an office, it has ways to share files between computers so users never know they're actually accessing another machine. Over longer distances, UNIX is good at trading information over phone lines. The networking system that has created the Internet (a network of computer networks) has been part of UNIX since the early 1980s.

➤ UNIX handles graphics well. A lot of industries (primarily engineering) that require excellent graphics use UNIX. Many UNIX systems in the early to mid-1980s were sold for engineering design. The engineers required the capability to display sophisticated and complex images. While not part of every UNIX system, many systems have quite sophisticated image processing programs.

➤ A lot of university graduates learned on UNIX systems in school and want to use UNIX in the real world. (I know it's not a technical feature, but don't underestimate those university graduates.)

➤ The capability to handle more than one user on each computer means the cost of the computer system can be spread over several people, which makes it cheaper. (And never underestimate the influence of the accountants.)

Why UNIX Is the Way It Is

The other parts of this book tell you how UNIX works and what to do. This little section tries to tell you why. If you understand why UNIX is the way it is, you can out-think it.

UNIX has a reputation for being complex and elitist and difficult to use. And I'm not gonna lie to you: it can be. But some of that reputation is undeserved. A lot of the "unfriendliness" of UNIX was forced on it in attempts to solve problems. For example, people thought it was a problem that the terminal took three seconds to print `Operation successfully completed` after every command. (Imagine, after *every* command!) So the solution was to keep the commands short and not print anything unless the command didn't work—which gave UNIX an "unfriendly" reputation.

In addition, the designers seem to have created UNIX based on these two premises:

➤ Don't design anything twice if you don't have to. Instead of writing two different programs that do the same thing in slightly different ways, try to write one program that can do the job both ways. This is why there are so many little programs in UNIX (a sort program, a count-words-in-a-file program, a find-a-file program) and why each program has so many options. The **ls** program lists the contents of a directory. It has almost two dozen options, and each option changes how **ls** behaves. These options are there because **ls** is trying to be the best single file-listing program there is (kind of like one-stop-shopping for file listings).

➤ Users know what they're doing. By assuming that all UNIX users would be computer experts like they were, the designers made life much easier for themselves. And although they created UNIX to let you do some very clever things, it also lets you do some very stupid things. If you want to do something stupid, UNIX will let you.

These two beliefs affected nearly *everything* in UNIX.

You're Not Alone

UNIX is a *multiuser* operating system. That means more than one person can use the computer at the same time. Remember the story at the beginning of this chapter, in which you were monarch of that little country? It turns out you have a whole bunch of second cousins (kind of like belonging to the U.N.).

As you might imagine, if UNIX can handle more than one user's programs at once, it can handle more than one program for each user. That capability makes it a *multitasking* system. UNIX does this by switching between programs so fast you don't notice. It spends a fraction of a second

Multitasking The capability to run more than one program at a time. The computer doesn't actually run more than one program at once; instead, it switches back and forth, devoting a bit of time to each job. (This is like a cook making multiple dishes for a meal: check this one to see how it's going, then check the next dish, and so on.)

15

Multiuser The capability to serve more than one user at a time. Of course, when you do this, you've got to identify each user and know what belongs to whom. In UNIX, you have a user id (your login name), and you have a number. You don't need to know your number, just your login name.

on the program you're running, then spends a fraction of a second on the program the next user is running, and so on. But the more programs being run on the machine (and the more people), the slower the machine gets. (A millionth of a second here, a millionth there—pretty soon it adds up to time you can notice.)

Despite the flexibility it provides, UNIX's multiuser capabilities also make it more complicated. You can't just turn the machine on and start giving commands; you have to login so the machine knows who you are. You even have to have permission to read a file or to use a program. Security of files and data is important when more than one person can login and use the system. (Logging in is discussed in detail in Chapter 3, "In the Beginning Was the Word: login;" file permissions are explained in Chapter 7, "The Root of the Matter: Files and Directories.")

In my opinion, the biggest advantage to a multiuser system is that somebody else does the hard stuff. This, in itself, is worth knowing about.

It's a Tough Job, but Somebody (Else) Has to Do It

There's a lot of housekeeping involved in making a computer system run right. (There's a lot of housekeeping involved in making a house run right, too. When I look at my chores list around the house, I'm glad my company doesn't depend on me to keep the computer system running.)

I'm a writer; that's what my company pays me to do. When there's a problem on our UNIX system, I call somebody else—somebody who is paid to look after that. I don't spend my time trying to figure out networks. I write. I like that. The person who keeps the system going is called the *system administrator* (or the Sys Admin, as the techies like to call him).

The system administrator makes sure that files are backed up. (Thank goodness. If it was left up to me, it would only get done twice a year.) The system administrator also makes sure that all the machines in the network are talking to each other, and that the printers work. You say the boss just bought you a fancy new terminal? The system administrator will hook it up for you.

In addition, the system administrator will help you if you get into trouble. You typed a command and removed all your files? Tell the system administrator immediately, and he or she will find yesterday's copies of your files and put them back up. (The details of this are up to your system administrator. Sys admins are paid to think about what files to back up and how often.) The printer's not working? Tell the system administrator. You can't figure out how to get the high score in that computer game you've become addicted to? Well, there are some things you should do for yourself.

The privilege of a system administrator is not to be taken lightly. Don't treat your sys admin as your slave. Be nice. Be thoughtful. Try to fix your problems yourself, but when you need a hand, it's really nice to have the system administrator around. Chapter 24, "Taking Charge," talks in a general way about what a system administrator needs to do.

 There are single-person UNIX systems out there, and you may have one. If so, you can't go to a system administrator for help; you are the system administrator. Fortunately for you, the UNIX manufacturers have tried to make things easier for users with single-person systems by providing tools for the system administrator.

There's usually a manual just for system administrators (with a name like *The System Administrator's Handbook*, for instance). The tools for system administrators are usually identified in the manual sections, too. See Chapter 5, "Won't You Please Help Me?," for information on how you can identify them.

More Flavors Than Baskin Robbins

The chocolate and vanilla of UNIX are System V and Berkeley Software Distribution (BSD). Almost all the different versions of UNIX are based on one or the other of these.

System V is based on the original (standard) UNIX. Over the years, AT&T released different versions of UNIX, adding improvements. Since 1983, all their UNIX versions have been called System V (usually abbreviated SV or SVR) and a release number; so SVR4 is System V Release 4. In 1988, AT&T released System V Release 4, in which they tried to merge the best features of BSD, System V, and others.

The Computer System Research Group at Berkeley released a number of Berkeley Software Distributions, all called BSD. The most popular versions are 4.2BSD and 4.3BSD. (It was the networking software in BSD—and not that of the original UNIX—that made the Internet.)

From a user's point of view, there weren't a lot of differences between flavors. The big differences involve how you print a file and which shells you have available. In this book, I talk mostly about System V, Release 4.2 UNIX. However, most of the commands will work on any system. Where there's a difference, I'll point it out in a "Techno Nerd Teaches" sidebar.

But wait, there's also POSIX, an important UNIX look-alike. POSIX is a checklist of requirements for an operating system (like the one that will be put in place for UNIX). However, POSIX is an international standard, endorsed by the Institute of Electric and Electronic Engineers (IEEE) and the International Organization for Standardization (ISO—the initials make sense in French). ISO is the organization that produces international standards; the IEEE works closely with them and with the National Institute of Standards and Technology. Federal purchasing regulations require that computer systems sold to the government have an operating system that meets the POSIX standards. An operating system that meets the POSIX rules looks and behaves like UNIX.

Incidentally, neither AT&T nor the University of California at Berkeley is involved in UNIX any more. AT&T sold the rights to UNIX to a company called Novell. Novell now sells SVR4.2 (System V, Release 4.2), which is also called Unixware. The Computer System Research Group was shut down in 1992 after releasing 4.4BSD, and today, the nearest thing to a BSD UNIX system is produced by a company called BSDI.

Which UNIX Do You Have?

You're probably wondering which flavor of UNIX you use and which shell program you have. (The three most common shell programs are the Korn shell, the C-shell, and the Bourne shell. I talk about them in Chapter 18, "The Shell Game.") When you login, look at your prompt. If it's a percent sign (%), you're probably using a BSD-like system and the C-shell. If it's a dollar sign ($), you're probably using a System V-like system. Enter the command **echo $SHELL** and look at the file name it displays. You're interested in the part after the last slash. If your prompt is ksh, you have the Korn shell. If it's sh, you have the Bourne shell. (If you get nothing or if it's csh, you have the C-shell.)

My examples in this book are almost all from System V Release 4 using the Korn shell. Most modern UNIXes provide both the BSD and System V versions of programs; if you have one of these UNIXes, you can use almost all of the examples in this book.

The Least You Need to Know

Well, that's your dose of high-level, sophisticated computer science. Basically, I've told you a bit about how the different designers of UNIX think, so when you're trying to figure out UNIX, you're at least playing the right game. Here are the chapter's highlights:

➤ UNIX is a computer operating system.

➤ Operating systems act as go-betweens for programs and the computer.

➤ The capability to support multiple users forced added complexity on UNIX.

➤ UNIX is good at handling multiple users, running more than one program at once, networking, and graphics.

➤ The UNIX philosophy assumes that you know what you're doing, and it's based on the idea that you can connect tools together.

In the Beginning Was the Word: login

Now that you understand some of what UNIX is, it's time to try using it. We'll assume someone has given you a UNIX account (kind of like a bank account). The first thing you have to do is tell the UNIX system who you are, and the second thing you have to do (because it's a great big, nasty, cynical world) is prove it by giving the system a password.

As you work the examples in the remainder of the book, note how I handle commands and the results. All UNIX commands appear in boldface, such as the **who** command. Commands you have to type at the command line start with a prompt character, usually $. Beneath the command, I'll show you the results; they are shown in a special font as they appear on-screen. Sometimes you need to specify some information, such as a file name or a login name. When you do, I'll use a variable to indicate it. For example, when I tell you to type **rm** *filename*, *filename* is the variable; you replace it with the name of the actual file you want to delete.

Getting Started

For your first session, you've got to be armed with your login name and your password. Whoever set up your account (probably the system administrator) should have told you what they are. Generally, your login name is just your first name or initials. My first login name was jhm; my current one is johnmc (we have several other Johns in our company). On some systems, especially school UNIX systems, they assign random login names made up of numbers and letters.

Account Your user relationship with the computer. Having an account just means you're an accredited user with a user id, privileges, and space on the machine.

Login name The short name used to identify you and everything you own on the computer. (It's like a CB handle.)

Terminal The device used for communicating with the computer. A terminal looks like a PC: there's a screen and a keyboard. There may even be a mouse. You can use a PC as a terminal if you have "terminal emulation programs" that make your PC behave as if it were a terminal. With these programs, you don't get the full features of your PC because it's trying to behave like a less sophisticated machine.

If no one is using a terminal (and the terminal is on), UNIX automatically runs a program called login that asks who you are. (It records—or logs—you as being on the system, hence the name.) As soon as you sit down at a UNIX terminal, there's the question waiting on the screen:

```
login:
```

This is called the *login prompt*. If your terminal has a mouse, your login prompt may be in a box on the screen. If your system is trying very hard not to look like UNIX, it may say something like username. The important thing is, the system wants to know who you are.

Now you're ready to login. At the login prompt, type your login name and press **Enter**. Note that UNIX distinguishes between upper- and lowercase letters: johnmc is a different login name than JOHNMC, or JohnMc. Usually your login name is all lowercase. The system responds by asking for your password, like this:

```
login: johnmc
password:
```

Type in your password. You won't see the letters as you type, but some systems will print pound signs (#) or asterisks (*) for every key you press so you know how many characters you've typed. You can't see your password for security reasons: anyone who knows your user id and password can get into the system and pretend to be you.

 What if the screen is blank? That might mean the screen has turned itself off. Press **Enter** (or jiggle the mouse, if you have one), and see if you get the login prompt. If you get something like the dollar sign ($), it means the last person didn't quit properly. You need to quit the session for him; check out "Quitting Your Session" later in this chapter for details.

The computer will check to see if you gave it the right password. If you didn't, it will ask you for the password again, or it may ask you to login again.

If you don't get the `password:` prompt, your account was set up without one. However, you should consider getting a password in order to prevent someone from damaging your data or reading your private files (or even to prevent someone from sending rude messages using your name). See "Changing Your Password" later in this chapter.

When you enter your login name and password correctly, the computer shows you a message of the day (if there is one) from the system administrator and indicates whether you have mail waiting.

```
login: johnmc
password:
I'm going on vacation next week so try not to have any problems. If
you have any, contact Lindsay.
—Your system administrator
You have new mail
$
```

If your terminal has a mouse, you might see the message in a box on the screen. It asks you to click on it, but there's no rush. Read it. Savor it. It's a bit of human communication in a technological world.

Prompt The character or characters that tell you the computer is ready for another command.

Cursor The box or underline that shows where the text you type will be inserted.

Once you have successfully logged in, you will see a line with the UNIX system prompt. That line, $, is called the prompt; it means the computer is waiting for you to enter a command. (It may not be a $; it might be a % or even your name or a number.) Beside it is a blinking block or underline. That's the cursor, which marks where characters will be inserted when you type.

```
$_
```

You type your UNIX commands at the prompt. The prompt is kind of like your own private slave: it's always ready and waiting for your command.

Changing Your Password

Sooner or later, you should change your password. A lot of system administrators set up accounts with no password or with the user's login id as the password. That's not very secure. There's certainly no guarantee that people won't read your private files. If you want to know how to make your files private, see Chapter 11, "More About Files (Some Useful Tips and Tricks)."

The command to change your password is called **passwd** (in keeping with the UNIX tradition of shortening words whenever possible). After you type **passwd**, the program asks you to prove who you are by typing your old password; it then asks you to enter your new password. Then it asks you to enter your new password *again* to prove you didn't make a typing mistake the first time, which is entirely possible, because you can't see what you're typing. A session of changing your password looks like this:

```
$ passwd
Enter old password: #####
Enter new password: #######
Enter new password again: #######
```

Dos and Don'ts on Password Security

UNIX is infamous for being an operating system with slack security—and it's true. Most system administrators don't go to the trouble to make their systems as secure as they can be. At its best, UNIX provides very good security, although it's not as secure as the computer systems used to store such vital information as national secrets, global banking information, and the formula for Coca-Cola. However, UNIX wasn't really intended for that: it was a system meant to be shared by everyone in the office. Security was an afterthought, and at its best, UNIX security is not bad.

As with any computer system, the weakest part of the system's security is the users. People who break into computer systems (called *hackers* or *crackers* depending on whom you talk to) know that. A good password helps stop them. So here are some hints for choosing passwords:

➤ Don't use a real word or name (like your spouse's name or your children's names). Some hackers just keep trying to login using a login name and a dictionary.

➤ Don't use a date that's important to you. People can figure that out.

➤ Don't write it down. This means you should choose a password that's easy to remember.

➤ Do include upper- and lowercase letters, punctuation, and numbers. A few years ago, I used the password "G'day,eh?" without a space.

➤ Do make the password more than a few letters long (some systems force you to make it more than eight characters).

➤ If you have accounts on more than one machine, don't use the same password on all of them.

➤ Do change your password frequently.

➤ Don't give your password out to others. If you must give your password out (maybe over the phone because you're on vacation and it's an emergency), change it as soon as possible.

Home Sweet Home

You're logged in. But what are you "in?" You're in your home directory, your personal space on the computer. Whenever you start a UNIX session, you start in your home directory.

Chapters 7, "The Root of the Matter: Files and Directories" and 8, "Branching Out: Working with Files and Directories" talk about files and directories in more detail, but all you need to know right now is that computers store information in *files*. A file is simply a bunch of related information that's stored in one place (like a paper file). A *directory* is a file that holds other files. (Some people also call them folders to make them seem more like file folders.) You can have a directory inside a directory. Each file and directory has a name, like the label on a file or a file folder. The entire file system is like one big filing cabinet.

On your system, there's a directory (like a file cabinet drawer) that's dedicated to users. This directory is called /usr, /u, or /home. Each user has his or her own directory, called a home directory, inside that big user directory. Your home directory is identified as /usr/*login name*. For example, my home directory is /usr/johnmc. To find out where your home directory is, type **pwd** and press **Enter**. (To give UNIX any command, you type the command name and press **Enter**.) The **pwd** command tells UNIX to print the home of the directory you're in.

```
$ pwd
/usr/johnmc
```

The computer's actual response to the command will vary depending on your system, but you'll see the name of your home directory.

Your home directory is your space to work with as you please. You own and, therefore, control any files and directories you make in your home directory. You can destroy any file or directory you own (although you might not be able to destroy one someone else owns). Among other things, your home directory contains:

➤ Files to personalize your programs. These files (called *startup files*) contain commands the programs should run whenever they start.

➤ Any directories you have created.

26

Anytime you're logged in, you're considered to be "in" a directory. The directory you're in is called your working directory, but you can change which directory you're in. Unless you say otherwise, UNIX looks for files in your current working directory. Every time you start a UNIX session, you start in your home directory.

Looking Inside Your Home Directory

Let's take a look inside your home directory to see what it's all about. To look at the contents of your home directory, you use the **ls** (for "list") command. If this is your first time logging in, there may not be any files in your home directory yet. Try the **ls** command and see:

```
$ ls
$
```

No response normally means no files. But in your home directory, there may be some *hidden* files. Your system administrator may have given you some startup files (which contain commands that are run every time you login). You don't want to change your startup files by accident, so they're usually hidden. In UNIX, you can hide a file simply by giving it a name that starts with a dot. I'll talk more about startup files in Chapter 19, "Environ-Mental Health."

If you want to see whether you have any hidden files, you can use an *option* to tell **ls** to behave differently. (I explain commands and options in more detail in Chapter 4, "Your Wish Is My Command Line.") The command **ls -a** shows all files, including hidden ones (**a** stands for "all"). Try **ls -a** and see if you have any hidden files.

```
$ ls -a
.            ..            .environ    .profile
$
```

In this example, there are four entries (named ., .., .environ, and .profile). The . entry is in every directory; it's short for the directory itself. The .. entry is in all directories but one; it's short for the directory that holds the directory you are in. (The directory that holds everything else, or root directory, doesn't have a .. entry.) The other two entries are for two hidden files.

If you want to know more about the files in a directory, such as who owns them, how big they are, how big each file in them is, and when each file was last changed, you can ask **ls** to give you a long listing by adding the -l option.

Instead of asking for a long listing for all the files in the directory, name the file you want to know about. For example, type the command **ls -l .profile** and press **Enter**. (If you don't have a .profile file, use the name of a file you do have, or use the file name /etc/passwd instead.) You should see something like this:

```
$ ls -l .profile
-rw-rw-r--  1 johnmc  pubs      37 Dec  9 11:12 .profile
```

(handwritten annotations: "all other users", "name (links)", "bytes", "owner", "owner's group", "owner", "group")

This line describes the .profile file. (If you don't name the file, **ls** lists all of the non-hidden files in the directory, one file to a line.) The first character on the line describes what kind of file it is: a - indicates a regular file, and a d indicates a directory. This example shows a file.

The next set of letters describe what permissions are attached to the file. Because more than one person uses a UNIX system, the users are broken down into groups. As a result, each file has three sets of permissions (in this order): one set for the person who owns the file, one set for people who are in the same group as the owner of the file, and one set for everyone else. For instance, at my company, all of the accounting people have been placed within the same UNIX user group so they can share files and information, but because I'm not an accountant, my company doesn't let me read accounting information. (I'm grateful.) The system administrator has set the permissions of the accounting group such that anyone not belonging to that group cannot read, write (change), or execute any of the accounting files. That is the purpose of the user group in UNIX: all of the people who are allowed to do the same sorts of tasks (accounting or system administration, for example) are put together in a *group*. So people inside a group may have different permissions for a file than the people outside the group.

Each permission is three letters long. An r means that that person or group can read the file, a w means the person or group can write (change or remove) the file, and an x means that the person or group can execute (run) the file. The x permission affects both programs and directories. To break down the permissions attached to the file shown above, the first rw- indicates that the owner has permission to read and change the file; the second rw- indicates that all members of the owner's group have the same permission; the r-- at the end of the series indicates that all other users can only read the file.

The ₁ after the permissions shows how many *names*, or *links* (covered in Chapter 11), a file has. Yes, in UNIX, a file can have more than one name! In this example, however, the file has only one name.

Next comes the name of the owner and then the name of the group to which the owner belongs. In this case, johnmc belongs to the group named pubs, so anyone who is a member of the pubs group can read or change johnmc's .profile file.

The next thing the list shows is the size of the file or directory. This file isn't very large; it's only 37 bytes long. (A byte is equal to one character; so this file has less than half a page of information.)

Next comes the date and time the file was last changed (Dec 9, 11:12 in this example), and last is the name of the file.

Some UNIX shell programs use the startup files .cshrc and .login. Those shells also have a logout file (.logout) that contains commands the system runs when you quit your UNIX session.

The **ls** command has a lot of options that change how it behaves, and you can even use two options at once. Try using **ls -al** on your home directory. (The **-a** tells UNIX to include hidden files; the l asks for the long listing.) In this example, I'm listing the contents of /usr/johnmc:

```
$ ls -al
total 12
drwxrwxr-x 32 johnmc  pubs     512 Dec  9 11;49 .
drwxr-xr-x 33 root    wheel   1536 Oct 11 10:12 ..
-rw-rw-rw-  1 johnmc  pubs      92 Dec  9 11:13 .environ
-rw-rw-rw-  1 johnmc  pubs      37 Dec  9 11:12 .profile
```

The only new piece of information here is the line total 12. It's an approximate measure of the size taken up by all the files; not all versions of the **ls** command show it. Even sophisticated UNIX users ignore this, and you can too.

See Chapter 8, "Branching Out: Working with Files and Directories," for more information on the **ls** command.

Changing Directories

How about a quick venture out of your home directory before you quit this session? You can change the directory you're in using the **cd** (change directory) command. Type **cd**, a space, and the name of the directory you want to go to. (For our example, type .. for the directory name; this tells the system you want to go the directory that holds the directory you're already in). Then press **Enter**.

```
$ cd ..
$ pwd
/usr
```

Because .. is a special directory name that stands for "the directory holding the directory I'm in," UNIX users call this process "going up a directory." You can keep typing **cd ..** until **pwd** shows you that the current directory is /. That's when you've gone up as far as you can go. The / represents the directory that holds all the files and directories in the UNIX system; it's called the root directory (because everything grows from it). To go back to your home directory, type **cd** and press **Enter**.

You can go straight to the root directory (/) by typing its name after **cd**:

```
$ cd /
$ pwd
/
```

Quitting Your Session

As confirmed smokers know, quitting can be tough. Fortunately, UNIX isn't as tough to shake as nicotine. (Although the discomfort at *starting* the habit is similar. I know. I started as a social UNIX user, but I digressed.)

To quit your session, simply type **exit** at the prompt and press **Enter**. You don't even have to be in your home directory. How much easier can it get?

The Least You Need to Know

Well, you've survived the first session. You got in, got on with it, got it over with, and got out. Get it?

➤ To start a UNIX session, you need an account, which comes with a login name (who you are) and a password (which proves who you are).

➤ You can start a session whenever you see the prompt login:. Type your login name, press **Enter**, type your password, and press **Enter** again.

➤ Every time you login, you start your UNIX session in your home directory, which is your personal space on the system.

➤ To change your password, use the **passwd** command.

➤ To quit, use the **exit** command.

Chapter 4

Your Wish Is My Command Line

> **In This Chapter**
>
> ➤ What a command looks like
>
> ➤ How options change a command
>
> ➤ What command arguments are
>
> ➤ How UNIX commands are described

How do you give the computer commands? In pretty much the same way you give commands to a dog or any other faithful servant. My computer's not as good at understanding what I want as my dog Molly is, but then Molly's not very good at math and printing. In this chapter, you'll learn how to tell your computer to "Fetch!" and perform other commands.

Death and Syntaxes

Computers aren't very smart, so their commands must be in a particular format. Every command has its own format, depending on what information it needs from you to carry out the command. This format is called the command's *syntax*. It's similar to the English syntax

Mrs. Hauser taught in fifth grade: there's a verb, an object, and modifiers. Computer scientists spend a lot of time thinking about languages, so they use a lot of terms you'll recognize from your fifth grade English class.

All UNIX commands start with the name of a program. For instance, when you enter the command **passwd**, you're really saying, "Go run the program named *passwd*." The rest of the command is information the program needs to carry out your command, and you separate the words on the line with spaces. A single command normally goes on one line (thus the name command line). After you enter any UNIX command, you press **Enter**; that's how UNIX knows you're done typing (and backspacing, retyping, and so on).

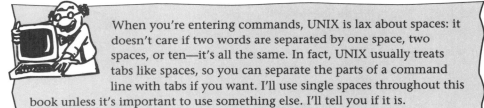

When you're entering commands, UNIX is lax about spaces: it doesn't care if two words are separated by one space, two spaces, or ten—it's all the same. In fact, UNIX usually treats tabs like spaces, so you can separate the parts of a command line with tabs if you want. I'll use single spaces throughout this book unless it's important to use something else. I'll tell you if it is.

If your command is very long, the command line will generally continue to "move over" so you can keep typing. Most UNIX systems will let you enter command lines a thousand letters long, counting spaces. Now that's a long command.

When you type a command name, you're typing the name of a file that happens to be a program. You could type the entire file name, including the directory where the file is located (such as /usr/bin/ls instead of ls), but that gets tiring, so UNIX has a mechanism for searching in a few known places for commands. This mechanism is called your *path*, and I talk more about it in Chapter 19, "Environ-Mental Health." Usually, where a UNIX command is located in the system is irrelevant to you; you just type the command name.

Many commands don't need any extra information. (A command like this for a dog would be "Sit." An example of a UNIX command that doesn't need any more information is **pwd**.) Other commands do something reasonable without any further information but will take information if you give it. For instance, the **ls** command lists what's in the current directory unless you tell it to list the files from another directory. (Usually when you say, "Fetch," the dog knows what to fetch.) Just as I can tell Molly to fetch the ball instead of the stick, you can tell **ls** which directory to list and how you want the contents of the directory listed by giving it an *argument*.

Most commands need that extra bit of information; they cannot perform the task or run the program without it. For example, how does a sort command know what to sort unless you tell it? Where should a mail program send mail? What should a printing program print? Why do fools fall in love?

The Last Word in Arguments

Let's move up from dogs to stockbrokers and look at an English sentence: "Sell." This is a command just as **ls** is. The sentence ends with a period; the command ends when you press **Enter**. Telling my broker what I want him to sell ("Sell my Jumbo Shrimp stock.") is the same as telling **ls** which directory I want to see listed:

```
$ ls /etc
```

This extra information (/etc) is an argument. An *argument* is like an object in English grammar: it describes what the command is acting on. In this case, I'm telling **ls** that I want a list of the contents of the /etc directory.

> **Argument** An argument is any part of a command line except the command. Like an adverb modifies the verb of a sentence, it can modify the command; or like an object in a sentence, it can represent the thing that the command will act on.

If a command takes arguments at all, it usually takes more than one. When you use arguments with a command, they're always the last thing on the command line. Nothing comes after the arguments—they're the last word.

Although the argument is optional with **ls**, you have to use an argument with some commands. An English-language example of such a command is "love"; you have to love someone or something. A UNIX example is the command **lp**. The **lp** command cannot print if you don't give it the name of a file to print. A file name is the argument the **lp** command needs to do its task.

Exercising Your Options

Remember back in Chapter 2 when I said that UNIX systems tend to have a lot of programs that are really good at one thing? If you're using a program for sorting, you may want it to be capable of sorting in alphabetical order or backward, or to ignore numbers. But how do you tell the sort command which way to sort?

You use a command line *option* with the command to tell it how to perform the task. An option is a special kind of argument that you use to tell the command how you want it to act. Just as I can tell my broker how I want him to sell my stock ("Sell short my Gulf Shrimp stock."), I can tell **ls** that I want to see all the files in the directory, even those that are usually hidden:

```
$ ls -a /etc
```

Options Instructions that change how a command behaves. They're called options because they're, well, optional. UNIX options begin with a dash (such as **-a**) and are sometimes called "flags."

The **-a** is an option. Options start with a dash, and most options are single letters. You don't have to use an option with a command; that's why it's an option. The option changes how the command works, usually by changing how the command presents information or where it puts information.

Not all commands have options, of course, and some commands have more than others. The **ls** command, which I keep using as an example, has approximately twenty options. To find out what a command's options are, you can check its usage statement (described later in this chapter) or read the manual page. I describe how to read a manual page in Chapter 5, "Won't You Please Help Me?"

You can use more than one option at a time, and it doesn't matter what order they come in (this is true for most UNIX programs). For instance, the -a option of **ls** shows all files, and the -F option shows what kind of file each one is. (Remember that case matters in UNIX; -F has to be a capital letter. If it exists, the -f option does something different than -F does.) You can combine the options like this:

```
$ ls -a -F
```

or smooshed together like this:

```
$ ls -aF
```

or even like this:

```
$ ls -Fa
```

With most UNIX commands, it doesn't matter what order the options are in, as long as they are all together and placed after the command and before the arguments (if there are any). The only programs in which the order matters are archiving programs, which are usually used to make backups of files. The only options you can't smoosh together are options that are more than one letter or options that take an argument (see the next section).

Every command knows what its options are, and it knows that a list of options starts with a hyphen. In the same way, it knows whether or not the option is supposed to have another word after it (an argument).

An Optional Argument

Some options take arguments because they need a bit of extra information. For instance, if you're telling **sort** (the sorting command) to store the output (the sorted information) in a file, you have to tell it the name of the output file, as this example shows.

```
$ sort -o sorted.text unsorted.text
```

Here's what each part means:

sort	This is the command. **sort** knows its options and which ones take arguments.
-o sorted.text	This is the option that asks **sort** to put the results of the sort into a file called sorted.text. When **sort** sees the **-o**, it knows that the next word is the name of the file in which to store the results. The argument is really part of the option.
unsorted.text	This is the name of the file you want sorted. It's the argument to the **sort** command.

In essence, you're saying, "Sort, use the output file sorted.text to store the results of the sort on the file unsorted.text."

Some commands need a space between an option and its argument; others don't. This has to do with how programmers used to write programs, and you don't want to know any more than that. All you can do is keep an eye out for it. I'll tell you if you need to know.

You can't group options that take arguments because the computer won't know which options the arguments go with. For example, if you wanted to tell the computer to sort a file in reverse order (with the **-r** option) and store the contents in the file sorted.text (with the **-o** option), you couldn't group the two options. You would have to use either **-r -o sorted.text** or **-o sorted.text -r**. If you did group the options (such as **-ro sorted.text**), the computer would be confused as to which option the argument went with. Although in this example it wouldn't be hard to figure out which option the argument goes with, this could be a real problem if both options take arguments.

Oh, What's the Usage?

Because all of this syntax is tough to remember, the UNIX people came up with a summary of the syntax for each UNIX command, which they call a *usage* statement. Here's what the UNIX usage statement for the **du** command looks like. (The **du** command shows you how much disk space you've used; I've left off the information that explains what each option does. Remember, your version of **du** may not have exactly the same options or usage.)

```
du [-a¦-s] [-krlx] [-l num] [pathname ...]
```

Look like a foreign language? Let's take a minute to break down what all of this mumbo-jumbo means.

➤ Everything in square brackets is optional. The **du** command is one of those commands that will work even if all you say is **du**.

➤ The ¦ means "or." It indicates options that contradict each other or that don't work together. For example, with the **du** command, you can use **-a** or **-s**, but not both.

➤ You can use any combination of the single-letter options **k**, **r**, **l**, and **x**.

➤ The *num* and *pathname* arguments are italicized to show that you should replace *num* with a numerical value and *pathname* with a real path name.

➤ If you use the -l option, it must have a number after it (as indicated by *num* in the usage statement).

➤ You can tell **du** which directory or file path it should describe (as indicated by the *pathname* in the statement). The ... after *pathname* means you can name more than one directory or path.

Here's an example of the **du** command in action:

```
$ du -k /home/johnmc
          24 /home/johnmc/.elm
         546 /home/johnmc/Mail
           3 /home/johnmc/News
         160 /home/johnmc/faxes
         101 /home/johnmc/releases
          90 /home/johnmc/labels
           9 /home/johnmc/bin
         150 /home/johnmc/letters
          27 /home/johnmc/letters/customers
          46 /home/johnmc/letters/private
         121 /home/johnmc/letters/suppliers
         902 /home/johnmc
```

du lists each directory and the space it takes up. The **-k** option tells **du** to list directory sizes in kilobytes (a kilobyte is a unit of storage that contains about a thousand letters, or two to three pages of a book). The value beside /home/johnmc (on the last line) is the total space used up by the directory and all of its subdirectories.

Any time you type a command with a bad option, the command gives you a usage statement. When I want to see a usage statement for a command, I use the -? option:

```
$ du -?
Usage:  du [-a¦-s][-krtx] [-l num] [pathname ...]
```

Accepting Exceptions

Of course, there are exceptions to these general rules of command lines. Sorry. Although UNIX was designed by only a couple of people, a lot of other folks got a word (or a program) in there, and all these programs are stuck to UNIX like barnacles. The bad thing about it is that those other folks didn't always make their programs consistent

39

with existing stuff, and needless to say, it would be too expensive to scrape them off now. We'd have to come up with new programs and retrain all the geeks.

First exception: A command doesn't have to end with the Enter key. For instance, if you want to put two commands on one line, you can separate them with a semicolon instead. UNIX responds to the ; character as if you had pressed the Enter key. So entering the command **cd /etc;ls** is the same as entering **cd /etc**, pressing **Enter**, and entering **ls**. (You still must press Enter at the end of the command line.) I talk about this exception in Chapter 25, "Neat Stuff."

Second exception: Some commands do so much that they have an extra kind of information called a *keyword* or a *directive*. (Nobody's quite sure what to call it.) Basically it's a kind of subcommand, and it goes between the command and the options. You won't run into these often; they're usually commands used for storing files. An example is the **tar** command, which creates one big archive file out of a group of files. The second argument to **tar** is the keyword that tells it whether you're reading an archive, writing an archive, or extracting information from an archive. For example, to unpack (extract) information from an archive, you use the command **tar x -f filename**. The **x** is the keyword that tells **tar** the options apply to an extraction operation. The **-f filename** option tells **tar** that the operation applies to the archive file named *filename*.

A Dozen Useful Commands

Now that you know how to give commands, here is an alphabetical listing of a dozen commands that you need to know. For now, I'm just telling you they exist. However, if you notice, most of them are about files and directories, and Chapters 7, "The Root of the Matter: Files and Directories" and 8, "Branching Out: Working with Files and Directories" describe almost all of them in greater detail. (Remember, if you forget the syntax of the command, just type the command and -? to view the usage statement.)

Command	Description
cd *newdirectory*	Changes current working directory. (See Chapter 7, "The Root of the Matter: Files and Directories.")

cp *originalname* *copyname*	Copies a file. See Chapter 8, "Branching Out: Working with Files and Directories."
chmod *permissions filename ...*	Changes who's allowed to read and write a file. Use this command if you want to prevent others from reading your files. See Chapter 11, "More About Files (Some Useful Tips and Tricks)."
logout or **exit**	Ends your UNIX session. It's very rare to find a system that doesn't accept both **logout** and **exit** as commands. See Chapter 3, "In the Beginning Was the Word: login."
lp (for System V systems) **lpr** (for BSD systems)	Prints a text file. If you have one of the newer UNIX systems, you can use either. See Chapter 9, "Printing Is Pressing."
ls [*directory*]	Shows contents of a directory. (**lc** is better if you have it.) See Chapter 8, "Branching Out: Working with Files and Directories."
more *filename ...*	Shows contents of a file. See Chapter 8, "Branching Out: Working with Files and Directories."
mv *oldname newname*	Moves (or renames) a file. See Chapter 8, "Branching Out: Working with Files and Directories."
passwd	Changes your password. See Chapter 3, "In the Beginning Was the Word: login."
pwd	Shows current working directory. See Chapter 7, "The Root of the Matter: Files and Directories."
rm *filename ...*	Deletes a file. See Chapter 7, "The Root of the Matter: Files and Directories."
vi [*filename ...*]	Creates and changes text files. **vi** is a text editor, a stripped-down word processor for programmers. Although **vi** isn't necessarily the best editor, it's sure to be available. See Chapter 16, "Viva vi!"

41

The Least You Need to Know

Well, that's fifth grade syntax for UNIX. And hey, Mrs. Hauser, if you're reading this, send me a note, huh? I'm still in town, and I'm in the phone book.

➤ A command is the name of a program somewhere on the system.

➤ Each command has its own particular format, called its syntax.

➤ At the beginning of each command line, you type the command, and at the end of each line, you press **Enter**.

➤ Options change how the command works.

➤ Options start with a dash (-), and you can group together as many single-letter options as you want.

➤ An argument tells the command what to work on.

Chapter 5

Won't You Please Help Me?

In This Chapter

➤ What help is available

➤ How to read UNIX man pages

➤ Reminding yourself of options for a command

➤ Finding out what command you need

Ancient Saying:
Give a man a fish, feed him for a day;
Teach a man to fish, feed him for life.

Modern response:
So who wants fish every night?

You're stumped. You're trying to use a command, but you just ain't gettin' it. Or worse, you know there's a command that does what you want (or there ought to be), but you don't know how to find it. I understand. Been there, done that, collected the bubble-gum cards. This is the chapter where you learn how to fish for the answers.

The standard online help program in UNIX is called **man**, short for "manual." (If I were designing a computer system, I'd call the standard online help command **help**. But since I wasn't even ten when they were designing UNIX, I don't think they would have listened to me.) The UNIX online help and manuals are very good if you need a memory-jog; they're not so good if you need to learn how it all goes together. **man** and the other help programs work best if you know which program you're having a problem with; they're not so helpful if you're trying to figure out which program to use. (In fairness to UNIX, this is a problem with most computer help systems.)

A **man page** is a manual section that usually describes one UNIX command or program. It may be more than one page long, but it's still called a man page. If two programs are very closely related, the same man page may describe both of them.

When something is **online**, it is available electronically through the computer, as opposed to being available on paper.

So UNIX doesn't really have a help command. It has a documentation command, the **man** command, that helps you wade through the volumes of man pages to learn about UNIX commands. The **man** command is designed to show you pieces of the manual, but you have to know what piece to look at. This shouldn't surprise you if you think back to who designed UNIX: real computer geeks (people who write operating systems just for the fun of it). These people didn't have to be told how the system was put together; they were the ones who put things there. They just needed a reminder once in awhile. As a result, the help features in UNIX are not so user-friendly for us non-geek types.

In addition to the **man** command, there are a couple of other commands that will help you find what you need. The **whatis** command shows you parts of the manual, and the **apropos** command tells you what part of the manual you might want to look at. I'll tell you all about these in this chapter.

What are your options if you're not a computer geek? If you know what program you're trying to use, you can read the UNIX man pages (or this fine book). You can "ask" the program. Your system might be blessed with any of the non-standard help tools. Or, as a last option (or maybe the first) you can ask a knowledgeable UNIX user. Let's walk through each one of these options.

O Lucky Man

There is a help program called **man** that comes with every UNIX system. When you type **man** and the name of a command you are unsure about, you get the manual page describing the command. For instance, if you type **man man**, you'll see the manual page for the **man** command itself. There's usually a special man page called **intro**, which tells you about how commands and man pages are organized on your system. So you might want to try the command **man intro**.

Even when a man page is more than one page long, it's still called a page (go figure). If a man page is more than one screen long, **man** runs it through the **more** program, which shows you files a screenful at a time. To go to the next screen, press the **Spacebar**. To quit the man pages, press **q**. I describe the **more** command in (ahem) more detail in Chapter 8, "Branching Out: Working with Files and Directories."

For historical reasons (which means nobody has bothered to change it), **man** formats pages with the **nroff** program so they can be printed on a line printer with 66 lines to the page. This means that in the third screenful of a man page, you'll suddenly see this page footer and then the header for the next page. It's a nuisance, but there's not much you can do about it.

The most important parts of the man page are at the beginning. The first three sections of the man page are always NAME, SYNTAX (also called synopsis or usage), and DESCRIPTION, which cover just what you think they cover. The Options sections (describing the options, of course) may be part of the DESCRIPTION, or it may be a separate section. Here's the man page for the **man** command itself.

```
/home/johnmc$ man man
man(1)                      USER COMMANDS                      man(1)
NAME
      man - display manual pages or find manual pages by keyword
SYNOPSIS
      man [ - ] [[ section ] title ... ]
      man -k keyword ...
DESCRIPTION
      Man displays information from the on-line reference manuals.
      Normally, you provide the title of the man page you want to
      see.  If you give a section, it applies to the titles that
      follow on the command line (up to the next section, if any).
      man looks in the indicated section of the manual for those
      titles.  section is either a digit or one of the words new,
      local, old, or public.  If you don't provide a section, man
      searches all reference sections and prints the first manual
      page it finds.  If man cannot find a man page, it prints an
      error.

      If you specify a keyword (-k) instead, man shows a  one-line
      summary of commands related to that keyword.

      The manual pages are usually  stored  in  subdirectories  of
      /usr/share/man.    Preformatted  versions  are  stored in sub-
      directories named cat1 through cat9, and  unformatted  ver-
      sions are stored in man1 through man9.

      If the output is to a terminal, man pipes its output through
      more  to  handle paging.  If output is not a terminal (or if
      the - flag is given), man pipes its output through cat.

Options
      The following options are available:

      -k keyword ...
         man searches the whatis database and prints all of  the
         one-line summaries that contain keyword.
ENVIRONMENT VARIABLES
      PAGER
         The  name of the command to use for displaying man pages
--More--(76%)
```

For you, the most useful parts of the man page are the command name, the usage statement (or statements), and the description.

➤ The NAME section contains a one-line description of the program. The description is usually accurate, but it was probably written by a programmer, so it may be misleading to you and me. (Remember, these are the same people who named the help command "man.")

➤ There may be more than one line in the SYNTAX section. If a command has several forms, each one will show up. For example, the **man** command can be used with a title or with the **-k** option, but not with both.

➤ The DESCRIPTION section describes the command in more detail than does the one-line summary under NAME.

➤ Each option is listed with a description of what it does. Some UNIX companies try to make sure that the options are in alphabetical order; others try to order the options by usefulness. Still others use a bowl of alphabet soup as their ordering technique. (Not really, but it often seems that way!)

There's more variation in the other parts of a man page. The order may be different than I tell you here, and not all parts will be found for every command in the man pages. Although the other sections are not as useful for understanding the command, they do come in handy once in awhile. Here's the rest of the **man** man page.

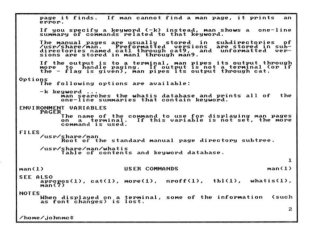

```
        page it finds.  If man cannot find a man page, it prints  an
        error.

        If you specify a keyword (-k) instead, man shows a  one-line
        summary of commands related to that keyword.

        The manual pages are usually  stored  in  subdirectories  of
        /usr/share/man.  Preformatted  versions  are stored in sub-
        directories named cat1 through cat9, and  unformatted  ver-
        sions are stored in man1 through man9.

        If the output is to a terminal, man pipes its output through
        more  to  handle paging.  If output is not a terminal (or if
        the - flag is given), man pipes its output through cat.

Options
        The following options are available:

        -k keyword ...
             man searches the whatis database and prints all of  the
             one-line summaries that contain keyword.
ENVIRONMENT VARIABLES
        PAGER
             The name of the command to use for displaying man pages
             on  a  terminal.  If this variable is not set, the more
        command is used.
FILES
        /usr/share/man
             Root of the standard manual page directory subtree.

        /usr/share/man/whatis
             Table of contents and keyword database.
                                                                   1
man(1)                     USER COMMANDS                      man(1)
SEE ALSO
        apropos(1), cat(1), more(1), nroff(1), tbl(1), whatis(1),
        man(7)
NOTES
        When displayed on a terminal, some of the information (such
        as font changes) is lost.
                                                                   2
/home/johnmc$
```

The SEE ALSO section at the bottom is useful when you're searching for a command that's related to the one you're reading about.

➤ If you're lucky, there will be an EXAMPLE section, which gives you an idea of how to use the command and what the results would be using some of the options or arguments.

➤ If a command checks for them, there's a section describing ENVIRONMENT VARIABLES: what they are and what values the command wants. (An environment variable provides a way to configure a command without using an option flag. I talk about them more in Chapter 19, "Environ-Mental Health.")

➤ Any data files or startup files are listed in the FILES part of the man page. For example, all of the manual pages in /usr/share/man are data files for the **man** command.

➤ Sometimes (especially on older man pages), you'll get the AUTHOR section, which tells you who to blame for all the cryptic descriptions of the commands.

Environment variable A piece of information specific to your system or environment (such as your home directory) that is given to all of your programs. If you use an environment variable instead of a command option, you don't have to retype the same information again and again to give it to all your programs.

Startup file A set of commands a program runs when it starts up. The commands often enable you to configure the program by setting options you want. Because of this, startup files are also called *configuration files*.

Bug An error or mistake in a program. Bugs can be unimportant (a spelling mistake) or serious (the program writes unusable data files). If a bug is really serious, it can cause the program to quit unexpectedly.

➤ The SEE ALSO section lists other man pages that are somehow related to the one you're reading. The numbers refer to the section of the manual. The note uucp(8) indicates that you can find related information under "uucp" in section 8 of the man pages.

➤ Different sections give hints, cautions, or warnings. If you're reading information in a NOTES section, it's probably not too serious, but you should avoid it. If you're reading information in a WARNING section, you should definitely be wary of what it says.

➤ Often, you'll see a section called BUGS. In geek-speak, a *bug* is a problem or an error. Obviously, nobody likes to put real errors such as "For no particular reason, erases all files in system" into print. Instead, the BUGS section talks about design flaws or limitations. You might see something like Program should understand Urdu and Sanskrit. (I think it's often a kind of reverse snobbery.) Don't expect to see these bugs fixed; some of them have been in man pages for more than a decade.

The Joy of Sections

Although you may never need to use this knowledge, you should know that the man pages are usually organized and categorized into the following eight sections (at least on the BSD-derived system):

Section 1: User commands and application programs. These are the commands you care about. You'll work with them every day.

Section 2: Operating system calls. These are used by programmers only.

Section 3: C library functions. A *function* is a standard piece of a program that does one little task and can be used inside a program. It's like a mini-program. These are used by programmers only.

Section 4: Device drivers. Only some programmers and system administrators need to worry about device drivers. (This section contains file formats on our Novell Unixware—System V—system.)

Section 5: File formats. Descriptions of certain file formats. You probably won't ever need these. (This section is miscellaneous files on our Unixware system.)

Section 6: Games and demos. These are the commands you *really* care about (but they don't let you get much work done).

Section 7: Miscellaneous. Various man pages that didn't go anywhere else. (This section contains device drivers on the Unixware system.)

Section 8: System administration. Programs that deal with system administration and networking. (This section doesn't exist on the Unixware system; the commands are put in section 1, but the man pages have a letter after the number to tell you what kind of program it is.)

If two different sections have man pages for the same command (the command name is the same but the commands may do different things), the man pages will always default to the most commonly used command. The most commonly used commands are found in the user commands (section 1) or games and demos (section 6). In most cases, all this will be obvious to you.

Sometimes, you may be looking for a command that was mentioned in a SEE ALSO section of a man page, which means you probably want the version of the command found in a lesser used section of the man pages. For instance, maybe you want to read the uucp man page from section 8—abbreviated uucp(8)—instead of the man page for the uucp command—abbreviated uucp(1). To tell **man** which section you want to read from, put the section number between the **man** command and the manual page title, like this:

```
% man 8 uucp
```

Some new UNIX systems use an **-s** option instead, such as:

```
% man -s 8 uucp
```

Either way, the man page for the **uucp(8)** command will be displayed. (Remember, you only need to include the section number if the **man** command doesn't give you the man page you want the first time you use the **man** command.)

Printing Man Pages

The quickest way to print a man page is to send the output of the **man** command directly to your printing program. You'll have to ask your system administrator which printing command you have (it will be **lp** if you're on a System V-derived system; it will be **lpr** if you're on a BSD-derived system). To use the output of one command as input for another, put a pipe symbol (¦) between the two commands. For example, my print command is **lpr**. I can send the man page for **passwd** directly to my printer using this command:

```
$ man passwd ¦ lpr
```

A Better Man Than I Am, Gunga Din

A lot of people have tried to come up with better versions of the man pages over the years. You might look for programs called **adam** (the premier man, of course) and **woman**. I've never found any of them to be so much better that I switched to using them, but you may feel differently. The only way to find out if they're on your system is to ask someone (or try them).

Pipe A method used to take the output of one command and use it as input for another. It's the same as saving the output of the first command in a file and then using that file as an argument to the second command—but it's faster. To use a pipe, connect the two commands with a vertical bar symbol (¦). You'll learn more about pipes in Chapter 11, "More About Files (Some Useful Tips and Tricks)."

If you have the X Windows system installed, you probably have the **xman** program. **xman** comes free with the X-Windows GUI, but not all UNIX vendors include it. The big advantage of **xman**, in my opinion, is that it shows up in its own window and displays a table of contents of all of the man pages available on your system. You can often guess what command you need by its name, but you don't know it's available until you see it on the list. The following figure shows part of the **xman** table of contents for our system. To use **xman**, you must be in the X Windows GUI. Enter the command **xman &**.

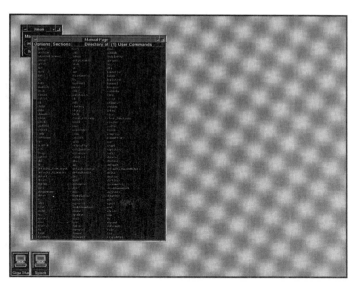

*An example of **xman**'s directory of man1 sections. To show a man page for a particular command, you click on the man page's title.*

Other Ways to Get Help

You don't have to rely on **man** and its variations to get help with UNIX. To help you find information, you can use other sources, such as the **whatis** command, program usage lines, and other users.

If you think of **man** as a way to read one page of the manual, the **whatis** command is a way to read one line of the table of contents. The UNIX programs themselves will offer up their usage lines if you ask them correctly. And because UNIX is a multiuser system, there's almost always someone else you can ask for help.

A **GUI** is a graphical user interface; it enables you to interact with the computer using pictures instead of commands. (See Chapter 6, "Surviving Window Pains," for more information.)

I'll also show you how to put it all together and use **man** and **whatis** to find out what time it is. (Don't laugh. It took me a year to figure this out, but I'll show you in a page and a half.)

The whatis Command

Some systems have a command called **whatis** that gives you the one-line description from the NAME line of the man page. You can use it when you're curious to know what a command does (specifically), but you don't want all the gory details. For example, here's what you would see if you used the **whatis** command to find out about the **man** command:

```
$ whatis man
man (1) - display manual pages or find manual pages by keyword
```

Ask the Program

Commands come with some built-in help, such as the usage statement I described in Chapter 4, "Your Wish Is My Command Line." If you type a command with a nonexistent option, you will almost always see a usage statement listing the available options.

In addition, some commands have a "help" option. However, (not surprisingly) there's no standard symbol or letter for this. Some commands use -?, some use -**H** or -**h**, some use -**x** (for *x*plain), and all the X Windows programs use -**help**. I always try the command with -? first to get the usage message and see if any options are described as giving help.

For example, there's a nonstandard command called **flip** that converts text files between UNIX format and MS-DOS format. To get help information, type **flip -h**. UNIX shows this help information screen.

```
/home/johnmc$ flip -h
File interchange program flip version 1.00.  Copyright 1989 Rahul Dhesi,
All rights reserved.  Both noncommercial and commercial copying, use, and
creation of derivative works are permitted in accordance with the
requirements of the GNU license.  This program does newline conversions.

    Usage:      flip -umhvtsbz file ...

One of -u, -m, or -h is required;  others are optional.  See user manual.

    -u      convert to **IX format (CR LF => LF, lone CR or LF unchanged,
            trailing control Z removed, embedded control Z unchanged)
    -m      convert to MS-DOS format (lone LF => CR LF, lone CR unchanged)
    -h      give this help message
    -v      be verbose, print filenames as they are processed
    -t      touch files (don't preserve timestamps)
    -s      strip high bit
    -b      convert binary files too (else binary files are left unchanged)
    -z      truncate file at first control Z encountered

May be invoked as "toix" (same as "flip -u") or "toms" (same as "flip -m").
/home/johnmc$
```

The information you get when you type a help option.

Again, all of this is great if you know what command you should use. But what if you don't?

Asking Other People

The least involved and most useful way to find out if a command exists is by asking somebody. Don't laugh; this is how most people learn, especially since so many UNIX systems have nonstandard commands that were put there by somebody who thought it was neat or useful, but never told anyone.

Ideally, you want to ask somebody who knows more about the UNIX system than you do, but not at the level of UNIX godhood. Even if the other person doesn't know the answer, you may be able to figure it out together.

If your system carries USENET news, see if they have a new-users newsgroup in which new users can discuss their problems. (USENET is a bunch of discussion groups carried by computers. When people say "Internet" they often mean news, because the two are closely connected. Your system might have local news without being on the Internet.)

If there's nobody around you can ask, you'll have to try some of the system's help programs.

Which Command Is Apropos?

The people at Berkeley who gave us BSD UNIX also added an extra command called **apropos**. **apropos** searches through the man pages for key words. (A synonym command is **man -k**.) Using this command and doing a small amount of searching through the SEE ALSO sections of the man pages, you can usually find the command you want.

Suppose you want to find a command that displays the time of day on your screen (you want to use your expensive UNIX system as a digital watch). You could use the **apropos** option to find the time command you want. As you will see in the following example, it sometimes takes persistence and a certain amount of knowledge of how to use the search tools at hand to find commands.

> Remember: The command **man -k time** would provide the same listing you see on the next page.

Using the **apropos** command, you search the man pages for all the commands in which the word "time" appears in the NAME line.

```
% apropos time
at, batch (1)        - execute a command at a specified time
clock (3)            - report CPU time used
crontab (5)          - table of times to run periodic jobs
profil (2)           - execution time profile
time (1)             - time a command
time (3)             - get date and time
times (3)            - get process times
touch (1)            - update file's access/modification times
uptime (1)           - show how long the system has been up
```

 Any NAME line that includes a form of the word "time" will be printed, even if the word is really "timer" or "pastimes." Make the keyword as specific as you can.

From the commands that are displayed, you would guess there are a couple candidates that could give you the information you want: **time**(1) and **time**(3). Let's try **time**(1).

```
% time
Time: Usage: time [-p] command ...
```

Well, that doesn't look like what you wanted. So **time**(3) must be the command you want, even though it's in section 3 of the man pages (which is not the place you would normally find user commands). Although Section 3 contains the man pages for library functions, remember that sometimes the SEE ALSO sections in section 3 of the man pages list commands that use a given library function. So, you tell **man** to show you the **time** man page in section 3 by typing **man 3 time**. Once you're inside the man page for **time**(3), space down to the SEE ALSO section. It should look something like this:

```
SEE ALSO
date(1), ctime(3) tzone(5)
```

Because **date** has a 1 after it, you know it's a command (the 1 means it is located in section 1, user commands, of the man pages). Because the other two commands are not in sections 1 or 6 of the man pages, you know neither is a command and, therefore, not likely what you're looking for. So go ahead and try **date**.

```
% date
Wed Sep 21 17:19:37 EDT 1994
```

There! You've outwitted a programmer! You found the command you wanted, and what you really wanted was the **date** command. Although this technique is baroque, it is sometimes necessary.

The Least You Need to Know

Okay, that's all the fishing you need to know. School's out! (There are lots of other fish puns I could make, but I've got a haddock.)

➤ The online documentation command is called **man**. You use it with the name of the command you want to know about, such as **man** *command*.

➤ If you want to know about a particular command, you can also use the command **whatis**.

➤ The most important sections of a man page are at the top (NAME, SUMMARY, DESCRIPTION, and OPTIONS).

➤ man pages are organized into sections; user commands are in section 1.

➤ Not all commands have manual pages.

➤ If you don't know which command you should be using, try asking somebody, using the **man -k** command, or using the **apropos** command.

THIS WON'T HURT A BIT...

Chapter 6

Surviving Window Pains

In This Chapter

➤ What is a GUI?

➤ What is X Windows?

➤ How to use X Windows

➤ GUI desktops

What if your terminal *isn't* like what I described in Chapter 3, and your login prompt is in a box on the screen? What if your terminal has a mouse, and after you login, your screen shows a box with a prompt in it? What's wrong?

Nothing's wrong. You've just got a modern UNIX terminal with a *graphical user interface* (or GUI, pronounced "gooey"). A graphical user interface enables you to communicate with the computer by using pictures instead of commands. The UNIX GUI is called X Windows, and it starts as soon as you login.

Each program written to use X Windows can create its own on-screen box, called a "window." A window is like a tiny terminal screen, and each terminal screen runs its own program. When a program ends, the window disappears.

You can move windows around the screen, even put one "in front of" another. You can change the size of a window to make it fill the screen or to shrink it down to a tiny picture, called an *icon*, at the bottom of the screen. Then you can turn an icon back into a window, or return a full-screen window to its original size.

A *command line interface* (or CLI, pronounced "see-ell-eye") is a system in which you use typed commands to control the computer. In a CLI system, you communicate with the computer through messages you type on the command line. Because so many UNIX programs were written for the command line, the most-used X Windows command is **xterm**, which creates a window that holds a command line! We'll talk about this command a little bit later.

UNIX Does Windows

Brace yourself for a little history. Even though the subject is terminals, I'll try not to make it terminally dull.

The first UNIX terminals were teletypes (which in those days were known as TTYs, when they were common). A teletype is a typewriter that takes the letters off a phone line and prints them on a roll of paper. (Remember that UNIX was created at AT&T. Because they are a phone company first and foremost, it's not surprising that the first UNIX terminals were linked to the phone lines.) UNIX still carries this heritage: a terminal device is still called a TTY. Screens didn't come along until later.

When screens did come along, they had something in common with teletypes: they knew how to draw the letters. For example, the computer system sent the terminal a signal that meant "A," and the terminal knew how to draw an "A." The letters looked like whatever the terminal designer figured the letters ought to look like. These screens were called *character displays* because they could only draw characters. (One reason for this was the Law of Layers. It was easier to let the terminal worry about drawing letters than to clutter the operating system with it.)

However, in the early eighties, more powerful computers were built, with a new feature called *bit-mapped graphics*. A bit map is a picture stored as ones and zeroes (that is, as bits). Instead of letting the terminal draw the letters, the computer program would describe which dots on the screen were supposed to be lit up to create the letter and which weren't. This is much more difficult (in a computing sense), but you can draw pictures with it.

So why not use pictures instead of letters to communicate with the user? Xerox's Palo Alto Research Center investigated this in the seventies; some of their results eventually led to the Apple Macintosh's graphical user interface and Microsoft Windows. In fact, why not treat the computer screen as a bunch of little terminals? (Which means you can have multiple UNIX programs running simultaneously.) Each terminal can run a program in its own miniscreen, called a *window*. And if you're using pictures, you need some way to point at a picture—thus the mouse. In fact, the arrow that indicates the mouse's position is called the *pointer*.

The Massachusetts Institute of Technology came up with a set of programs that do all of these things. They called it X Windows. (Probably because it's the one that came after a windowing system called "W." No kidding.) In addition, they gave X Windows away free of charge, which helped make it popular.

> A **character display** is a terminal display that shows only letters. (A typewriter is a character display device.) Old computer terminals were usually character display devices. Even if X Windows is installed, you cannot use it if you have a character display device.
>
> A **bit-mapped display** is a terminal display that can show pictures. (Your television is a bit-mapped display device.) The position of every dot on the screen has been calculated. You need a bit-mapped display in order to use a GUI. The screens for almost all personal computers (but not all terminals) are bit-mapped.

Other programs do the same thing X Windows does. The NeXT computer has its own GUI, for example, and so do Sun's computers and Hewlett-Packard's. However, the most common graphical user interfaces available for UNIX are built using X Windows' parts. (I have never seen a graphical user interface for UNIX that wasn't based on X Windows, though I know they exist.)

Popular User Interfaces

X Windows is a graphical user interface in the same way that a pile of lumber and nails is a log cabin or a Southern mansion. X Windows is all the pieces that go into building the graphical user interface. But programmers had to actually take these pieces and design and program how the windows would look, how the mouse buttons would work, what the menu bars and commands would be, and all the other details that give the GUI its look and feel. Two standard GUIs have been created using X Window parts: Motif and Open Look. The most common is Motif. Here's a picture of Motif windows:

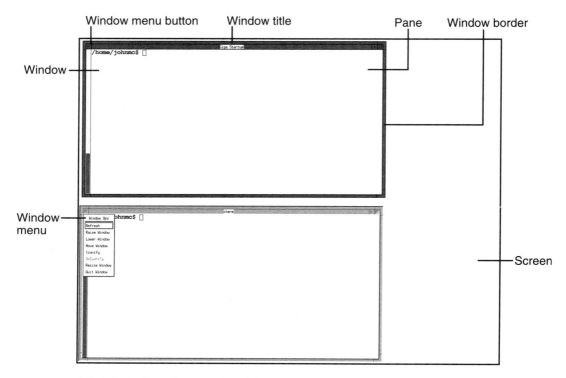

Motif windows have colored borders with two buttons in the upper right corner.

Here's a picture of an Open Look Window:

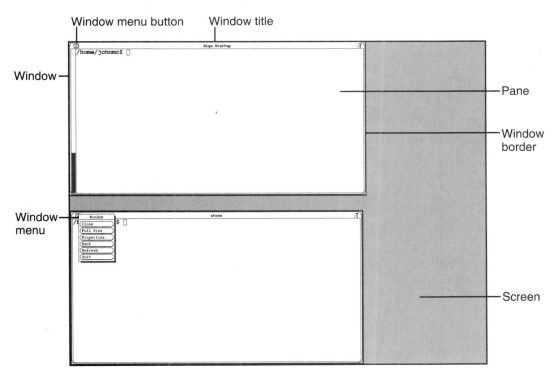

Although the Open Look window has a different appearance, it has most of the same parts.

When your UNIX account was set up, the system administrator chose a GUI for you. Most UNIX systems use a GUI like Motif or Open Look to give you lots of little terminal screens. You still type commands in the terminal windows. Some systems go further than that: they actually try to eliminate as much typing as possible.

This type of GUI is called a desktop GUI. A desktop GUI like this might, for example, show a directory not as a name, but as a picture of a file folder. A file might have a picture of a sheaf of papers. Program files have a third kind of picture. By using pictures, you can tell the directories from the files just by the way the pictures look. If you "open" the file folder (by double-clicking on it with the left mouse button), the picture turns into a window containing pictures of the files, programs, and directories in that directory.

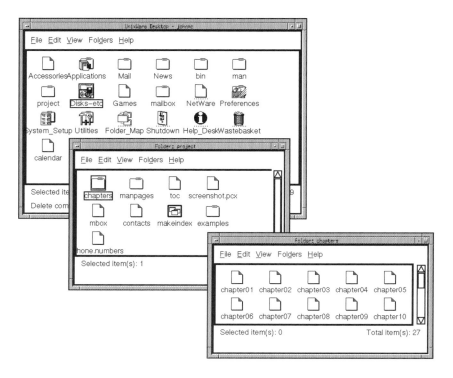

In this shell, each window is a directory, and each item in the directory has a picture.

If you double-click on a program picture (that's how you start a program), the program asks you to enter the command arguments or select options, and then the program runs.

As much as possible, a desktop GUI tries to replace your command line shell program with pictures. (For more about what a shell program is and does, see Chapter 18, "The Shell Game.") A GUI shell usually shows your home directory as your main window—kind of like your desktop. The UnixWare GUI shell even calls itself the Desktop program. The following figure shows what it looks like:

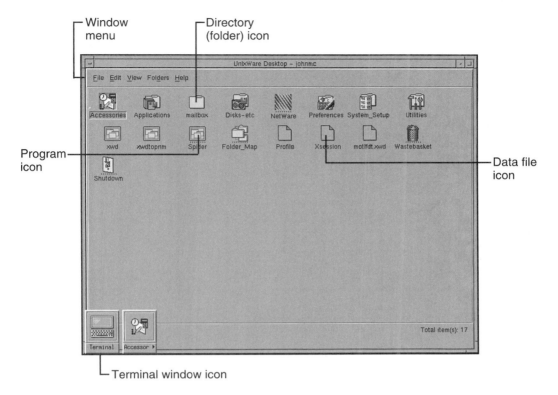

This desktop replaces a command line. The terminal program provides a command line, when needed.

Because in UNIX you sometimes have to use a command line, all GUI shells provide a terminal program that makes a window containing a command line.

Working with a Mouse

How do you use an X Windows GUI? What are the basics? First let's talk about the mouse, since that's new. I'm going to discuss the left and right mouse buttons, but in fact, most UNIX mice have three buttons. And you can swap left for right if you're left-handed (ask your local UNIX guru to help you with this).

When you move the mouse on your desk or mouse pad, the pointer (usually an arrow or a vertical line) moves on-screen. When you press the left mouse button and let go, you are *clicking* the mouse. You click the mouse to select something, such as a window, an item in a window, or an item in a list. Clicking on an empty part of the screen will often show you a list of commands as well. (A list of commands is called a menu.) If you click on the iconify button (I'll explain which one that is in a moment), the window turns into an icon.

When you press the left mouse twice quickly, you are *double-clicking* the mouse. For instance, double-clicking on an icon is a short-cut for a longer sequence of mouse commands that turns the icon back into a window. The effects of double-clicking depend on what program you're using and what you're double-clicking on.

If you have a GUI shell, double-clicking on a directory icon opens a window showing the contents of the directory; double-clicking on a program icon runs the program; and double-clicking on a file icon opens a window showing the contents of the file.

When you hold down the left mouse button, move the mouse, and then release the button, you are *clicking and dragging*. You click and drag on the move bar (also called a title bar) in order to move a Motif window. You also use clicking and dragging to move icons around the screen.

That's the basics of the mouse. Now about windows.

Working with a Window

Motif and Open Look windows have basically the same parts, although there are some differences, and they behave differently. For instance, in Motif, you click the left mouse button on the Window menu button to access the Window menu; in Open Look, you click the right mouse button.

Here's a Motif window with the important parts labelled:

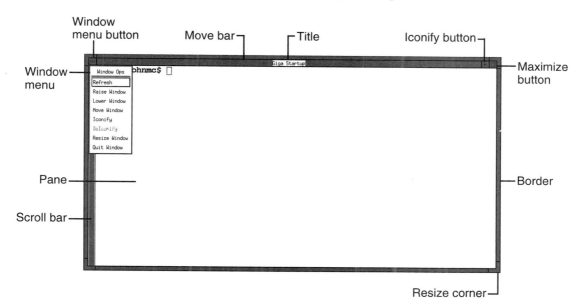

These are the parts of a Motif window. Not all parts have to be in every window.

Around the window is a *border*. Across the top is a *title bar* (or *move bar*), which in this case contains the (cryptic) title "Giga Startup." Each corner is its own little area. To the left of the title bar is the *Window menu button*. If you click on this button, you'll see a menu of commands that you can use to control the window. To the right of the title bar are the *iconify button* and the *maximize button*. (Don't blame me; these are their names!) The iconify button shrinks the window to an icon, while the maximize button makes the window grow to fill the whole screen.

Not every window has all of these parts or capabilities. A programmer could design a program with a window that couldn't be resized, for example. In addition, Open Look windows don't feature the iconify or maximize buttons; you perform those actions using the commands on the Window menu (which you access with the Window menu button).

The following guidelines explain how to handle windows under Motif. Experiment with these methods on your system, especially if it's not Motif.

➤ To make a window the active window, click on it. (Some systems make the active window the one that contains the mouse pointer.)

➤ To make a window wider or narrower, click on and drag the left or right border.

➤ To make a window shorter or taller, click on and drag the top or bottom border.

➤ To change a window's size in two directions at once, click on and drag a corner.

➤ To move a window, click on and drag the title bar.

➤ To shrink a window down to a tiny block (called an icon), click on the **iconify button**. Double-click on the icon to bring the window back.

➤ To make a window fill the screen, click on the **maximize button**. To return it to its original size, click on the **maximize button** again.

➤ To delete an existing window, end the program that's running the window, or click on the **Window menu button** and then click on **Close**.

If you have X Windows on your system and have a terminal that can display windows, you have configuration files for your window system in your home directory. Don't mess with them, and especially don't delete them. You probably have these files:

.Xdefaults   This is the configuration file that describes the properties of your X Windows. Settings in this file are true no matter which window manager you use.

.mwmrc (or something similar that ends in rc)   This file describes your settings for one particular window manager. (It's an old UNIX tradition to name configuration files with a period at the beginning and *rc* at the end.)

.xsession   The set of commands to be run when your personal session of X Windows starts.

Every window is attached to a program: when you start the program, the window appears. To create a new window, start the appropriate program. When you end the program, the window disappears.

Running X Windows Programs

To run X Windows, you need a UNIX system with X Windows installed and a bit-mapped display terminal. If you have these, your system administrator has probably set up your system so X Windows starts when you login.

As I said earlier, in most systems, X Windows is used to provide terminal windows—a command line in a window. You can run any UNIX program inside one of these command-line windows.

Programs that "know" about X Windows can make their own windows and can take full advantage of the mouse. Programs that understand X Windows and work with it are called *X programs* or *X commands*. This section will tell you a bit about X commands.

If you're using a terminal with X Windows, you can run any X program from the command line or from a menu. (Your system administrator will have set up a menu for you to start X commands.) If you have a menu, it appears when you click on an empty part of the screen. You may have no menu, one menu, or a different menu for each mouse button.

Here's a picture of one of my menus. It lists some common X programs that I sometimes want to start.

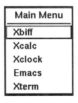

Main Menu
Xbiff
Xcalc
Xclock
Emacs
Xterm

This menu is a convenient way to start these X programs.

For example, to start a new command-line window, I only have to click on **Xterm** in this menu.

You can configure your menu yourself. The menu is usually defined in the resource file for your window manager (that's the .mwmrc file if you use the MWM window manager). You can edit your .mwmrc file (or any other window manager resource file) to add commands to your menus. For instance, here are some of the entries for my main menu (the one that comes when I press down the left mouse button):

```
Menu Main
{
  "Main Menu" f.title
  "Emacs"    ! "emacs"
  "Xcalc"    ! "xcalc"
  "Xbiff"    ! "xbiff"
  "Xterm     ! "xterm -name Spock"
}
```

The section Menu Main { indicates the beginning of the list of contents for this menu; the list ends with the } character. Each line describes a menu entry. On the left of each entry is the word or phrase that appears in the menu; on the right is the instruction that goes with the menu entry. So the phrase "Main Menu" is an f.title (which means it's a menu title). A command is indicated by ! and the command is put in double quotes: ! "emacs" runs the **emacs** program.

When I click on Emacs in the menu, the **emacs** program starts; when I click on Xcalc, the **xcalc** program starts; when I click on Xbiff, the **xbiff** program starts; and when I click on Xterm, another **xterm** program starts with the option **-name Spock**.

These are some of the common X programs; there are more, but they vary from system to system.

xterm   The X program used most, this gives you another command line window, and it provides you with an easy way to run two programs at once: you have one in each window.

xbiff   Shows you when you have mail waiting. This is an X Windows version of the **biff** program. When you get electronic mail, **biff** writes a few lines on the screen, messing up whatever you're looking at. **xbiff** is much less obtrusive—it's just a window with a picture that changes when you get mail.

xcalc   A calculator program.

emacs   The latest version of the **emacs** editor makes full use of X Windows if it's available. (For more information on **emacs**, see Chapter 17, "Circus Emacs-Imus.")

There are also games and demos, of course, including **xeyes** and **xroaches**. In the **xeyes** program, a pair of eyes appears on-screen and watches the mouse. Try to put the mouse pointer between the eyes. In **xroaches**, little computer roaches run around the screen and hide under your windows. Move a window and watch them scurry to another window. Some versions let you squash the bugs, too.

For your convenience, almost all X programs will give you a wordy help message if you run them with the option **-help**.

The Least You Need to Know

Those are the basics of GUIs. Although there's a lot more, this is enough to get you started.

➤ X Windows is a set of programming tools that provide windows, buttons, and mouse control for programs.

➤ X Windows can only be used on terminals with bit-mapped displays.

➤ To provide a standard look to windows, there are programming packages that describe how windows should look and how the mouse should behave. The most common packages are Motif and Open Look.

➤ Any program that works with X Windows is called an X program. To start an X program from the command line, type the X program's name and any options; end the command with an ampersand (&).

➤ X programs can also be started from menus; you can see a menu (if you have one) by clicking a mouse button while the mouse pointer is on an empty section of the screen.

The Root of the Matter: Files and Directories

Every year just before income tax time, I am forced to admit that I am organizationally challenged. My idea of a file is the big manila envelope into which I empty all the little slips of paper that accumulate in my wallet and any governmental mail that isn't a summons.

Despite this, I'm fine with computer files. A file is just a place to store related information, such as all the words that make up this chapter, or all my phone numbers, or a program. And a directory is just a place to store related files. Because I produce my letters using the computer, I store all of my work-related letters in one directory and all my personal letters in another directory. That way I don't get them mixed up.

Files and Paths and Directories

Let's start at the very beginning (a very good place to start). A file holds information. Like that box in your closet, it's a place to store things. You open it up, you throw something in, you close it. Just as you can put boxes inside of boxes, you can put files inside of files. A file that holds other files is called a *directory*.

The complete set of files on your computer is called the *file system*. The directory that holds all files and all other directories on the computer is referred to as the *root*, because all of the files and directories sprout from it, like a tree from its root. The file system (shown in the following figure) is sometimes called the file tree.

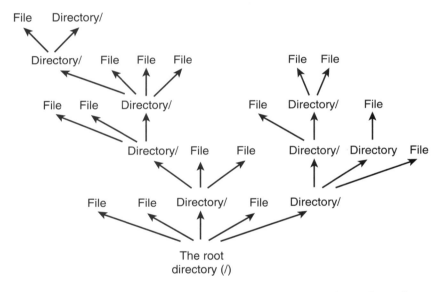

The file system spreads from the root directory like the branches of a tree.

Every file and every directory has a name to help you tell them apart. Two files can have the same name if they're in different directories because the computer looks at the *entire* path name of each file, and a file's entire name describes the path you take to get to that file. So we call a full name the *path name* or sometimes the *absolute path name*. An absolute path name always starts with a slash, because it describes the full path from the root (/) to the particular file or directory.

Think of your closet as a directory in which you store your belongings. Let's say you put last year's French maid Halloween costume in the closet. If you stored it in a shoe box inside a green box in your closet, you might tell someone looking for the costume to "Open the closet, get in the green box, and look in the shoe box for the French maid costume." To put these directions into UNIX language, instead of using words to say "in the box" or "in the directory," you use slashes for the words "in the." So if the French maid costume were a file you were looking for, the absolute path name would look like this:

/green box/shoe box/costume

If you were trying to find the file called costume, you'd start in the root directory (/), which is the equivalent of the closet. (Because root is at the beginning of every name, we don't bother to write it, but we keep the slash there. Any file or directory name that starts with / starts at the root directory.) So, in the root directory, you'd look for a subdirectory called green box. The next / tells you to move into a subdirectory below green box named shoe box. The next / means we're going into the directory shoe box to look for the file named costume.

You're always considered to be in a directory when you're in a UNIX session. The directory you're in is called your *current working directory*. You can also describe a file's path in terms of where you are now. For instance, if you already have the green box open, you could just say, "in the shoe box." Since you're giving the path relative to where you are now, this path name is called the *relative path name*.

If you're in a directory and you give the command **ls -l afile**, it's a

File A bunch of related information stored together. In UNIX, a file can also be a device that can receive or produce a stream of information.

Directory A file that contains other files and tells you how to find them. A directory contains only the list of file names and numbers where the information *about* those files can be found. You should use directories to store related files.

Absolute path name A path name that specifies exactly where a file is in the file system. An absolute path name starts with a slash (at the root directory). This is the equivalent of a AAA map for the file system.

Relative path name A path name that specifies where a file is in terms of your current directory. A relative path name never starts with a slash. This is the equivalent of directions given only in terms of right and left turns.

relative path name: you really mean the file named afile in your current directory. Relative path names never start with a slash, which distinguishes them from absolute path names.

An absolute path name is like a AAA map for the file system: it tells you both where to start and how to get to where you're going. A relative path name tells you how to get there based on your current position (or current working directory): it's like a set of directions consisting only of left and right turns.

Although the absolute path name always stays the same, a file can have different relative path names depending on what your current directory is. For example, take the path name /usr/ella/scores/gershwin. If your current directory is /, the relative path name is usr/ella/scores/ gershwin (with no leading /, because that's your current directory). Here are some possible combinations of current directory and relative path name for this file (as shown in the following figure):

If your current directory is:	The relative path name is:
/usr/ella	scores/gershwin
/usr/ella/scores	gershwin

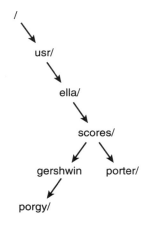

The directory structure described in the text.

Another way to look at this is that you can re-create the absolute path name by joining your current directory and the relative path name.

A directory that contains another directory is called the *parent* directory; the directory it contains is its *child*. A directory inside another directory is also called a *subdirectory* because it's under another directory. See the following figure:

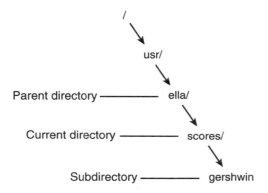

The parent and subdirectory of /usr/ella/scores.

The UNIX Differences

If you're a DOS user, you're already familiar with files, directories, and file names. However, there are some differences between files and directories on DOS and UNIX.

➤ UNIX uses the slash (/) instead of the backslash (\) to separate directories in a path name.

➤ UNIX distinguishes between uppercase and lowercase letters in path names.

Parent directory A directory that holds another directory. In the directory name, two dots (..) always refer to the directory that holds your current directory. (The root directory doesn't have a parent.) I talk more about this in Chapters 3, "In the Beginning Was the Word: login," and 8, "Branching Out: Working with Files and Directories."

Subdirectory Also called a *child directory*, this is a directory that's in another directory.

➤ In UNIX, names can be longer than eight characters, and you can put the dot anywhere in the name.

➤ There are no drive letters in UNIX path names. In DOS path names, the drive letter tells DOS to look on a different disk drive. (In fact, it's the colon that tells DOS this; that's why devices like printers have names that end in a colon.)

➤ UNIX systems can have more than one disk drive. The way that a disk drive is added to the file system hides the fact that it's a different drive. As a user, you never have to know what disk drive you're using.

➤ Like DOS, UNIX has **mkdir** (make directory) and **rmdir** (remove directory) commands. Unlike DOS, there are no **md** and **rd** commands.

What's in a Name?

What can you name your files and directories? Almost anything you want.

In theory you can use any letter in a UNIX file name except /. In practice, you should avoid any character that's special to your shell. Basically this limits you to all the letters and numbers, and some of the punctuation (including +, =, -, _, ., and ,).

You must remember that upper- and lowercase letters are different. A file named AARDVARK is different from one named Aardvark, which is still different from one named aardvark. Here's a rundown of the characters you can and cannot use when naming files:

DOs:

    ABCDEFGHIJKLMNOPQRSTUVWXYZ0123456789_-
    ,.abcdefghijklmnopqrstuvwxyz0123456789+=

DON'Ts:

    ~'""!%:;&*()?><[]|{}\ (space) (tab) (newline)

76

DON'T EVEN TRY IT:

/

Also remember these file naming guidelines:

➤ While you can use such characters as spaces and brackets in your file names, they turn out to be a nuisance. Because the command line tries to interpret them specially, you have to tell the shell not to treat them specially. (This is called escaping or quoting, and I talk about it in Chapter 25, "Neat Stuff.")

➤ If you're using a UNIX system derived from System V, the maximum length of any individual file or directory name is 14 characters.

➤ If you're using a UNIX system derived from BSD, the maximum length of any individual file or directory name is 255 characters.

➤ Because most UNIX vendors now provide features from System V and BSD, your system will probably accept file names of up to 255 characters.

➤ Use all this freedom to give files and directories names with some meaning. There's nothing worse than looking in a directory six months later and wondering what the file called ch4 is related to. You can save yourself a lot of mental anguish by using a name like chap04.command_line.

➤ Use directories to organize the files. Create a directory with a clear name, and put all the related files into it. It will make your life a lot easier in the future. For example, I stored all of the files for this book in a directory named CIG_UNIX. Each chapter had a name like chap07.root_of_files and chap01.least_you_need_to_know; all screen shots were stored in a subdirectory named screenshots. When I look at these directories in a year's time, I'll know what the files contain.

Isn't That Special?!

Some file names contain special characters that you should know about. If your file names starts with a dot (.), the file is a *hidden* file. (Only a dot at the beginning of the file name makes it hidden; a dot anywhere else doesn't have that effect.) Regular directory listings don't show hidden files; you have to use the **ls** command with the special **-a** option to see them.

To simplify typing, you can use UNIX's two special directory names: dot (.) and dot-dot (..)—or double-dot. The dot (.) represents your current directory; dot-dot (..) represents the parent of your current directory. (Of course, every directory except the root directory has a parent.) That means that two directories in the same directory are siblings. Using an example from earlier in this chapter, consider these combinations of current directories and relative path names for the file /usr/ella/scores/gershwin using dot (.) and dot-dot (..).

If your current directory is:	Your relative path name is:
/usr/ella/scores/gershwin	.
/usr/ella/scores/gershwin/porgy	..
/usr/ella/scores/porter	../gershwin

The relative path name ../gershwin means "go up one directory from the current directory and then go into the directory gershwin."

Here's another example of how to use this shortcut:

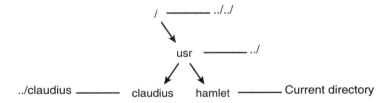

Relative pathnames, if your current directory is /usr/hamlet.

Let's say your current directory is hamlet (that is, you're currently in hamlet, which is in usr, which is in /). The directory, claudius, is a sibling of the hamlet directory under /usr. If you want to go to the directory /usr/claudius from /usr/hamlet, you can type either **cd /usr/claudius** or **cd ../claudius** to get there. From /usr/claudius, you can list the contents of /usr with the command **ls ..** or with **ls /usr**.

The tilde (~) is also considered a special character when it shows up at the beginning of a path name. It means "home directory." If there's a login name right after the tilde, the whole thing stands for "the home directory of *user*" (for instance, ~johnmc represents my home directory, /home/johnmc). If you don't specify a login name, UNIX assumes you mean your own home directory. If you want to copy a file to the directory named stuff in your home directory, you can specify the destination as ~/stuff. For me, ~/stuff is the same as /home/johnmc/stuff.

Making a File or Directory

Now you know (almost) everything about files and directories, but how do you make one?

You usually create a file with some other tool, such as an editor or an application program. You can create a new file which is a copy of an existing file with the **cp** command (discussed in Chapter 8, "Branching Out: Working with Files and Directories"). You can also create a new file using the **cat** command and file redirection. (I discuss **cat** in Chapter 8 and file redirection in Chapter 11, "More About Files (Some Useful Tips and Tricks)." For now, take them on faith.)

To create a file named memo, type the command **cat > memo** and press **Enter**. (You could use any file name instead of memo.) The cursor moves to the next line and waits. Now, everything you type, including Enter, goes into the file memo. To quit entering text into the file, press **Control+D**.

This is a pretty crude technique for creating files, but it works well for text files that are only a couple of lines long. If you want to create (or edit) longer files, it's easier to use an editor. (See Part III, "A Textbook on Text.")

You can also create a file with file redirection. I talk about file redirection in Chapter 11. Go there for more information.

mkdir will fail if you don't have permission to create a directory where you are. If you have trouble, go to your home directory to test the command. (For more about permissions, see "Changing Your File's Permissions" later in this chapter.)

To make a directory, you use the **mkdir** command. For example, to create a directory named reports in your home directory, enter the **cd** command to go to your home directory (you don't have to if you're already there). Then type **mkdir reports**. If the command works, you won't see a message. Use the **ls -F** command to see your new directory (the -F option tells UNIX to indicate directories by putting a / after the directory's name). UNIX responds by showing you the name of the directory you just created. (Your home directory may have other files and directories in it, of course.)

```
$ mkdir reports
$ ls -F
reports/
```

Some versions of **mkdir** let you make more than one directory at a time. For example, the command **mkdir reports minutes** creates two directories, one named reports and one named minutes, in the current directory. With these versions of the **mkdir** program, you can even create a directory and its subdirectory with the same command. For example, you can create the directory, called reports, and then the subdirectory august (under the reports directory) by typing **mkdir reports reports/august**. You'll notice that in order to tell **mkdir** that august is a subdirectory of reports, you must include the name of the parent directory, which is reports.

```
$ mkdir reports reports/august
$ ls
reports
$ cd reports
$ ls
august
```

One thing you should note, however, is that you can't put these arguments (**mkdir reports reports/august**) in the opposite order. The **mkdir** command cannot create the reports/august subdirectory until it creates the reports directory. The reports directory must exist first.

Some **mkdir** versions have an option that enables you to automatically create intermediate directory levels if they don't already exist.

The option is usually **-p**. So, in the previous example, if you typed the command **mkdir -p reports/august** and the reports directory didn't already exist, UNIX would create it first, and then create the august subdirectory under it.

Destroying a File or Directory

What happens when your directory becomes cluttered with a lot of unwanted files? The command **rm** (for "remove") gets rid of any unwanted file. Just type **rm** *filename* to blow the file away. You can even remove as many files as you want on one command line and remove files from more than one directory at a time, as this example shows:

```
$ rm minutes.txt minutes.bak minutes.ps ../minutes.other.doc
```

If you're really brave, you can get rid of all the files in the current directory with the * wild card (for more about wild cards, see Chapter 8, "Branching Out: Working with Files and Directories"):

```
$ rm *
```

You can remove directories with either the **rmdir** command or the **rm -r** command. The **rmdir** command removes only empty directories. For example, if the minutes directory contains no files or subdirectories, you can remove it with:

```
$ rmdir minutes
```

Use **rm *** with caution. Make sure you really want to get rid of all the files in the current directory. It doesn't hurt to list the contents of the directory first before you delete everything—just to be sure. You can also use the **-i** option to remove, which I discuss later in this chapter. The **-i** option makes **rm** ask you if the file should be deleted. (The i is for "inquire.")

If, for example, the minutes directory isn't empty but you want to eliminate everything in it, you can use **rm -r minutes**. The **-r** option makes **rm** "recursive": it removes all the files and subdirectories under the minutes directory, and then deletes the minutes directory. The only way you can delete a directory with the **rm** command is if you use the **-r** option with it.

Something that is *recursive* repeats itself until some condition is met. The command **rm -r** is recursive; when **rm** finds a non-empty directory, it goes into the directory and removes every file it finds (including hidden files). If it finds a non-empty subdirectory there, it goes into that and removes every file it finds. It continues this cycle until **rm** succeeds in deleting all the files in all the subdirectories. It then moves up a level to the next directory. Because everything in that directory has already been deleted, it can be deleted. It continues at this level until it's back where it started and can delete the directory you originally requested.

Everything I said about using **rm *** with caution goes *double* for **rm -rf ***. You probably had a good reason for making those files read-only, so you don't want to blow them away without thinking about it. Around the camp fire at UNIX techno-nerd summer camps, they tell horror stories of the system administrator who typed **rm -rf *** while he was in the root directory. It gives me shivers.

If some file you own is set to be read-only, **rm** asks you if you're sure you want to get rid of it. To delete it, press **y**; to keep it, press **n**. If you don't want to be asked, use the **-f** (for "force") option. For example, **rm -rf minutes** deletes the minutes directory and everything in it without asking your permission.

If you're the careful type (and you're smart), you can force **rm** to ask you if a file should be deleted by using the **-i** option. Normally, **rm** asks you for permission to delete a file only if it's a read-only file; the **-i** option makes **rm** ask you for every file. For example, suppose you're cautiously deleting the files project-notes-1 through project-notes-3. For the sake of this demonstration, you decide not to delete project-notes-2:

```
$ rm -i project-notes-1 project-notes-2 project-notes-3
Remove project-notes-1? y
Remove project-notes-2? n
Remove project-notes-3? y
$ ls
project-notes-2
```

The **-i** option is most useful with wild cards, which are a short form for specifying more than one file. (I discuss wild cards in Chapter 8, "Branching Out: Working with Files and Directories").

Changing Your File's Permissions

As I said earlier, every file is owned by somebody, and it has permissions. As far as files are concerned, there are three groups of people who might want access to the file, and they can each have different permissions: the owner of the file, the members in the same group as the owner of the file, and everyone else. You can see a file's permissions with the **ls -l** command.

UNIX lets you change the permissions for each of those groups using the **chmod** (change mode) command. (A file's permissions are sometimes called its mode.) You can only change permissions on a file you own. You can change who owns a file with the **chown** (change owner) command, however, on some systems, only the super-user can use **chown**.

> Sooner or later, you'll need to remove a file with a weird file name, and no matter how you type the command, it won't seem to work. This is probably because the file has an invisible character in its name. (Trying to track down file names with a backspace in the name is difficult.) Instead of having a fit, use **rm -i ***. For each file, **rm** asks you if you want to keep it; say yes until you get to the offending file.

Changing Read and Write Permissions

The **chmod** command changes the permissions assigned to the file for each of the three groups, the owner (or user who created it), other members of the owner's group, and everyone else (the others). A **chmod** command looks like this:

```
$ chmod ugo-w phonelist
```

This command takes away write permissions from the file phonelist. The permission change is the `ugo-w`. Let's look at each of the parts of this in detail.

> ➤ The `ugo` part indicates whose permissions we're changing: `u` stands for user, `g` stands for group, and `o` stands for other. Therefore, `ugo` tells UNIX that we want to change the permissions for everybody. (In fact, if you're changing everybody's permissions, you could also use the short form `a`, for all.)

83

➤ The - tells UNIX how we're changing the permission. The - indicates that we want to take away the permissions. On the contrary, a plus sign (+) adds permissions. If you want to make the permissions exactly equal to the specification in the next part, use an equals sign (=).

➤ The **w** shows which permissions we're changing. The **w** indicates that we're working with write permission, the ability to change a file. Other permissions include read (r) and execute (x). (Execute is only important for programs and for directories.) These are the same abbreviations the **ls -l** command uses to show permissions.

So, the example command above removes everybody's write permission from the file called phonelist. No one can change the file. When you list the file with **ls -l**, the permissions will be shown as **rw-rw-rw-**.

Let's say, however, that you decide you want to change the phone list after all. Because you're the owner, you're allowed to change the permissions; so you give yourself write permission again. You add your write permission back to the file with this command:

$ chmod u+w phonelist

As you learned above, the **u** indicates the user, the + adds permission, and the **w** shows that it's write permission. Once again, the owner of the file can make changes to the file.

Here's a summary of the parts of a permission:

Who Has Permission

u	User (individual)
g	Group (individual's group)
o	Other (everybody)
a	All users (everybody)

How to Change Permissions

+	Add a permission
-	Take away a permission
=	Make a permission equal to

84

Kind of Permission

r	Read file
w	Write (change) file
x	Execute program file

Now that you've got those basics under your belt, you can make a file (such as job.reviews) unreadable and unwriteable by everyone but you:

```
$ chmod go-rw job.reviews
```

- takes away the **rw** (read and write) permissions from **go** (group and others).

Here are some of the most common permissions.

Make read-only for everyone: **a-w**

Give everyone read and write permissions: **a+rw**

Take away write permission for others: **o-w**

Take away permissions from everyone but you: **go-rw**

If you want to make multiple changes to a file's permissions, you can use the **chmod** command more than once (which, frankly, is what I do), or you can join multiple changes in one command by separating them with commas. Here's how you take away everyone else's read, write, and execute permissions from a file called printpic, and add execute permission for yourself:

```
$ chmod go-rwx,u+x printpic
```

Even if you take away your own write permission on a file you own, you can still delete the file with the **rm** command. (However, UNIX will confirm the deletion with you first.)

 You can also represent the permissions as *numbers*. Suppose you have a file that has read and write permissions for everyone—**ls -l** shows the file's permissions as **rw-rw-rw-**. You can also represent this as a three-digit number, where the first number is the user's permission, the second number is the group's permission, and the third number is the "other" permission. Each of the letters in the **ls -l** permission listing has a numeric value—an r is worth 4, a w is worth 2, and an x is worth 1. If a group's permission is rw-, the numeric equivalent is 4 (r) + 2 (w) + 0 (-) = 6. The numeric equivalent of rw-rw-rw- is 666. (Ooooh, scary.)

You can give this number to **chmod** to *set* the permission. Instead of using **chmod a-x,a+rw** to make sure the permission is rw-rw-rw-, you can give the command **chmod 666** *filename*.

You can change permissions for directories, too. Give **chmod** a directory name instead of a file name. If I want to keep other people from reading files in a directory named private, I can take away their permissions to read and write there:

```
$ chmod go-rwx private
```

This keeps them from reading files in the directory private, writing files in the directory, or using **cd** to go into the directory. (You could then go in and change permissions on some files in the directory so other people could read and write them.)

When you're changing permissions on directories, remember these rules:

➤ You have to be able to execute a directory to access it with the **cd** command.

➤ You have to be able to read a directory to list its contents with the **ls** command.

➤ You have to be able to write in a directory to create or change files there.

Some Useful Directories

This section is intended to give you some idea of what the main directories are. Different systems may use different names, and your system administrator may have customized the system, but here's a starting point.

Directory	Description
/	The root directory.
/bin	Contains many of the programs.
/dev	Contains devices; never go here.
/etc	Contains system configuration files, control files. You don't need to go here either.
/etc/passwd	Contains your login information. (Don't worry; your password is encoded so no one can figure it out.)
/home	Some systems use this for users' home directories.
/lib	Program libraries; these are of interest to programmers only.
/opt	Optional packages on some systems. Sometimes called /usr/opt.
/tmp	Contains temporary files.
/u	Some systems use this for home directories.
/usr	Things for users; may contain home directories.
/usr/5bin	Contains System V programs.
/usr/local/bin	Contains programs added to the system locally.
/usr/man	Contains directories containing manual pages.
/usr/ucb	Contains BSD programs.

The Least You Need to Know

So that's the storage system here at Chez UNIX. Everything is in boxes, but we've labelled them all, and you can bring in your own boxes, fill them, empty them, and throw them out as you please.

➤ Every file has a name. Although the file's full name (or path) is unique on the system, any individual part of it may not be unique. A directory is a kind of file that holds other files.

➤ On System V systems, the name of a file or directory must be 14 characters or less. On BSD systems, it must be 255 characters or less.

➤ In a file or directory name, upper- and lowercase letters are different. You can use any character except / in a name, but you should stick with letters, numbers, and the comma, period, underline, or dash characters. (The symbols $, ~, and + are okay as long as they're not the first character.)

➤ To create a directory, use the **mkdir** command. To delete an empty directory, use the **rmdir** command.

➤ To delete a file, use the **rm** command. To delete a directory that isn't empty, use the **rm -r** command.

➤ To delete a file with a funny character in the name, use **rm i *** and say yes when you are asked to confirm deletion of the offending file.

➤ To change the permissions on a file or directory, use the **chmod** command.

Branching Out: Working with Files and Directories

In This Chapter

➤ Showing the contents of a directory

➤ Showing the contents of a file

➤ Copying a file

➤ Moving or renaming a file

➤ Using wild cards to specify files and directories

You can make a file; you can remove a directory. But can you see what's in a file or a directory? Can you list only the files that start with *z*? Can you move everything into another directory? Can you change your mind about a file or directory name? Can you find a file or directory even if you don't know exactly what you're looking for?

Of course you can! And I'm going to tell you how.

Listing Directory Contents

To list the contents of a directory, use the **ls** command, which is one of the most important commands in UNIX. You can't work with files if you don't know they're there. With **ls**, however, you can see what files you have, and you can get a lot of information about your directories and files. **ls** has a lot of options, and I'm going to tell you about the most used options and the kind of information each option gives you.

ls is short for "list," which is what **ls** gives you: a list of what's in the directory. If you don't specify a directory, **ls** lists the contents of your current working directory. Here I've specified the directory /u/rhood:

```
% ls /u/rhood
Mail                    bin                     maps
News                    bows                    notes
archery.contest         feathers                plans
arrows                  lincoln.green.suppliers sherwood
```

The files are normally listed in columns of equal width and in alphabetical order (although you probably noticed that all uppercase letters come before any lowercase letters).

When you use the **ls** command by itself, there's no way to tell whether something is a file or a directory. One way to do this is to use the **ls -F** option; the -F flag tells **ls** to add an extra character to the end of certain file names to tell you what kind of file it is.

```
% ls -F
Mail/                   bin/                    maps@
News/                   bows                    notes/
archery.contest         feathers                plans/
arrows/                 lincoln.green.suppliers sherwood*
```

Here's what the extra characters mean:

/   A directory

*   A program you can run (called an executable, because you can execute it)

@   A symbolic link (see Chapter 11 for information on links)

These two characters aren't shown in the previous example, and you won't see them very often, but I'm including them to be complete:

| | represents a named pipe

=   represents a socket

So Mail, News, arrows, bin, archery.contest, notes, and plans are all directories; bows, feathers, and lincoln.green.suppliers are files; sherwood is an executable program; and maps is a symbolic link.

There's no way to ask **ls** to show only files or only directories.

If you want to see all the files in a directory, including any hidden files, use the **-a** option with either the **ls** or **lc** command. (Most versions of **lc** have **-a**, and it does the same thing as **ls -a**.)

```
% ls -a
.                       News                    lincoln.green.suppliers
..                      archery.contest         maps
.cshrc                  arrows                  notes
.login                  bin                     plans
.logout                 bows                    sherwood
Mail                    feathers
```

The example above shows three hidden files: .cshrc, .login, and .logout. I'll tell you about these files in Chapter 19, "Environ-Mental Health."

Everything You Ever Wanted to Know (About Your Files)

Sometimes you need to know more about a file or files, like how big it is, or how old it is, or who owns it. To find out this type of information, ask **ls** for the long listing (**ls -l**). The following figure shows an extract from the listing for the /u/rhood directory:

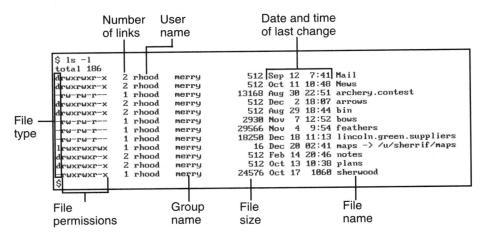

```
$ ls -l
total 186
drwxrwxr-x    2 rhood    merry         512 Sep 12  7:41 Mail
drwxrwxr-x    2 rhood    merry         512 Oct 11 10:48 News
-rw-rw-r--    1 rhood    merry       13168 Aug 30 22:51 archery.contest
drwxrwxr-x    2 rhood    merry         512 Dec  2 18:07 arrows
drwxrwxr-x    2 rhood    merry         512 Aug 29 18:44 bin
-rw-rw-r--    1 rhood    merry        2930 Nov  7 12:52 bows
-rw-rw-r--    1 rhood    merry       29566 Nov  4  9:54 feathers
-rw-rw-r--    1 rhood    merry       18250 Dec 18 11:13 lincoln.green.suppliers
lrwxrwxrwx    1 rhood    merry          16 Dec 20 02:41 maps -> /u/sherrif/maps
drwxrwxr-x    2 rhood    merry         512 Feb 14 20:46 notes
drwxrwxr-x    2 rhood    merry         512 Oct 13 10:38 plans
-rwxrwxr-x    1 rhood    merry       24576 Oct 17  1060 sherwood
$
```

Number of links · User name · Date and time of last change · File type · File permissions · Group name · File size · File name

*The **ls -l** command shows you a long listing of information about each file.*

Link An extra name for a file. In UNIX, a file can have more than one name attached to it. Links are very useful if you need the same file in two places at once. Suppose the file /my/file has an extra name (a link) called /your/file. Any changes that are made to /my/file show up automatically in /your/file because they're secretly the same file. When you use **rm** to remove a file, you're really taking away a link (or a name). When the last name is taken away, the file is deleted. You'll read more about links in Chapter 11, "More About Files (Some Useful Tips and Tricks)."

You can safely ignore the total line. After that, each line describes one file, telling you seven things about that file: the file's type, permissions, and number of links; the login name of the user who owns the file, the name of the group to which the owner belongs, the size of the file in bytes, the date the file was last changed, and the file's name. Look in Chapter 3 in the section "Home Sweet Home" for an in-depth breakdown of what all this information means. It can be very helpful if you know what you're looking at.

Another command you can use to get information about a file is the **file** command, which I describe in Chapter 12, "The Search Is On." **file** tries to guess what kind of file you have.

92

Show Me More!

And after all this, I still haven't told you how to look at the contents of a file. There are two commands that you can use to look inside your files: **cat** and **more**.

I mention the **cat** command here because you can use it to view files on the screen. However, as you see in the following figure, with a long file (such as /etc/passwd), the text just streams up and off the screen. Try it on the /etc/passwd file, which lists all of the users on the system. Your command should look like this:

```
$ cat /etc/passwd
```

cat is good for very short files, but not so good for longer ones. The **cat** command has some other useful purposes that I will tell you about in Chapter 11, "More About Files (Some Useful Tips and Tricks)."

For reading longer files, I suggest using a program called **more**. The program is called **more** because it shows you one screenful of the file and, at the bottom of the screen, asks if you want to see more. To look at a file or files, just type **more** and the name of the file or files you want to look at. For example, if you want to look at the password file on your system, you can type **more /etc/passwd**. You'll see a screen something like this one. Note the bottom line on the screen.

```
root:y3gGfnsXis1B6:0:1:Operator:/:/bin/csh
supervisor:*:0:1:Operator:/:/bin/csh
nobody:*:65534:65534::/:
nouser:*:25000:25000:Dummy user:/usr/nobody:/etc/nosh
daemon:*:1:1::/:
sys:*:2:2::/:/bin/csh
bin:*:3:3::/bin:
uucp:1DGSZRHhD/AGg:4:8:MKS UUCP:/var/spool/uucppublic:
operator:*:5:5:System Operator:/usr/opr:/bin/csh
onews:*:6:6::/var/spool/news:/bin/csh
ingres:*:7:7::/usr/ingres:/bin/csh
sync::1:1::/:/bin/sync
sysdiag:*:0:1:System Diagnostic:/usr/diag/sysdiag:/bin/csh
news:BZ3N0NJDvl63I:9:9:Usenet news:/usr/lib/news:/bin/csh
nuucp:*:10:1:UUCP dialin:/usr/spool/uucppublic:/usr/lib/uucp/uucico
Uucp:W4c9wKo7pEzWU:10:1:UUCP dialin:/usr/spool/uucppublic:/usr/lib/uucp/uucico
Udecvax:pnNpYZNhESSzI:10:1:UUCP:/usr/spool/uucppublic:/usr/lib/uucp/uucico
Umkseast:009Yg1p2sPYow:10:1:UUCP:/usr/spool/uucppublic:/usr/lib/uucp/uucico
Uposty:6bgtNITQ8018Y:10:1:John Postma,UUCP:/usr/spool/uucppublic:/usr/lib/uucp/u
ucico
Ujnana:yMfI7zJE.6IkY:10:1:Scott McCurdie,UUCP:/usr/spool/uucppublic:/usr/lib/uuc
p/uucico
Umickey:tbp.Jo7nwxXPU:10:1:Michael Ding, UUCP:/usr/spool/uucppublic:/usr/lib/uuc
[/etc/passwd](41%)
```

*This mess is a password file. You are not expected to understand it, but it's certain to be long enough to test the **more** command.*

93

The `[/etc/passwd]`(41%) line tells you that what you see displayed on-screen is 41 percent of the passwd file. If you want to see the remaining 59 percent, do one of these two things:

➤ To show one more line, press **Enter**.

➤ To show another screenful of text, press **Spacebar**. It doesn't actually advance an entire screenful; two lines of the old text are left so you can keep the thread of what you're reading.

If you don't need to see the remaining 59 percent of the file, simply press **q** to quit. (You probably recognize **more** as the program that shows you man pages.)

Once you're reading a file with **more**, you can search ahead in the file for a particular word or phrase. (This is a big help when you're trying to get through some really big man pages.) Instead of pressing **Spacebar** or **Enter**, type **/*text*** (where *text* is the word or phrase you want to find) and press **Enter**. In fact, the phrase can be any regular expression. See Chapter 13, "Matchmaker, Matchmaker (Regular Expressions)" to learn about regular expressions.

Let's say you want to search for the word "alex." To find the next mention of "alex," type:

```
/alex
```

If **more** can't find the word, it complains with a message at the bottom of the screen. If it can find the word, it adjusts the screen so the word you're searching for is on the third line of the screen, as in the following figure.

```
Uwalter:HdN3E1rxMFVkc:10:1:GRW Enterprises:/usr/spool/uucppublic:/usr/lib/uucp/u
ucico
Ualex:CqHyZrxMVBg06:10:1:alex at home:/usr/spool/uucppublic:/usr/lib/uucp/uucico
Utestia:H0tU0mrIO7OBI:10:1:chrisk's testing machine:/usr/spool/uucppublic:/usr/l
ib/uucp/uucico
Umksia:A7rqtts73YonA:10:1:mksia server:/usr/spool/uucppublic:/usr/lib/uucp/uucic
o
Ulapchuck:2kpu7nqT/Y6cA:10:1:Chuck's Laptop:/usr/spool/uucppublic:/usr/lib/uucp/
uucico
Ulapterr:thwiYBt0a99mY:10:1:Terry's Laptop:/usr/spool/uucppublic:/usr/lib/uucp/u
ucico
Ulaplesl:tF9bP/mhNKn8E:10:1:Lesley's Laptop:/usr/spool/uucppublic:/usr/lib/uucp/
uucico
Uguppy:PogBEQoIQxGe.:10:1:Kevin D:/usr/spool/uucppublic:/usr/lib/uucp/uucico
Uatoy:jfwKQSScYchLw:10:1:andy at home:/usr/spool/uucppublic:/usr/lib/uucp/uucico
Uuutest:Kif58FAC4I4q.:10:1:UUCP testing:/usr/rd/spool/uucppublic:/usr/rd/lib/uuc
p/uucico
alex:Pt1LXtvphcFDo:16:32:Alex White,InterOpen,4311,8860812:/u1/alex:/usr/rd/bin/
sh
andy:9/rjhq75peduA:64:10:Andy Toy,CS,4333,5717035,119 John Street East, Waterloo
, Ontario, CANADA N2J 1G2:/u2/andy:/bin/csh
+::0:0:::
[/etc/passwd](EOF)
```

more shows you where it found the word you asked for. In this case, we asked for "alex." It's on the third line of the screen.

This screen shot illustrates two of the problems with searching in **more**. First, most versions of **more** won't highlight the text once they've found it. (Some do. I don't have one of those.) Second, when **more** displays the text on the third line, it's not on the third line of text, it's the third line of the screen. In the figure, the word "alex" is actually on the *second* line of text, but because the first line wraps, the word "alex" is on the *third* line of the screen. (It took me three years to figure that out; until then, I just figured text searching in **more** was broken and pointless.)

Moving and Renaming Files and Directories

Sometimes you want to move a file from its current directory to another directory. Maybe you've been working on a document in your home directory, but now it's time to put it in your company's official document directory. Or maybe you're just reorganizing the files in a directory, and you want to move a bunch of related files into a subdirectory. Or maybe you want to change file names to make them more meaningful. You do all this with the **mv** command (which stands for you-know-what). You can do three things with the **mv** command: move a file or files into a different directory, change the name of a file or directory, or do both things at once (move a file or directory someplace else and change its name).

When you move a file, the file takes on a new path name, because you've changed its location. Therefore, the **mv** command essentially changes the file's path name. And just as the **mv** command can change the path name, it can also change the file name because the **mv** command treats path names and file names in the same way. You tell **mv** what you want it to do by the arguments you give it. Keep reading; I promise this will all make sense very soon.

If you want to move a file or files into a different directory, give **mv** the name of the file (or files) you want to move and then the name of the directory into which it's going. The file's name stays the same. To move a file called shortcake into the directory /usr/johnmc/recipes, type:

```
$ mv shortcake /usr/johnmc/recipes
```

If you do an **ls**, shortcake is no longer in the current directory; if you do an **ls** on /usr/johnmc/recipes, you'll see /usr/johnmc/recipes/shortcake. The file name is the same, but the *path* has changed because you now get to it in a different way.

This works even if shortcake is a directory, because **mv** moves directories, too. When you move a directory, all the files contained *in* that directory are moved with it. Suppose shortcake is a directory, and it contains a file called strawberry. To move the shortcake directory, you would type **mv shortcake /usr/johnmc/recipes**. If you then did an **ls** of the directory /usr/johnmc/recipes/shortcake, you would find the file strawberry. So the file that used to be shortcake/strawberry has become /usr/johnmc/recipes/shortcake/strawberry.

You can move as many files as you want into a directory by typing **mv *file1 file2 pathname*.** For example, I have two files named blackberry and elderberry in my current directory, which is /usr/johnmc. To move these files to /usr/johnmc/recipes/shortcake, I type:

```
$ mv blackberry elderberry /usr/johnmc/recipes/shortcake
```

96

To move every file in one directory to another directory, you can use wild cards (I talk about wild cards later in this chapter). Using wild cards makes this task easy and quick. For example, let's say your current directory is /project/solar/notes/tom. All the files within the tom subdirectory really belong one level above tom in the notes directory (in this case, the notes directory is the parent directory of the tom subdirectory). To move all the files from the current directory into the parent directory, use this command:

```
$ mv * ..
```

The * is a wild card that represents everything in the tom directory. As you remember from Chapter 7, dot-dot (..) is just another name for the directory above tom, which is the notes directory.

As I mentioned earlier, you can use the **mv** command to change the name of a file. If you want to change the file's name from LIST to list, just move the file to the new file name:

```
$ mv LIST list
```

In this example, you're changing (or moving) the file LIST to the new name list in the current directory. When you use the **mv** command to change the name of a file, it is important to remember that the original file goes away with the creation of the new file name. This is different from the **cp** (copy) command, in which the original file stays intact and a copy is created with a different name. (I'll talk about the **cp** command later in this chapter.)

You can use the **mv** command to rename only one file at a time. If the new name is the same as that of an existing file, the new one replaces the old one. You should be careful doing this because UNIX does not warn you before it overwrites the existing file. (However, a file can't replace a directory; if the file name you enter is the same as that of a directory, you'll get an error message from **mv**.)

Well, you've learned how to move a file, and you've learned how to rename a file. What if you want to move a file to a new location and give it a new name at the same time? You would type **mv *oldname* / *newpathname/newname*. UNIX moves the file to the new location and changes its name. For example, to move and rename the file /library/books/overdue to the new location of /bills/paid and change its name to library, type:

```
$ mv /library/books/overdue /bills/paid/library
```

The directory /bills/paid must already exist for this to work; **mv** won't create it for you. People often make the same mistakes when using **mv**.

Even though you may have done it using DOS, don't try to rename a whole bunch of files from one file extension to another using wild cards. This works in DOS; it doesn't work in UNIX. There is a way around it, but it involves a little bit of shell programming. If you've got a whole lot of files to move from one file extension to another, ask a guru to explain the **for** loop and variable substitution.

Copying Files and Directories

The process for making a copy of a file is almost identical to that for moving a file, except the original file doesn't go away. The command you use is called **cp**. To make a copy of a single file or directory, give **cp** the names of both the original file and the new file in the format **cp *oldname newname*.**

```
$ cp valuable.data temporary.copy
```

If you were to do an **ls** on your directory, you would see both of the files. You can make a copy of any file you can read.

Unlike **mv**, **cp** doesn't copy subdirectories inside a directory unless you tell it to with the **-r** option. (The **-r** stands for "recursive" or "repeat.") The format for the command is **cp -r *olddirectory newdirectory*.** For instance, a system administrator might use a command like this to create the home directory for a new account:

```
$ cp -r /u/guest /u/dana
```

This makes a copy of /u/guest, including all of its subdirectories, and calls it /u/dana. /u/dana now contains copies of all the subdirectories of /u/guest.

To copy a file or files into a directory, use the **cp** command. The format for the command is **cp *file ... directory*.** (The *file ...* means that you can name more than one file in the command; it's common in usage statements, which I described in Chapter 4, "Your Wish Is My Command Line.") For example, the command to copy /etc/passwd into your current directory looks like this:

```
$ cp /etc/passwd .
```

Another option of **cp** that's very useful is **-i**. When you copy a file into a directory, your new file replaces any old file that has the same name. The **-i** option tells **cp** to ask you if you want to replace the existing file. To replace a file, press **y** (yes). If you press **n** (no), **cp** doesn't copy the file.

Wild About Wild Cards

I've told you already that UNIX users are lazy typists. Instead of typing multiple file names, they want to use shortcuts called *wild cards*. You almost always use these wild cards with parts of file names. Wild cards are shortcuts that make it possible for you to name more than one file at a time or to name just one file without typing the entire file name.

There are three wild cards you can use: *, ?, and []. Each one does something different:

> **Wild card** A character that represents one or more unknown characters in a file name. It's called a wild card because it stands for other characters, just as a wild card in poker (and even some games of rummy) stands for another card. The three wild cards are * (which represents multiple characters), ? (which represents any one character), and [] (which represent any character you put between the square brackets).

Wild Card	Description
*	Matches any text string in a file name.
?	Matches any one letter of a file name.
[ ]	Matches only the letters you specify to be matched.

Generally you use * to cover as many files as possible on one command line, and you use ? and [] to eliminate as many files as possible from the list.

You will use the * wild card the most because it represents any combination of characters. For example, **ls *** lists all the files in the current directory, and the command **rm /project/cancelled/*** removes all the files in the directory /project/cancelled/.

Wild cards come in very handy when you're looking for a file but you can't remember its exact name. If you only know part of a file's

If you follow some consistent file naming procedures, wild cards are much more useful. For example, if you name all your letters with file names that end in ltr, you can use the command *ltr to access all your letters.

name, you can use * to find the file. Let's say you're looking for a file that you know starts with A. To list all files with names that start with A, you would use the command **ls A***. Because the * stands in for any letters that might come after A in a file name, **ls** shows you all files that begin with A. Then you can look for the one particular file you need. If you know more information about the name to begin with, you can narrow down the list of file names that **ls** returns by providing all the information you know. For example, if you know the file name starts with a and ends with doc, use **ls a*doc**.

The * is an inclusive sort of wild card; you use it to affect as many files as possible. However, sometimes you need to be a bit more restrictive. Because the ? wild card stands for only one letter in a file's name, the result of its use in a command would be much more limited. Let's suppose your directory has these files:

```
intro.doc       part1.text      test.doc

parking.doc     parties.doc     part1.doc

part2.doc
```

How do you name only part1.doc and part2.doc without typing both names? In this example, there's no easy way to use * because it matches the characters in several of the file names: if you typed part*doc, you would get parties.doc and parking.doc, as well as part1.doc and part2.doc. This is where the ? wild card comes in handy. Because it stands for only one character, it returns only those file names that have one character in that position, as you see here.

```
$ ls part?.doc
part1.doc part2.doc
```

Because there are only two file names in the listing above with one character after part (part1.doc and part2.doc), the ? in this case stands for 1 and for 2. (If there were a file called party.doc in the listing, it would match too; in that case, ? would also also stand for y.)

You can use more than one ? wild card character in a row. If you typed par????.doc, **ls** would match parking.doc and parties.doc but not part1.doc and part2.doc (because they don't have four letters between the par and the .doc). However, in order to use multiple ? wild cards successfully, you have to know exactly how many characters the file name contains.

Sometimes you have to be even more restrictive with your search techniques in order to save time. When a wild card that stands for all letters is too broad, the [] wild card lets you name specific letters to match as search criteria for finding the files you want. To illustrate this, let's add party.doc to the directory. Now when you type part?.doc, you see three file names: part1.doc, part2.doc, and party.doc. If you don't want to include party.doc in your command, you have to go back to typing all the file names (ugh!). Or, you can use a new wild card to name the letters you want to see between part and .doc. This wild card, [], is a bit different: you put the letters you want to match between the square brackets.

If you want to name only the files part1.doc and part2.doc, you can use the form part[12].doc. On the other hand, if you want to name only the files part2.doc and party.doc, you can use part[y2].doc.

Remember that no matter how many letters you put between the square brackets, they still only match one letter in a file's name. The form part[y2].doc would never match a file named party2.doc because the [y2] tells **ls** to search for either a y or a 2 in that position.

If you're putting a range of consecutive characters into square brackets, there's a short form for that. (Yes, in UNIX there are even short forms for short forms.) You indicate a range in square brackets with a dash; [0–9] tells **ls** to accept any number zero through nine in that position. For example, suppose you now have nine files, part1.doc through part9.doc in the directory. You want to include them all in a command, but you still don't want to name party.doc. Instead of typing part[123456789].doc, you can type part[1–9].doc. You can use any of the following ranges with the square bracket wild card. You can even put more than one range in the brackets. The form [A-LN-Z] represents all capital letters except M.

[A–Z] Represents all capital letters

[0–9] Represents the numbers 0 through 9

[a–z] Represents all lowercase letters

[A–l] Represents all capital letters and lowercase letters from a to l.

By mixing these three wild cards in file names, you can name files very succinctly. For instance, if you wanted to remove all files that started with capital letters, **rm [A-Z]*** would do it.

Wild Cards Going Wild

Here are some things to be aware of when using wild cards.

➤ Remember that * by itself doesn't include the hidden files. You have to specify those with **ls -a** if you're doing a file listing or with **.*** otherwise.

➤ If you're a long-time DOS user, you're probably used to the idea that *.* matches all the files. Not in UNIX. In DOS, every file secretly has a dot in its name, but that's not true in UNIX. In UNIX, the wild card pattern *.* matches all files that have a dot somewhere in their names. To really match all the files in the directory, use *.

➤ Some commands can have dangerous side effects if you use them on the wrong file. For instance, it's almost impossible to get back a file after you've deleted it with **rm**. (I talk about this in Chapter 10, "When It Goes Wrong.") If a command is hard to undo, be careful when using it with a wild card like *.

The Least You Need to Know

➤ To list the contents of a directory, use **ls**. The three most useful options for **ls** are **-a** (show all files), **-F** (show the types of files), and **-l** (show a long list of information about files).

➤ To move a file or directory, use **mv** *oldpathname newpathname*. To rename a file or directory, use **mv** *oldname newname*.

➤ To copy a file or a directory, use **cp** *original copy*. To copy a directory and any directories inside it, use **cp -r** *original copy*.

➤ Wild cards stand in for one or more unknown characters and can be used as shortcuts to avoid typing out multiple similar file names. The three available wild cards are *, ?, and [].

Part II
UNIX Tips and Trix

You've got the moves. You can get in there, get on with it, get it over with, and get out. Now it's time to get fancy. You'll learn how to print a file, fix some problems that might crop up, search for information on the UNIX system, and hook programs together with pipes to create new commands. This is real work!

You ain't no silly rabbit: these trix definitely aren't for kids.

MOMENTS IN COMPUTER HELL #607:

MISSING THE SAVE

Chapter 9

Printing Is Pressing

In This Chapter

➤ How the printing system works

➤ Sending text to a printer

➤ Finding out the status of a print job

➤ Cancelling a print job

➤ Formatting text for printing

Working with all these files doesn't help much if you can't get your work down on paper (the paperless society is just somebody's pipe dream). This chapter talks about how you get words from inside the computer onto paper. Of course, first you have to have a printer.

The printing commands on UNIX are for printing text files, files you've created using an editor such as **vi** or **emacs** (see Chapters 16, "Viva vi!," and 17, "Circus Emacs-Imus"), mail messages you've received, or the output of commands. Although text files may look pretty plain to those who are used to using word processing packages, there are some things you can do to make text files look more presentable. I'll tell you about these formatting commands in this chapter as well.

These printing commands cannot be used with files created in applications such as a word processor or spreadsheet, because those files are usually not text files—they contain hidden control characters that mess up the printing. Fortunately, most applications have a print command inside them that will handle all the details of printing for you.

(This is similar to DOS applications—you can print text files from the DOS command line, but to print files from applications, you need to be inside the application to take advantage of these extra printing features.)

The Printing Business

How do you go about printing something on a UNIX system? It's like taking documents to a copy shop. When you drop off the document at a print shop, the clerk takes your name and other information (such as "How many copies?" and "Is it really *that* urgent?") and places your document in the stack of things to do. Another clerk picks up your document and makes the copies according to the instructions the first clerk wrote down. You go back to the copy shop to pick up your copies.

Spool directory A directory used as a storage queue, where files (which are jobs-to-be-done) are stored until they're printed. There are spool directories for mail, printing, network news, and certain kinds of file transfers. The name comes from the fact that in the old days, files to be printed had to be stored on a spool of tape to be taken to the printer.

Similarly, in UNIX, the **lp** command serves as the clerk, taking all the necessary information about your file. As the clerk queues your work in a stack of copies to be made, **lp** puts your file in a special directory, called a *spool directory*, where your file stays until it can be printed. Spool directories are usually subdirectories in /var/spool or /usr/spool (if you care).

Another program, called a *scheduler*, keeps looking in the spool directory for files to print. When it finds your file, it sends it to the printer to print according to your specifications.

This entire system assumes that you can send text files directly to your printer without any special formatting. Although that used to be the case with the old line printers (since printing plain text was their forté), with today's laser printers, color printers, fax printers, and what-have-you, that's not really a reasonable assumption. Most laser printers require that the files be "processed" in some way. The information in the file has to be translated into a language the printer understands.

 The two most popular printer "languages" right now are Hewlett-Packard's PCL (printer control language) and Adobe's PostScript. PCL tends to be used more for business applications, and PostScript is more for graphics and desktop publishing; but that's just a tendency. In my experience, PostScript is more popular for UNIX systems (even though it's more expensive) because the PostScript language files are simply text files, like so much else on UNIX.

Not to worry, most UNIX systems provide a command to translate files into the appropriate printer language for you. For example, our company uses a command called **hpr** (instead of the **lp** command) to send text to a Hewlett-Packard printer. Ask your system administrator if you need a special command.

If you use a BSD system, the commands have different names, but they behave the same. This list shows you the System V UNIX commands and their BSD equivalents. You'll find out how to use each of these commands later in this chapter.

UNIX Command	BSD Equivalent
lp	lpr
lp -dprinter	lpr -Pprinter
lpstat	lpq
cancel	lprm
LPDEST	PRINTER

Printing a File

Before we start, you should know that every printer has a name. This is so you can choose which printer to print on—you can give the printer's name, but you don't *have* to.

The simplest way to print a text file is to use the **lp** command followed by the name of the file you want to print. Here's how to print a file called violet.blue.

```
$ lp violet.blue
job id: crayon-100a
```

Each time you use the **lp** command, it gives you a *job id*, which, in this case, is `crayon-100a`. The job id is like your receipt from the copy shop: it identifies this particular print request. (The format of the job id number varies with the brand and version of UNIX you have.) You only need the job id if you have to cancel the job later. You can usually ignore it, since there are other ways to get the number if you need it.

If you need to, you can print more than one file at a time by entering multiple file names on the command line. *When you do, you must include a space between file names in order for the **lp** command to understand that you want to print two files.* For example, if you wanted to print the files blue.green and red.orange, your command would look like this:

```
$ lp blue.green red.orange
job id: crayon-101a
```

You can also print multiple files using wild card characters (as discussed in Chapter 8, "Branching Out: Working with Files and Directories"). For example, the command below prints all files in the current directory that have names ending with the extension .txt.

```
$ lp *.txt
job id: crayon-102a
```

If you change a file between the time you use **lp** to send the file and the time it prints, the change may show up in the printed copy. This is because **lp** just stores a request to print a particular file. When the scheduler gets around to fulfilling the request, it prints the file as it is at that time. Likewise, if you give the **lp** command and then delete the file, it may not print. You can get around this with the -c option: **lp-c** file includes a copy of the file directly with the printer request.

Selecting a Printer

When your system administrator sets up the printing system, he or she selects a default printer. The *default printer* is the printer that is used if you do not name or request a specific printer. If your UNIX system has more than one printer, you may not want to use the default printer (maybe it's downstairs or in the basement or in another building). You may want to print using a different printer. To do so, you must tell UNIX what printer you want to use.

As I told you in Chapter 7, "The Root of the Matter: Files and Directories," every hardware device in UNIX (even your terminal) has a name. That's because UNIX thinks that hardware devices are files. Following that rule, every printer also has a name. You can get a list of all available printers on your system by typing the command **lpstat -p**. This command is not always useful because you don't know which printer goes with which name. Somehow, you'll have to find out the name of the printer you want. Your best bet is to ask around.

Here's an example of **lpstat -p** output:

```
$ lpstat -p
printer crayon is idle. enabled since Wed Nov  9 18:49:05 EST 1994.
available.
printer ink is busy. enabled since Thu Nov 10 09:32:16 EST 1994.
available.
```

Your version may have different output. Notice that the printer named ink is both "busy" and "available"—on this system, that means it's currently printing something (it's busy), but it is accepting new requests (it's available).

Another command, **lpstat -a**, shows you only the printers that are accepting printing requests:

```
$ lpstat -a
printer crayon accepting requests since Wed Nov  9 18:49:05 EST 1994.
printer ink accepting requests since Thu Nov 10 09:32:16 EST 1994.
```

Suppose there are two printers available named ink and crayon. The default printer is ink; that is, when you use the **lp** command and don't specify a printer, the file prints on the printer named ink. However, today you want to print on the printer named crayon (crayon

109

Notice that there's no space between the option and the name of the printer. That's true for the options you use with all of the commands in this chapter: **lp**, **lpstat**, **fmt**, and **pr**.

prints in color). If you only use this printer once in awhile, you simply specify the name of the printer on the command line. To specify a printer other than the default printer, use the **-d** (for destination) option with the **lp** command. For example, to send the file proposal to the printer named crayon, your command would look like this:

```
$ lp -dcrayon proposal
job id: crayon-205
```

If you always want your files to print to some other printer, you can permanently change your default printer by changing the **LPDEST** environment variable. To give this information to the **lp** command, change your **LPDEST** environment variable so it is the name of the printer you want to use. For example, suppose your company just added a new printer called pencil, and it's right next to your desk. You'd rather print on pencil because it's convenient. Therefore, you want to set your **LPDEST** environment variable to be pencil. Use the following command:

```
$ export LPDEST=pencil
```

Now your default printer is pencil. You don't need to use **-d** to print on pencil. However, if you want to print on any other printer (even ink, which was originally the default), you *do* need to use the **-d** option.

If your company has a number of printers, chances are your system administrator has already set your **LPDEST** environment variable to be the default printer that you want. For more information about environment variables, see Chapter 19, "Environ-Mental Health."

Printing Multiple Copies

What if you want to print more than one copy? You could just use the **lp** command several times, but it's more efficient to tell **lp** how many copies you want. (This turns your UNIX system into a very large photo-copier.) Use the **-n** option to tell **lp** how many copies you want. Put the number right after the **-n**. For example, to print five copies of the file minutes.Dec.12, use this command:

```
$ lp -n5 minutes.Dec.12
request id is 947
```

What's Waiting to be Printed?

PROBLEM: You sent the file off to be printed twenty minutes ago, but you have yet to hear the hum of the printer and the familiar cry of the office neat freak: *"Please* don't leave your printouts on the printer!" What could be going on?

If **lp** or **lpstat** tells you the scheduler is not running, you need to get the system administrator to restart it.

ANSWER: Maybe the printer isn't working. Maybe somebody has a really big file just ahead of yours. Maybe the office neat freak is busy adding more paper to the printer's paper tray. Whatever it may be, you need to see what's waiting to print, to see if your job has gone to the printer yet. In UNIX, this is called "checking the print queue."

The command for checking the print queue is **lpstat** (for lp status). Without options or arguments, **lpstat** shows you the status of your print requests on the default printer. For example, if your login name was ohenry, you might see something like this:

```
$ lpstat
101 ohenry      19237 bytes gift-of-magi
```

You'll see the job id, your login name, the size of your file, and finally, the name of the file that you sent off to be printed. The list only shows files that haven't printed (or finished printing) yet.

Usually, however, you want to see everything in the print queue (so you know what jobs are ahead of you). To see jobs for all users on the printer you are using, use the **-u** option (for users).

```
$ lpstat -u
pencil-100 mproust    21735478 bytes things-past.txt
pencil-101 ohenry        19237 bytes gift-of-magi
```

The top job in the list is the one currently printing. Here, the user mproust has a big job ahead of yours. In a situation like this, you might want to use a different printer. You can look at the status of all printers on the system with the **-o** option.

```
$ lpstat -o
crayon:
pen:
pencil:
pencil-100 mproust    21735478 bytes things-past.txt
pencil-101 ohenry        19237 bytes gift-of-magi
```

From this, you can see that there are no files waiting to print on the printers crayon and pen. Hurry! Send your print job to one of those printers before someone beats you to the punch.

If you want to see what's queued up for some of the printers but not all of them, you can list the printers you want to know about. (This is useful if your company has a lot of printers.) Put the list of printers after the **-o** option. If the list has more than one printer, put the list in double quotes, like this: **lpstat -o"crayon pencil"**.

Stop the Presses!

Well, you've gone and done the inevitable: you sent the wrong file to the printer. It wouldn't have been so bad if it wasn't 150 pages worth of the wrong information. You can just hear the spotted owls screeching at you for unnecessarily killing the tree they live in, and you're cringing with guilt thinking, "How do I stop the printer?!" To stop a print job, use the **cancel** command.

Without any other information, **cancel** ends all the print jobs you have waiting, including the one currently going to the printer. If you want to stop one print job out of many, specify the job's id number. (The number may still be visible on your screen from the **lp** command, or you can get it with the **lpstat** command.) For example, this command cancels job 102:

```
$ cancel 102
189vila9283102 dequeued
190vila9283102 dequeued
```

Note that you can only cancel print jobs that you sent. If you need to cancel somebody else's print job, you'll have to ask the system administrator or someone else with super-user access to do it (and you'll probably have to have a darn good reason).

Formatting for Printing

When you go pick up your printed files (don't worry, I'll wait), one thing you'll notice is the complete lack of formatting. That's because **lp** just dumps your text file into your printer without inserting any page-break or formatting commands into the file. Don't lose heart; there are a couple of commands and some options you can use to improve the appearance of your printed files.

To format the paragraphs in your file so all the lines are about the same length, you can use the **fmt** command. In longer files, you'll sometimes have problems with where the page breaks: for example, text runs to the bottom of the page and sometimes onto the next page, text gets chopped off the page, and so on. To insert blank lines into your file so the pagination works correctly, use the **pr** command. You'll learn about these commands in the following sections.

Formatting with fmt

The **fmt** command formats text so all the lines in a paragraph are about the same length. **fmt** isn't very sophisticated, though; it doesn't even know about hyphenating words. **fmt** is intended for simple files like mail messages. If you have a very complicated document to format, you should use a word processing program. (The word processing program will contain its own print command.)

fmt joins short lines and breaks long lines. It fits text into a maximum line length of 72 characters (which fits comfortably on most screens that are 80 characters wide). However, **fmt** doesn't join two lines if:

➤ The indent changes from one line to the next (there are more or fewer spaces at the beginning of one line than there were at the beginning of the previous line).

➤ One of the lines is blank.

➤ A line starts with a dot (.).

You can separate paragraphs with a blank line or a change in indent (such as by starting a paragraph with a tab or some spaces), or by starting a line with a dot to ensure the **fmt** command formats your paragraphs correctly.

For example, if you use the **lp** command to print a file with very short lines like this poem:

```
Jack (not Jill)
Went up the hill
To fetch a pail of water.
Jack fell down
And sued the town
For damages, the rotter
```

the file prints with short lines. That's great if you're printing poetry, but most of us don't write poetry (not at work, anyway).

However, if you run **fmt** on the poem (as in **fmt nursery**), your output will look like this figure.

```
/home/johnmc$ fmt nursery
Jack (not Jill) Went up the hill To fetch a pail of water.  Jack fell
down And sued the town For damages, the rotter
/home/johnmc$
```

*An example of **fmt** output.*

The **fmt** command is limited in the sense that it can only write the formatted text to the screen. That's not very useful because, typically, you want to print the formatted text. One way to print a formatted file is to save it in a new file and then print that new file. For example, to save the formatted version of nursery in the file nursery.formatted, use the > symbol.

```
$ fmt nursery > nursery.formatted
```

The > symbol tells the UNIX system to put the output in the file you name after the >. This is called file redirection, and I cover the topic in more detail in Chapter 11, "More About Files (Some Useful Tips and Tricks)."

Notice that I said "one way" to print a formatted file is to save it in a new file. However, you don't have to save the output in a file; you can skip the file step entirely with this command:

```
$ fmt nursery | lp
job-id: 204
```

The ¦ symbol is a *pipe*, which is like an abbreviated way of telling UNIX to "save the output in a temporary file and then use that file as input for the next command." In this example, the file called nursery is temporarily saved and then sent to the printer for printing. (I talk about pipes in Chapter 11, too.)

If you want the maximum width of lines to be something other than 72 characters, use the **-w** option. (On some systems, the option is **-l**; it works the same.) Here's how you'd tell UNIX to format the file nursery so the lines are no more than 50 characters wide.

```
$ fmt -w 50 nursery
Jack (not Jill) Went up the hill To fetch a pail
of water. Jack fell down And sued the town For
damages, the rotter
```

Now that you know how simple **fmt** really is to use, use it. It can make your printed files much easier to read.

Inserting Page Breaks with pr

The **pr** command inserts blank lines into your text so that there are five-line margins at the top and bottom of each page. One of the lines in the top margin has a header line that describes the file and the page number. The header line tells you when the file was printed, the name of the file, and the current page. In the following example, the **pr** command is used to print the contents of the minutes.txt file to the printer. I've numbered the lines to make it easier for you to see the top margin and header line.

```
$ pr minutes.txt ¦ lp
 1
 2
 3   Dec 12 09:47 1994  minutes.txt  Page 1
 4
 5
 6   MINUTES OF COMMUNICATIONS COMMITTEE
 7
 8   December 12, 1994
 9
10   Present: Alexa
11
12   Absent: Tom, Rudy, Becky, Nicholas, Karen, Murray
13
```

```
14    I showed up at 9:04.  I waited until 9:35, and
15    then I left. Meeting postponed because we failed
16    to reach quorum.
17
18
```

If your file is short (maybe it only takes up a third of the page), **pr** adds blank lines at the end of the text so the file fills a printed page. Unless you say otherwise, **pr** makes each page 66 lines long. It was designed this way because most line printers (including dot-matrix printers) print six lines to the inch, and standard letter size in North America is 8.5 by 11 inches. (In the example above, I don't show lines 19 through 66 in order to save space.) Because laser printers use different font sizes, however, 66 lines may not be a page. You may find the top of your text is not starting at the top of the page. To change how long **pr** thinks the page is, use the -l option. For a laser printer, try 60 lines per page:

```
$ pr -l60 minutes.txt ¦ lp
```

If that doesn't work, you'll have to experiment with your printer and try different numbers of lines per page.

When you print with **pr**, you'll notice that **pr** only inserts top and bottom margins. The text is still jammed against the left side of the page. Most (though not all) versions of **pr** will also insert a left margin (or offset) if you use the **-o** option. The argument to **pr -o** is the number of characters you want to shift. On my dot-matrix printer, 10 gives me a 1-inch left margin, so I often use **pr -o10** to finish formatting files for printing.

It's quite difficult to get rid of the header line. There is a **-t** option to **pr** which removes both the header and trailer, but then **pr** doesn't paginate the file at all—it never inserts the blank lines. (I've never been able to figure out why anyone would want it.)

Putting It All Together

To make your files readable on paper, you'll probably use **fmt** and **pr** with **lp** quite frequently. With pipes, you can easily use any combination of these three commands on one command line. As an example, I keep a file of UNIX hints handy; it contains the locations of useful files, information on how to fix my display fonts if they get weird, and things like that. When I print this file, I connect all the commands using pipes (¦). To print my hints file on a laser printer, I use this command:

```
$ fmt -w65 hints ¦ pr -o10 -l60 ¦ lp
```

fmt -w65 formats the file hints so no line is longer than 65 characters. (My printer prints 10 characters/inch, so that gives me a 6.5 inch margin.) The first pipe takes the *results* of the **fmt** command and sends it into the **pr** command. **pr** paginates the text, and **-o10** inserts a left margin of 10 spaces so my document has reasonable margins. (Not all versions of **pr** have the **-o** option, but many do.) The last pipe sends it to **lp** for printing.

If you're environmentally-minded, you may want to print your documents double-sided. That's handled by your printer, not by UNIX (although the printer manufacturer may have supplied a command to turn double-sided printing off and on).

The Least You Need to Know

That's how you put words on paper in UNIX. If that seems too complicated to remember right now, just concentrate on these things:

➤ To send a file or files to the printer, use the **lp** command. The **lp** command leaves a request to print in a queue; another program prints these requests in order.

➤ To send the file to a different printer, use the **-d** option, like this: **lp -d***printername file*.

➤ To see the files you have waiting to print, use the **lpstat** command.

➤ To see the list of printers, use the **-p** option: **lpstat -p**.

➤ To see all the print requests waiting at your printer, use the **-u** option: **lpstat -u**.

➤ To see the jobs you have waiting on all printers, use the **-o** option: **lpstat -o**.

➤ To cancel a print job, you have to know the job id number, which you can get using the **lpstat** command. Then use the command **cancel *job-id***. You can only cancel jobs you sent.

➤ To format a file, use the **fmt** command; to paginate a file, use the **pr** command.

➤ Both **fmt** and **pr** write to the screen, so you have to send the output somewhere useful using redirection or pipes, both of which are explained in detail in Chapter 11, "More About Files (Some Useful Tips and Tricks)."

Chapter 10

When It Goes Wrong

In This Chapter

➤ Getting back to the prompt

➤ Killing a job

➤ Finding out which job you should kill

➤ Clearing up your terminal

➤ Can you get back a file you've just deleted?

➤ Stopping a print job

This chapter deals with some problems that are common to all UNIX users. So don't feel like an idiot, you're not alone. I've identified some common symptoms below. Then we'll talk about the probable causes for each of them, and I'll give you solutions for fixing them. So, what happens if one of the following occurs:

You press **Enter** and can't get your prompt, or you get a prompt you don't recognize. See "Getting Back to the Prompt" in this chapter.

A program is still running, and it won't go away. See "Kill, Not Execute" in this chapter.

You get a message that says something like Another version of this program is already running. Cannot start. See "Kill, Not Execute," and read the section on **ps** in this chapter.

You've got a 400-page file going to the printer, and you've discovered an error on page 1. How do you stop it? That was covered in Chapter 9, "Printing Is Pressing," but it's summarized under "Stop the Presses" in this chapter.

Your terminal is printing funny characters, or lines start all the way across the screen in a zigzag pattern. See "Terminal Cases" in this chapter.

You've just deleted a file that's important! How do you get it back? See "Undeleting a File" in this chapter.

Getting Back to the Prompt

So your program has gone off into space, somewhere. It's boldly going where no one has gone before, and you're left staring at the screen. When you press **Enter**, lines show up on the screen, but you don't get a prompt. Here are the most common causes:

➤ If there's a new prompt, such as >, the shell thinks the command you typed takes more than one line.

➤ If there's no prompt at all, wait a few moments. When a lot of people are using a UNIX system, it runs more slowly. If you've waited and it's still not doing anything, look at the command you typed. Does it need a file name or something else as an argument, and did you remember to type it in?

If you look at usage statements for UNIX commands, you'll notice that many of them treat a file argument as optional. **lp** is one of these as shown in the following line:

```
$ lp
```

If you don't supply a file name, **lp** takes the text to be printed from your keyboard—you can type it in directly. (Try it; type **lp** and then press **Enter**.) When you do this, the command (**lp** in this case) treats your keyboard as if it was a file, but you need a way to tell **lp** (and other programs taking input from the keyboard) that you've come to the end of the file. You can't use Enter because you might want to print the file. Instead, you use a special key combination that says, "Here's the end of the file." The key combination is **Control+D** (press the **Control** key and the **d** key simultaneously).

So this means that if you forget to type the name of a file argument, the program takes whatever you type as the contents of the "file." The way to quit is to press **Control+D**. Then type the command again, correctly. If Control+D doesn't work, you may have to kill the program. See "Kill, Not Execute" later in this chapter.

If you get an odd prompt like >, look back to see if the command contains a ' or " character or ends with \. These characters tell the shell to treat this command line in a special way. Remember, when you use a ' or " character, you must always use it in pairs. Therefore, if you forgot to type the last quote on the command line before you pressed Enter, you would get the > prompt. For example, consider this command:

```
$ rm "Tom's File
>
```

The greater than sign is a prompt, but it's not the one you're waiting for. It's a sign that the shell is waiting for more to come. Even if you type the missing ' or " character, the command probably won't work because you've already pressed the Enter key. Kill the command with **Control+C** and start over.

In the same way, the command **cd** \ won't work:

```
$ cd \
>
```

Using the ', \, and " characters is called *shell quoting*, and I talk about it in Chapter 25, "Neat Stuff."

Kill, Not Execute

In the English language, when we talk about blowing someone away, "kill" and "execute" mean about the same thing. However, one of the odd things about UNIX geek-speak (yes, another odd thing) is that "execute" means to run a program, but "kill" means to stop a program from running.

121

Because UNIX can run more than one program at a time, it has built-in ways for programs to send signals to one another. There's a fairly simple set of signals, which range in meaning from "I'm hanging up the phone; clean up and put everything away" to "Die *now!* And I don't care about the consequences!"

You can usually kill a running program by pressing **Control+C**. (Hold down the **Control** key and press **C**; it doesn't have to be capital C.) This sends the message "interrupt what you're doing" to the program. Most programs then clean up (they close any files they have opened and "put back" any system resources they're using) and go away.

Process A running program. One of the reasons for giving each process a different ID number is that it's got other stuff attached to it, like who's running it, what the options are, what other files are involved, and what its environment is.

However, some programs, such as an editor (see Part III), are designed to ignore control characters like Control+C. In an editor, pressing Control+C might do something else, such as center a line. If Control+C doesn't work, you need to try the **kill** command. The **kill** command always works—well, almost always. While Control+C sends only one signal to a program, the **kill** command can send different signals ranging from polite to urgent. The problem is, to use the **kill** command, you have to have a command prompt: $ or %. If you have a program that's really gone nuts on you (it's been churning away for a while), login at another terminal and kill the sucker. (If you've got a graphical user interface, you only have to open another terminal window. See Chapter 6, "Surviving Window Pains," for more on graphical user interfaces.)

When you have a command line, you can kill the program. How do you tell the **kill** command which program you want to kill? You use a number. Every running program (called a *process*) has an identification number, called its *process ID number* (or PID, if you want to get really geekish). I'll tell you how to find the PID for a process in the following section.

You indicate which program to kill with a number instead of a name because UNIX is a multitasking and multiuser operating system. More than one person can be running the same program at any time, so the name isn't of much use. For that matter, a single user could be running two versions of the same program at the same time. (How you do that is discussed in Chapter 20, "A Little Background Music.")

Therefore, the **kill** command wouldn't know which process you wanted to kill if all you gave was the name.

Using **kill** is easy. Let's say you know the PID number is 1961. First you try the default kill signal:

```
$ kill 1961
$
```

> *Double-check your process numbers!* It can be disconcerting and annoying to discover you've just killed the wrong program. You can't kill a program you don't own—but you'll hate yourself if you kill your shell and have to login again.

If you managed to kill the varmint, you will get your command prompt back at the terminal or window from which you originally executed the die-hard program. The default signal (it's called "terminate") is polite; it gives the process lots of time to clean up. However, if that didn't kill the program (for example, the terminal is still "hung up"), you'll have to move up to the tough stuff. There are two higher grades of kill signal. The next one is **-2**, which is the "interrupt" signal.

```
$ kill -2 1961
```

The interrupt signal still allows for cleanup, but it's more urgent than the terminate signal. If **kill -2** doesn't work, you can pull out the big guns: the kill signal, **kill -9**:

```
$ kill -9 1961
```

Normally you won't need to go all the way up to **-9** to kill the process—which is good, because not all programs clean up properly after a **kill -9**; **kill -9** can also cause you other problems, like corrupted data files.

Finding Your Process Number

The **ps** command shows you what processes you have running. Here's what the basic **ps** command looks like.

```
$ ps
  PID TTY      TIME COMD
 3228 pts002   0:01 ksh
 3262 pts002   0:00 ps
```

The first column shows the PID number; the second column gives your terminal's name, or TTY (which in this case is pts002); the third

Zombie process A process that should be dead but isn't. If a parent process doesn't make the proper arrangements before shutting itself down, its children can become zombie processes. In the **ps -ef** listing, zombie processes are identified with a Z status. Some versions of **ps** use the status `<defunct>` instead of Z.

column (TIME) tells you how long the program had been running when you executed the **ps** command; and the last column (COMD) is the command being described. This information lets you know what PID number goes with each process so you know which process to kill.

Unfortunately, **ps** by itself only tells you about programs you've been running since you logged in. It won't tell you about processes left over from the last time you logged in, and if you use an X Windows interface, **ps** may not even tell you about processes you're using in a different window! (Under X Windows, there's no convenient option to get a listing of *all* the programs you're currently running.)

Sometimes you need to find the process ID number of a program you started last time you logged in (because it hasn't died yet). Because the basic **ps** command won't show you these "old" processes, you need to use some command options. The only option that will show you the old processes is the **-e** option ("e" stands for everything). There are a lot of processes on your system; one Sunday afternoon, when I was the only user on our computer, I counted: there were 60 processes running, and I was responsible for only three of them.

In order to know which of your processes you need to kill, you also have to use the **-l** (for long) option, which shows each process' status in the second column. You want to kill any commands with a status of Z. (Z stands for zombie.)

But the **-l** option doesn't tell you the owner's name! To add the owner's login name to the output, you have to give the **-f** option. The **ps -fl** output is so wide, every line folds at the end of the screen, making it even harder to read. How are you going to find your processes in that mess?

You use an old UNIX trick: use the **grep** command to strip out all of the lines that don't contain your name. It sounds complicated, but all you have to do is type the command: **ps -efl ¦ grep** *loginname*. (The ¦ is called a *pipe* and I talk about them in Chapter 11, "More About Files (Some Useful Tips and Tricks)." **grep** is explained in Chapter 12, "The Search Is On.")

To show you the difference in output, here's a figure that shows the first 7 processes in the **ps -efl** output (**head -7** shows only the first 7 lines; I talk about **head** in Chapter 11), and the results of this command for my name. (Sorry, I didn't have any zombie processes available.)

```
/home/johnmc$ ps -efl | head -7
 F S     UID  PID PPID  C PRI NI    ADDR    SZ   WCHAN   STIME TTY      T
IME COMD
39 S    root    0    0  0   0 SY c0feb000     0 d01aafe6  Dec 06 ?       0
:03 sched
10 S    root    1    0  0  39 20 c0feb048    37 e0000000  Dec 06 ?       3
:08 /sbin/init
39 S    root    2    0  0   0 SY c0feb090     0 d107a800  Dec 06 ?       5
:36 pageout
39 S    root    3    0  0   0 SY c0feb0d8     0 d0031300  Dec 06 ?       7
:21 fsflush
39 S    root    4    0  0   0 SY c0feb120     0 d01df720  Dec 06 ?       0
:00 kmdaemon
39 S    root    5    0  0   0 SY c0feb168     0 d00cf9a0  Dec 06 ?       0
:00 sd01dkd
/home/johnmc$ ps -efl | grep johnmc
10 O  johnmc 16072 15930 80  95 20 c074a368    71           18:55:23 pts/0  0
:01 ps -efl
10 S  johnmc 16073 15930  1  26 20 c074a2d8    17 d1347500  18:55:23 pts/0  0
:00 grep johnmc
10 S  johnmc 15930 15928  0  30 20 c0febee8    97 d1119400  18:39:13 pts/0  0
:03 -ksh
/home/johnmc$
```

The final result of the commands you use to see a list of all your currently running processes.

Some versions of **ps** use different options. If **ps -efl** doesn't work on your system, try **ps -ax**. If you do have to use **ps -ax**, make a note that you've got a BSD system. (The different systems were briefly described in Chapter 2, "Operating on Systems.")

Although all of this might seem like a lot of work to kill one command, sometimes you may not have a choice.

Terminal Cases

A number of things can go wrong with your terminal, but almost none of them are your fault. Unless your terminal was never correctly config-ured, terminal problems are usually caused by programs that end without cleaning up after themselves. (Sometimes this happens if you kill a program with **Control+C**.)

There are three common terminal problems:

➤ Your terminal is printing funny characters like ^[7m^[before some words.

➤ Keys don't do what you expect. Maybe Backspace prints as ^H, or the @ key erases the entire line.

➤ Every letter prints twice, lines are double-spaced, or they crawl across the screen.

The following sections address each of these problems and their solutions in detail.

My Terminal Doesn't Speak My Language

If you've never had an understandable screen (you see funny characters like ^[7m^[appearing in front of words), your terminal isn't configured correctly. Your **TERM** environment variable may be set wrong. Ask your system administrator to check this for you. (See Chapter 19, "Environ-Mental Health" for more about the **TERM** environment variable.)

The Mighty stty Command

The **stty** command enables you to reset the current values of your terminal's control characteristics. When used without options or arguments, the **stty** command shows you some of your terminal's settings. The following figure shows my settings, both those that **stty** shows without an argument and those that **stty -a** (for all) shows.

```
/home/johnmc$ stty
speed 38400 baud; -parity hupcl
erase = ^h; swtch = <undef>; dsusp = <undef>;
brkint -inpck icrnl -ixany onlcr tab3
echo echoe echok
/home/johnmc$ stty -a
speed 38400 baud;
intr = DEL; quit = ^|; erase = ^h; kill = @;
eof = ^d; eol = <undef>; eol2 = <undef>; swtch = <undef>;
start = ^q; stop = ^s; susp = ^z; dsusp = <undef>;
rprnt = ^r; flush = ^o; werase = ^w; lnext = ^v;
-parenb -parodd cs8 -cstopb hupcl cread -clocal -loblk -parext
-ignbrk brkint ignpar -parmrk -inpck istrip -inlcr -igncr icrnl -iuclc
ixon -ixany -ixoff -imaxbel
isig icanon -xcase echo echoe echok -echonl -noflsh
-tostop -echoctl -echoprt -echoke -defecho -flusho -pendin -iexten
opost -olcuc onlcr -ocrnl -onocr -onlret -ofill -ofdel tab3
/home/johnmc$
```

*An example of the settings you can adjust with the **stty** command. You could adjust all of these, but it's not worth the trouble.*

126

There are two types of settings here: control character settings and communications settings. The control character settings contain equals signs: they assign keys to particular control signals. For instance, backspace is a control signal called erase—it erases the character to the left of the cursor. The erase signal can be assigned to any control key (Backspace and Delete are control keys). In this case, you can see that the erase signal (what we think of as backspace) is assigned to the key that sends a Control+H signal.

The other settings (-onlcr, for instance) all deal with communications between the terminal and the computer: how fast signals are sent, how they're to be interpreted, whether all output is uppercase or not, and so on. Understanding those settings requires a fairly in-depth knowledge of computer communications over a phone line. You can ignore those settings most of the time (and you probably want to).

Let's explore the **stty** command a little further.

If the control keys don't do what you think they should, you can adjust the settings. Every control key has a name for what it does. When you set control keys with the **stty** command, you supply the name of the function and then the key you want to perform that function. For instance, if the Backspace key just prints ^H on the screen, that means that UNIX doesn't know you want the Backspace key to back up the cursor a space. This is easy to fix. Simply type this command:

```
$ stty erase ^H
```

This command tells UNIX that when you type a Control+H, you want it to mean "erase." You're changing the key that does the "erase" function.

There's no way to guess this; you just have to know that (a) "erase" is "erase the character immediately to the left of the cursor" (what we all think of as "backspace") and (b) the Backspace key sends the signal Control+H.

To make this a permanent part of your UNIX sessions, add that line (**stty erase ^H**) to your shell's startup file (.profile if you're using the Korn shell, .login if you're using the C-Shell). Startup files are discussed in Chapter 18, "The Shell Game." If you don't put it in your shell's startup file, you'll need to re-type the **stty** command every time you login.

There are three other control signals I discuss throughout this book; their names are "intr" (for "interrupt"), "eof" (for "end-of-file"), and "susp" (for "suspend"). If your system uses different control-key combinations for these signals than the ones I describe in this book, here's how to change them:

➤ To assign the "interrupt" signal to the key combination Control+C (which is the key combination I described earlier in this chapter), use the command **stty intr ^C**.

➤ To assign the "end-of-file" signal to the key combination Control+D (which is the key combination I described earlier in this chapter), use the command **stty intr ^D**.

➤ To assign the "suspend" signal to the key combination Control+Z (which is the key combination I describe in Chapter 20, "A Little Background Music"), use the command **stty intr ^Z**.

To make these changes permanent, put them in your shell startup file as I described earlier.

Going Sane

If your terminal is producing strange output (lines are double spacing as in the following figure), there's something wrong with some other terminal settings. There are a lot of different settings that control how your terminal handles the Enter key and shows lines; you don't need to know them, and you shouldn't have to. However, there is one command you may find useful: the **stty sane** command.

```
/home/johnmc$ ls
              Accessories    Games           Preferences    Wastebasket   man
                                                                                Appli
cations  Help_Desk      Shutdown      bin              netware
                                                                 Disks-etc    Mail
          System_Setup  calendar      project
                                              Folder_Map    News              Utilities
     mailbox        termio.7
                              /home/johnmc$ stty sane
                                                       /home/johnmc$ ls
Accessories    Games         Preferences    Wastebasket   man
Applications   Help_Desk     Shutdown       bin           netware
Disks-etc      Mail          System_Setup   calendar      project
Folder_Map     News          Utilities      mailbox       termio.7
/home/johnmc$
```

*The **stty sane** command can solve the problems caused by an ill-behaved program.*

You can tell **stty** to set everything to reasonable settings with one command:

```
$ stty sane
```

This tells **stty** to use a set of defaults that work in a lot of cases. Some systems have another similar option called **crt**. If **stty sane** doesn't work for you, try **stty crt**. If that doesn't work, logout and log back in. If that doesn't work, logout, turn off your terminal, turn it on again, and log back in. And if even that doesn't work, definitely call your system administrator.

Undeleting a File

You've just deleted a very important file and you want it back. How do you retrieve it? The short answer is, you can't. On UNIX, when a file is gone, it's gone forever. The long answer is, maybe you can get something back.

➤ If you created the file in an application, did the application keep a backup? Some programs keep the last saved version in the directory. Although it won't have all your work in it, it's better than starting from nothing.

➤ Was the file more than a day old? Check with your system administrator to see if he or she may have made a backup of that file. If there is a backup, your system administrator can restore that copy of the file. Again, it may not be updated, but it's better than nothing.

If you're really prone to this sort of accident, MIT's Project Athena produces (free of charge) a set of utilities that handles deleting and undeleting files. Ask your system administrator to get and install these utilities.

Here's what you tell your system administrator if you want the Project Athena commands: The package with **delete**, **undelete**, **purge**, and **expunge** was posted to the Usenet group comp.sources.misc, volume 17, issues 023–026. If you have Internet access, you can get them via FTP or through a mailserver.

If your system administrator refuses to get the files (because you don't have electronic mail or Internet access), there's one more possibility. After you've logged out, the files are gone; but until then, you can get them back.

Stop the Presses

Although I covered this in Chapter 9, "Printing Is Pressing," here's a quick summary. To cancel a print job, you need to know the job request number. The **lp** command prints the job request number when you submit the job, so you might still see it on your screen. If not, use the **lpstat** command to identify the print job you want to cancel, as shown in this example:

```
$ lpstat
pr2000   1st jklein 4802338 quarterly.wks Printing
pr2001   2nd amorton 281331 comm-minutes
```

Suppose the number of the print job you want to cancel is pr2001. To cancel the print job, use this command:

```
$ cancel pr2001
job cpr2001 dequeued
job xpr2001 dequeued
```

The Least You Need to Know

This chapter talked about how to fix some common problems. Here's the short version:

➤ If you can't get a prompt, try pressing **Control+D**. If that doesn't work, try **Control+C**. Control+C will stop most running programs.

➤ Inside UNIX, running programs are identified by a number called a process ID. To find the process IDs of the programs you've started this login session, use the **ps** command. To find the process IDs of all the programs you're running, use the command **ps -efl ¦ grep** *loginname*

➤ You can kill a running program with the **kill** command: **kill** *processID*. The ones you want to kill have a Z (for zombie) in the second column.

130

➤ If the running program is still there after a straight **kill** command, you can increase the urgency of the **kill** command with the -9 option: **kill -9** *processID*.

➤ You can often fix your terminal display problems with the command **stty sane**. If that doesn't make your terminal display correctly, it's often easier to logout and then log back in.

➤ The only way to get back a deleted file is with a backup. The application program in which you created the file might have a backup, or your system administrator might have made one. If you just created the file today, the chances of having a backup are slim.

➤ You can cancel a print job with **cancel**, but you need to know the number of the print job. You can find the number of a print job with the **lpstat** command.

Chapter 11

More About Files (Some Useful Tips and Tricks)

> **In This Chapter**
>
> ➤ Other ways to look at files
>
> ➤ Saving the output of a program
>
> ➤ Using one program's output as another program's input
>
> ➤ Changing a file's ownership and permissions

Even though you now know the basics of working with files, some-times there are quicker or easier ways to accomplish a task. This chapter provides some alternative techniques for doing things (including a few advanced file tricks) and introduces you to a couple of UNIX utilities for scheduling.

Less Is More

In Chapter 8, "Branching Out: Working with Files and Directories," I told you to use the **more** program to look at the contents of a file, but the **more** program isn't the only way to look at a file. UNIX provides you with several other ways to look at a file's contents, depending on what you want to do. Each of these programs meets a need slightly different from that of **more** or provides you with a slightly different style of working.

For instance, **more** only lets you go forward through the file you want to view. You can't back up and look at something you've already passed. However, there's an alternative program called **less**, which does let you back up in the file you're reading. (It's called **less** because it's the opposite of **more**.) With **less**, you can browse through the entire file instead of just reading it sequentially. Unfortunately, not all UNIX systems have **less**.

You view a file with **less** in exactly the same way you do with **more**. For example, to read the file schedule.09.18.94, use this command:

```
$ less schedule.09.18.94
```

Once you're inside that file, you can navigate around using all of the keyboard keys that the **more** command uses. In addition, there are some keys that are used only with the **less** command. All of the keyboard navigation keys for the **less** command are listed here.

Press	To Perform This Action
q	Quit
#f, #Spacebar	Move forward # lines (no number: one screen) (Same as **more**)
#e, #j, #Enter	Move forward # lines (no number: one line) (Same as **more**)
*n*d	Move forward # lines (no number: half screen or last # used for **d** or **u**) (Same as **more**)
#b	Move backward # lines (no number: one screen)
#y, #k	Move backward # lines (no number: one line)
#u	Move backward # lines (no number: half screen or last # used for **d** or **u**)
#/word	Search forward for #th line containing *word* (Same as **more**)

Press	To Perform This Action
#?word	Search backward for #th line containing *word* (Same as **more**)
#n	Repeat previous search (for #th occurence) (Same as **more**)
#g	Go to line # (no number: line 1)
#G	Go to line # (no number: last line in file)
#p, #%	Move to # percent in the file (**50%** is half-way)
H	Display the help screen(s) (**h** in **more**)
r	Redraw screen
m*c*	Mark the current position with letter *c*
#N	Read next file listed on command line (**:n** in **more**)
#P	Read previous file listed on command line (**:p** in **more**)
=	Print name of current file
!command	Run *command* outside **less** (Same as **more**)

You can look at multiple files just by naming them on the command line. For example, to read the files list.1 and list.2, use this command:

```
$ less list.1 list.2
```

less displays the first file given on the command line; to see the next file, use the **N** command. Once you're in a file, use the regular **less** movement commands to move around. To go to the next file in the list, press **N**. To go back to the previous file, press **P**.

If you don't want to look at an entire file, there are programs that let you look at only the first few or last few lines. For example, to see the first 10 lines of a file, use the **head** program:

```
$ head schedule.09.18.94
```

With **tail**, you can name only one file on the command line. However, all of the other programs discussed here will accept more than one file name on the command line.

To see the last 10 lines of a file, use the **tail** program:

```
$ tail schedule.09.18.94
```

There's another program, called **cat**, that also copies a file or files to the screen. I prefer **more** for looking at the contents of a file because it lets you pause when reading long files. However, **cat** is useful for joining short files into one longer file, which is where the name comes from: "catenate" is an old word meaning "to join, like a link in a chain."

For example, this command displays the contents of the files line1 and line2 (each of which is one line long):

```
$ cat line1 line2
What a curious bird is the pelican
His beak can hold more than his belly can
```

File Redirection (A Cat-Copy)

Most programs in UNIX display the results on-screen. Sometimes you may want to save that output in a file so you can print it later or look at it again. UNIX enables you to do this with a feature called *file redirection*. The file redirection instruction goes at the end of the command line, like this:

```
$ ls -l > directorylist
```

In this example, the > tells UNIX to put the output of the **ls -l** command into a file named directorylist. If you were to run the **ls -l** command again on this example, the newly created directorylist file would *replace* or *overwrite* the old one.

You can also use > to copy files. If you were to use > with a file named phone, UNIX would make a copy of the phone file and name it list:

```
$ cat phone > list
```

Besides standard input and standard output, every program in UNIX also has a place to send errors. This is called, logically enough, standard error. Normally errors just print to the screen. When you redirect output with >, you're just redirecting the standard output. (In fact, standard output is **1>**, but it's used so often that you can leave the 1 off.) However, error messages will still print on the screen. To redirect error messages, use **2>**. Redirecting standard error with **2>** is useful if somebody asks you to save the error messages from a command.

You're probably saying, "So what? I know how to use the **cp** (copy) command." The advantage is that you can use this to turn a bunch of small files into one large file. Suppose several co-workers have sent you comments on a new contract proposal. You've saved each mail message in a separate file: comments.bob, comments.chris, and so on. (Using electronic mail and saving mail messages are described in Chapter 22, "Send Me a Letter.") Let's say you want to combine those comments files into one file named comments, so you can print them all at once and compare them. You type:

```
$ cat comments.* > comments
```

The * wild-card character tells UNIX you want to copy all comments files (both Bob's and Chris's) into the file called comments.

If you want to, you can add a file to a file that already exists using >> instead of >. (The >> tells UNIX to append the new information to the end of the existing file.) For example, suppose Dana, another co-worker, tells you that her comments are in the file proposal-thoughts in her home directory. You can add the contents of her file to your comments file (which already contains Bob's and Chris's comments) with the >> redirection:

> **Input** The information that goes into a program; literally what you put into it. Most UNIX programs expect this to come from the keyboard, unless you tell it otherwise. In fact, the keyboard is called standard input, or stdin.
>
> **Output** The information that comes out of a program. In UNIX programs, this is usually written to the screen, so the screen is called standard output, or stdout.

```
$ cat ~dana/proposal-thoughts >> comments
```

File redirection
Using a file as input or output instead of the screen or the keyboard. Output redirection puts a program's output into a file, while input redirection tells a program to take input from a file instead of the keyboard. The symbols for output redirection include > (send output into a file), >> (add output to the end of a file), and 2> (send only error messages into a file). The symbol for input redirection is < (take input from the file).

(Remember that a ~ before a login name stands for that user's home directory. I mentioned that in Chapter 7, "The Root of the Matter: Files and Directories.")

In addition to redirecting output, you can redirect input, too. Almost any UNIX program that accepts input from the keyboard can also take it from a file. Since > redirects output, it's only reasonable that the < character redirects *input*.

As an example, let's say your boss now wants you to mail her a copy of everyone's comments (which you gathered in the examples above). You could start the mail program and spend the whole day (or week) typing in all the comments, or you can use file redirection again. To mail the comments file, for instance, you would use this command:

```
$ mailx boss < comments
```

Thus, the comments file replaces a mail message you might have otherwise typed from the keyboard (input).

Pipe Down!

Well, if you can put output from one program into a file and take input for another program from a file, why not get rid of the file entirely? That's what a *pipe* does (shown on the command line by ¦). A pipe enables you to use the output of one program as the input for another program. You can use a pipe anywhere you might use a temporary file.

Back in Chapter 9, "Printing Is Pressing," I implemented pipes to use the output of **fmt** as input to **pr**, and to use the output of **pr** as input to **lp**:

```
$ fmt manual ¦ pr ¦ lp
```

The "pipeline" takes the output of the **fmt** *manual* command and puts it directly into **pr** instead of storing it in a file (like *temp1*). Then it takes the output of **pr** and puts it directly into **lp** without storing it in a file (like *temp2*). This "pipeline" of commands is equivalent to:

```
$ fmt manual > temp1
$ pr temp1 > temp2
$ lp temp2
```

Pipes are one of the features that make UNIX so flexible: you can join individual commands to make new ones specific to your task. Basically, pipes are the nuts and bolts of a computer user's Erector set.

The most common use of the pipe is to see the output of a command that's longer than a full screen of information. Anytime a program's output runs off the screen, you can view it by adding ¦ **more** to the end of the command:

```
$ ls /bin ¦ more
```

> **Pipe** A method for taking the *output* of one command and using it as *input* for another. This works the same as if you saved the output of the first command in a file and then used that file as an argument to the second command—but it's faster. To use a pipe, connect the two commands with a vertical bar symbol (¦). Pipes are meant to work with commands that send their output to the screen.

In this example, you can view the directory listing of the /bin directory (which is usually very long) one screen at a time.

Changing Your File's Permissions

In Chapter 9, I described how every file is owned by somebody, and that it has permissions. As far as files are concerned, there are three groups of people who can have different permissions: the owner of the file, the members in the same group as the owner of the file, and the others.

UNIX lets you change the permissions for each of those groups using the **chmod** (change mode) command. (A file's permissions are sometimes called its mode.) You can only change permissions on a file you own. However, you can change who owns a file with the **chown** (change owner) command.

Changing Read and Write Permissions

The **chmod** command changes the permissions assigned to each of the three groups, the owner (or user who created it), other members of the owner's group, and everyone else (the others). A **chmod** command looks like this:

```
$ chmod ugo-w phonelist
```

139

The **ugo-w** is the permission change. Let's look at each of the parts of this in detail.

➤ The **ugo** part indicates whose permissions we're changing. To break it down even further, **u** stands for user, **g** stands for group, and **o** stands for other. Therefore, **ugo** tells UNIX that we want to change the permissions for everybody. (In fact, you could also use the short form **a**, for all.)

➤ The - part tells UNIX how we're changing the permission. The - indicates that we want to take away the permissions. On the contrary, a plus sign (+) adds permissions. If you want to set permissions exactly, use an equals sign (=).

➤ The **w** shows which permissions we're changing. The **w** indicates that we're working with write permission, the ability to change a file. Other permissions include read (**r**) and execute (**x**). (Execute is only important for programs and for directories.)

So, the example command above removes everybody's write permission from the file called phonelist. No one can change the file.

Let's say, however, that you decide you want to change the phone list after all. Because you're the owner, you're allowed to change the permissions; so you give yourself write permission again. You add your write permission back to the file with this command:

```
$ chmod u+w phonelist
```

As you learned above, the **u** indicates the user, the + adds permission, and the **w** shows that it's write permission. Once again, the owner of the file can make changes to the file.

Now that you've got those basics under your belt, you can make a file (such as job.reviews) unreadable and unwriteable by everyone but you:

```
$ chmod go-rw job.reviews
```

You can join multiple changes in one command by separating them with commas. Here's how you take away everyone else's read, write, and execute permissions from a file called printpic and add execute permission for yourself:

```
$ chmod go-rwx,u+x printpic
```

140

Even if you take away your own write permission on a file you own, you can still delete a file with the **rm** command. (However, UNIX will confirm the deletion with you first.)

 You can also represent the permissions as *numbers*. Each permission is a three-digit number: the first digit shows the user's permissions, the second digit shows the group's permissions, and the third digit shows other people's permissions. 0 = no permissions, 1 = execute permission, 2 = write permission, and 4 = read permission. You can add the digits to get combinations of permissions; for example read and write but not execute is 2+4=6. Therefore, a permission of 666 gives read and write permissions to everyone; 644 gives the owner read and write permissions, but gives everyone else read permission only. 700 indicates a program that only the owner can run, read, or write. Get the idea? With numbers, you specify the entire permission at once. The command **chmod 644 phonelist** sets the permissions so the owner can read and change the phonelist file, but everyone else can only read it.

You can change permissions for directories, too. Changing the permissions for a directory affects who can read the directory, who can go into the directory, and who can create or change files in the directory.

➤ You have to be able to execute a directory to access it with the **cd** command.

➤ You have to be able to read a directory to list its contents.

➤ You have to be able to write in a directory to create or change files there.

A Link in the Chain

Sometimes you need a file to be in two places at once, and a copy just won't do. For instance, a co-worker might need an up-to-date copy of a file you're responsible for. You don't want to give her a copy because you'll have to recopy it every time you change it. On the other hand, you don't want to put it in her directory because it's your file. What do you do?

You give it another name. The new name is sort of a "pointer" back to the real file—kind of call forwarding for files. Just as someone calling a call-forwarded number gets re-routed to the number you're really at, anyone trying to use the new "file" gets sent back to the file you really want them to see. This pointer or re-routing connection is called a *link*. In almost every way, the link cannot be told apart from the "original" file. The command to create a link is **ln**, and this is how you use it:

```
$ ln originalfilename newname
```

So if you wanted to create a link between the original file named procedures.manual and the file you want to call /home/leslie/hand-outs/proc.man, you would use this command from the directory where procedures.manual will reside:

```
$ ln procedures.manual /home/leslie/handouts/proc.man
```

In this example, a "file" named procedures.manual is created in the current directory. This new "file" is really just another name for /home/leslie/handouts/proc.man. When anyone tries to read procedures.manual, they're really reading /home/leslie/handouts/ proc.man. When you make changes in procedures.manual, they show up in proc.man. And, if Leslie makes a change in proc.man, you'll see it in procedures.manual.

If you delete one of those file names with **rm**, the name disappears. When the last name is removed, the file goes too. This kind of link is called a *hard link*. A hard link is an extra name for a file that cannot exist without the file. (In this way, it's different from a *soft* or *symbolic* link, which can remain after the file is gone.)

You can't hard-link a directory, but you can hard-link a set of files to a directory. For example, let's say you've turned procedures.manual into a bunch of smaller files called proc.1 through proc.9 in the directory called manual in your current directory. How do you link them to Leslie's handouts directory? The same way you'd copy them all there. (The question mark is a wild-card character that represents any single character that might appear in that position.)

```
$ ln manual/proc.? /home/leslie/handouts
```

All of the proc files that were in in your directory manual are now also in the directory /home/lesie/handouts:

```
$ ls manual/*
proc.1    proc.4    proc.7
proc.2    proc.5    proc.8
proc.3    proc.6    proc.9


$ ls /home/leslie/handouts/*
proc.1    proc.4    proc.7
proc.2    proc.5    proc.8
proc.3    proc.6    proc.9
```

Not all systems have **ln**, but most modern UNIXes do.

Sometimes, however, **ln** can't make a hard link. If that's the case, you'll usually see a message that says something like cannot create link across file systems. This is because the directory for the link is on a different computer or hard disk. (In UNIX, you can join the file systems for different computers. I talk about this in Chapter 21, "Everybody's Talkin'.") In that case, there's a second kind of link you can make, called a *soft* or *symbolic link*. To make a symbolic link, you use the **ln -s** command.

Suppose you want to create a link between the file proc.1 and the directory /nfs/gyro/howto/man1, which is on another computer (called gyro). (It's a common practice on UNIX systems to put directories that are on other computers in a directory called /nfs. Each directory in /nfs is named after a computer—gyro in this case—and all the directories and files in /nfs/gyro are actually on gyro. I talk about this more in Chapter 21.) You're in your manual directory. The command you use would look like this:

```
$ ln -s proc.1 /nfs/gyro/howto/man1
```

If you were to do an **ls -l** on the man1 directory, which is on the computer called gyro, the first letter of the listing would be l (for link), and under the file name it would show you where the original file is. (This was described in Chapter 8, "Branching Out: Working with Files and Directories.")

A soft or symbolic link behaves slightly differently than a hard link does. When you **rm** a symbolic link, it behaves the way you'd expect: the linked name disappears. If you **rm** the original file instead of the link, the file goes away—but the symbolic link remains. The lc

143

 This example shows the kind of trouble you can make for yourself with symbolic links. Although pamphlets is in your directory, it's really in /home/leslie, yet it contains files that are really in your directory. This is worse than trying to figure out what really happens in the *Back to the Future* movies. Be careful when you use symbolic links.

command will show you this with the category `Unresolved symbolic links`. These are symbolic links that don't connect to anything anymore. You can delete an unresolved symbolic link with the **rm** command.

Unlike hard links, you can make a symbolic link from one directory to another directory. For example, you could make Leslie's handouts directory a directory named pamphlets in your home directory with this command:

```
$ ln -s /home/leslie/handouts pamphlets
```

Now when you **cd** into pamphlets in your home directory, you're really changing to the directory /home/leslie/handouts.

The Least You Need to Know

This chapter has been broad-ranging. You've learned four new ways to look at a file's contents, how to save program output in a file, how to use a file as program input, and a bit more about files. Here it is in a not-so-little nutshell:

➤ Some systems have an alternative to **more** called **less**. **less** enables you to move back and forth in a file instead of just from beginning to end.

➤ Use the **head** command to look at the first 10 lines of a file, and use the **tail** command to look at the last 10 lines of a file.

➤ To use a file as input or output instead of the screen or keyboard, use the file redirection symbols >, >>, or <.

➤ To use the output of one command as input for another, connect the commands with a pipe symbol (¦).

➤ To change a file's permissions, use the **chmod** command. You can only change permissions on files you own.

➤ You can create alternative names for files using the **ln** (hard link) and **ln -s** (soft link) commands.

144

BLAAAP

The Search Is On

Because there are a lot of files on a computer system, it's easy to lose track of one particular file—and hard to find one you want. Heck, I'm constantly losing pieces of paper on my desk, and compared to a file system, my desk is tiny.

The developers of UNIX must have lost files too, so they created a program that enables you to find a file whether you know its name or not, as long as you know what it's about. They also created a file comparison program that enables you to compare the contents of two files or directories. So when you find two files with the same name, you can see how they differ. (What insight and generosity those UNIX creators had!)

Sometimes you find a file, and you have no idea what it's for. You try to read it, but it's not a text file; if it is a text file, it's full of lines that are obviously meant for some kind of program to understand, and not a person. Have no fear, UNIX even has a command that can tell you what kind of file that file is.

Even Sherlock Holmes didn't explore every alley way in London by himself: he had the help of Watson, and the Baker Street Irregulars. So come, Watson! The file's afoot!

Finding the Lost File by Name

How do you find a file if you know its name but nothing else? You could list the contents of every directory on the computer, but that would take time (and besides, it would be boring). However, you're in luck! There's a command to find files called **find**. (Imagine that! For once a command name that makes sense.) **find** is a detective: it hunts for files. **find** starts in a directory that you choose, looks for the file, and then checks every subdirectory contained in the specified directory. Then **find** checks every subdirectory of those directories, and so on until it has checked all of the subdirectories. **find** leaves no stone unturned. Note that there's one big disadvantage to **find**: because it is so thorough, it can be slow.

To use **find**, you have to provide three pieces of information, in this order: where to start looking, what to look for, and what to do when it finds the file. Here's how you'd find the file customer.list starting in the directory /home/you:

```
$ find /home/you -name customer.list -print
/home/you/marketing/notes/customer.list
```

➤ "Where to start looking" is the directory /home/you. It always has to be a directory name, although it could be a short form like . or .. or ~. If you want **find** to check all the files on the system, tell it to start in the root directory, /.

➤ "What to look for" is usually a file name, so you use the **-name** option followed by the file name. It doesn't have to be a file name. There are other options besides **-name**, but that's what you'll use most often. (Other options include **-mtime**, which lets you pick files based on the last time they were changed, and the option **-user**, which lets you pick files based on the owner's login name.)

146

➤ "What to do" is almost always to print the name on-screen. You tell **find** to print to the screen with the **-print** option. Although not all versions of **find** need the **-print** option, it doesn't hurt to include it as part of the command. There are other options for what to do besides **-print**, but they're more for system administrators.

In this case, the result of the search tells you that the file is in /home/you/marketing/notes. If **find** can't find the file, it doesn't print anything.

You don't have to specify the full program name with **find**; you can use wild cards to specify part of the file's name. In order to make the wild cards work correctly, though, you need to put them in quotes. For instance, this command finds all the files on the system with names ending in ".temp":

```
$ find / -name "*.temp" -print
```

The **find** man page says you can use more than one criteria for searching files if you group them with parentheses. What most **find** man pages don't tell you is that the parentheses have to be in quotation marks. For instance, this finds all files that start with "temp." or end with ".temp":

```
$ find / "(" -name "temp.*" -o -name "*.temp" ")" -print
```

The **-o** tells UNIX to search for a match in this criteria or that one.

Searching Files for Content

Often you can't remember the name of the file you want, but you know what the file is about. The **grep** program searches files and tells you which files contain a particular word.

Perhaps you want to know if the file called procedures.3 discusses the proper procedure for ordering stationery. You can print it and search for the information on stationery, or you can look through it with the **more** program and search for the information on stationery, or you can let **grep** search for you. So, you use the **grep** program to search for the word "stationery" within the /doc/procedures directory with this command:

```
$ grep stationery procedures.3
```

```
/doc/procedures$ grep stationery procedures.3
supplies required by all in-office personnel, including stationery and
 * stationery (paper, pens, envelopes)
 * letterhead (Note that letterhead is *not* considered stationery.)
All orders for stationery must be made through the deparmental
/doc/procedures$
```

*This **grep** command found four lines in the file procedures.3 that contained the word "stationery."*

To give you the context, **grep** shows you the line or lines that contain the word you're looking for. Here four lines match. (Some of the lines are too long to fit on the screen, so they fold over to the next line.) If the word "stationery" had not been in the file, **grep** wouldn't give any output at all.

grep's search is normally case-sensitive. If you entered the search command given above and the word "Stationery" or "STATIONERY" was in the file, **grep** wouldn't report it. To make **grep** case-*insensitive*, use the **-i** option.

```
$ grep -i stationery procedures.3
```

```
/doc/procedures$ grep -i stationery procedures.3
        3.3.1 STATIONERY
supplies required by all in-office personnel, including stationery and
 * stationery (paper, pens, envelopes)
 * letterhead (Note that letterhead is *not* considered stationery.)
3.3.1 Stationery
All orders for stationery must be made through the deparmental
/doc/procedures$
```

*The **-i** flag tells **grep** to ignore the case of the letters in the file it's searching.*

This time, **grep** found "STATIONERY" and "Stationery," as well as "stationery."

grep isn't really looking for words, it's looking for patterns of letters. Therefore, if you want, you can even search for a phrase. The pattern of letters can contain spaces, if you want, but you must put it in quotes on the command line. For example, if you had wanted to search for the phrase "ordering stationery," you could have used this command:

```
$ grep -i "ordering stationery" procedures.3
$
```

The fact that **grep** doesn't give any ouput indicates that there are no lines in the file that contain the phrase "ordering stationery."

Remember, though, **grep** is searching the file line-by-line. So if one line ends with "ordering" and the next starts with "stationery," **grep** won't find it.

You can look for more than one word or pattern in a file, but each pattern must be an argument to the **-e** option, or **grep** can't tell when one pattern ends and the next begins. To show all lines that contain either the phrase "order form" or the word "stationery," for example, use this command:

```
$ grep -e "order form" -e stationery procedures.3
```

You can search as many files as you'd like. Usually, I search an entire directory at once, as this figure shows. When you name more than one file, **grep** puts the name of the file containing the word at the beginning of the context line.

```
/doc/procedures$ ls
procedures.1        procedures.4        procedures.7        table_of_contents
procedures.2        procedures.5        procedures.8
procedures.3        procedures.6        procedures.9
/doc/procedures$ grep -i stationery *
procedures.3:     3.3.1 STATIONERY
procedures.3:supplies required by all in-office personnel, including stationery
and
procedures.3: * stationery (paper, pens, envelopes)
procedures.3: * letterhead (Note that letterhead is *not* considered stationery.
)
procedures.3:3.3.1 Stationery
procedures.3:All orders for stationery must be made through the deparmental
procedures.9: * stealing stationery is punishable by demerits
procedures.9: * making inappropriate remarks on corporate stationery or in the
table_of_contents:                    3.3.1 Stationery
/doc/procedures$
```

*You can use **grep** to search an entire directory at once. For each line that matches, **grep** prints the name of the file and the matching line.*

One thing you should note is that **grep** won't search subdirectories for you; you have to specify each directory on the command line. Suppose your company stores documents in /doc and in two subdirectories: /doc/reports and /doc/letters. You want to find all of the documents that mention UNIX. Here's the command you would use:

```
$ grep -i UNIX /doc/* /doc/reports/* /doc/letters/*
```

What's the Diff?

There may come a time when **find** finds two files with the same name, and you don't know if they're the same. I often make extra copies of files so I can change the text somehow; then a week later I can't remember how I changed the text. How do you tell the differences between two files? Instead of spending most of my life printing out copies of files and comparing them, I let the computer do the work. The **diff** program compares two text files and reports on the differences.

To use **diff**, supply the names of the two files you want to compare in the format **diff *file1 file2***. For instance, here are two phone lists, side by side. The left column I saved in a file called phone1, and the right column I saved as phone2.

```
Alto Eager (music) 508-5608        Aaron's Aquariums 508-2345

Bagley, Martin 518-7421            Alto Eager (music) 508-5608

Crowe's Nest 508-0900             Crowe's Nest 508-0900

Czerny, Ann & Bob 508-6492        Czerny, Ann & Bob 518-2139
```

The following figure shows what you get when you compare them using **diff**.

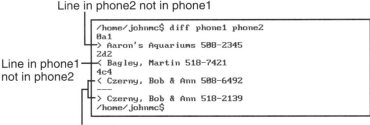

*The **diff** program compares two text files and shows you the differences.*

When **diff** returns a line with a c, it means the line is somewhat the same but has changed (see the lines after 4c4 in the figure). An a means the line was added in the second file (see the line following 0a1), and a d means the line was deleted from the second file (see the line following 2d2).

diff is actually showing you how to change the first file to make it identical to the second. Each change begins with the line number in the first file, the type of change (add, delete, or change the line) necessary to make it match the second file, and the line number in the second file. Therefore, the first difference **diff** showed in the figure:

```
0a1
> Aaron's Aquariums 508-2345
```

means that you have to add this line after line zero in the first file, and that it's line 1 in the second file. The > indicates that this line is from the second file. Likewise, the **diff** result

```
2d2
< Bagley, Martin 518-7421
```

means you have to delete line 2 of the first file to get line 2 of the second file. The < indicates this line of text is from the first file.

The last two changes **diff** reports look like this:

```
4c4
< Czerney, Ann & Bob 508-5492
---
> Czerney, Ann & Bob 518-2139
```

4c4 means you have to change line 4 in the first file to get line 4 in the second file. The contents of the line in the old file are shown above the ---; the new file's version is shown below the ---.

Like **grep**, **diff** has its limitations. First, it works best on text files; there's not much point in running **diff** on spreadsheets. Second, **diff** compares files line-by-line, so changes in formatting show up as differences even if no words have changed. If you

> **Regular expression**
> A way to describe a pattern of letters. The simplest pattern is a word, but a regular expression can also include wild card characters (like the ? in the shell, which stands for any single letter). If a word or phrase is described by a regular expression, we say it matches the regular expression. And "regular" is just an expression. You'll never find an irregular expression in UNIX.

> To remember which file is meant by < and >, I imagine which file name in the command line they point to: < points to the left one, and > points to the right one.

151

format a text file with **fmt** (see Chapter 9, "Printing Is Pressing"), save it in a new file, and compare the two files with **diff**. **diff** will show differences on almost every line—even though none of the words have changed.

If you want to compare two binary files, you can use **cmp**, but it will only tell you if the two files are different (not how they differ). This is useful for comparing two data files. Suppose you saved a copy of a spreadsheet worksheet in your directory, and you want to know if the original has been changed. Use this command to find out.

```
$ cmp /1Q94.wks /FirstQ94.wks
/1Q94.wks /FirstQ94.wks differ: byte 97
```

cmp compares the two files and tells you if they differ. The `byte 97` part tells you where **cmp** found the difference. However, unless you're a programmer, you won't need to know where the difference is. Once **cmp** has found a difference, it stops. If **cmp** doesn't find a difference, it ends and you get the command prompt again.

If you want to compare the contents of two directories, use the **dircmp** program. **dircmp** shows you which files are unique to each directory, and then compares the files the directories have in common. The output of **dircmp** is quite long, and many versions automatically use **pr** to format it for printing (**pr** is described in Chapter 9, "Printing Is Pressing").

You use **dircmp** just like **cmp** or **diff**, giving it the names of the directories you want to compare. Suppose you have directories named clients and CLIENTS, and they contain the following information (clients on the left and CLIENTS on the right):

Anne.Bosch	Anne.Bosch
Becky.Hatcher	Becky.Hatcher
Chris.Deutch	Chris.Deutch
Jan.Anderhooven	Ken.Arron
Jim.Harriss	Les.Passmore
Ken.Arron	Maria.Callen
Lynne.Klein	Ray.Bobb
Maria.Callen	

I used the command **dircmp clients CLIENTS ¦ more -s** and got the results shown in the following figure. (The **more -s** command turns consecutive blank lines into one blank line, so I could fit the output on one screen.)

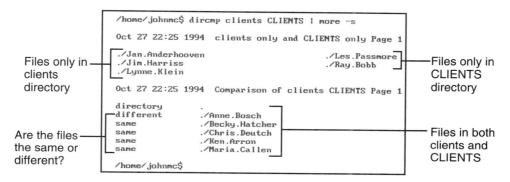

Files only in clients directory

Files only in CLIENTS directory

Are the files the same or different?

Files in both clients and CLIENTS

```
/home/johnmc$ dircmp clients CLIENTS ¦ more -s

Oct 27 22:25 1994   clients only and CLIENTS only Page 1

./Jan.Anderhooven                    ./Les.Passmore
./Jim.Harriss                        ./Ray.Bobb
./Lynne.Klein

Oct 27 22:25 1994   Comparison of clients CLIENTS Page 1

directory        .
different        ./Anne.Bosch
same             ./Becky.Hatcher
same             ./Chris.Deutch
same             ./Ken.Arron
same             ./Maria.Callen

/home/johnmc$
```

dircmp compares the contents of two directories.

The left column at the top gives the names of files that are only in the directory clients; the right column gives the names of files that are only in CLIENTS. Below that, **dircmp** shows whether files with the same name that are found in both directories are actually the same.

What Kind of File Is It?

While looking around the file system for a particular file, you're bound to run into files you can't identify. These are files that are obviously *for* something, but you can't figure out what. UNIX has a program called **file** that guesses what the file is for. If **file** can't make a guess, it prints the file's name but nothing else.

Here's an example of how **file** can be useful. I once received an electronic mail message that I was told was a document. (Electronic mail is discussed in Chapter 22, "Send Me A Letter.") I'd never seen a document quite like it before; the first line was \documentstyle[12pt,twocolumn]{article}. I could guess it was meant for some kind of formatting program, but which one? I needed to know so I could print it properly. To find out, I saved the mail message as a file called mystery.document and ran the **file** program. Here's what it said:

```
$ file mystery.document
mystery.document:   LaTeX program code
```

153

After I read the LaTeX manual page, I was able to print the document. (See Chapter 14, "Write Like the Prose," for more about LaTeX.)

To use the **file** program, name the file (or files) after the command. **file** looks at the first 500 or so characters and then "guesses" what kind of file it is. The guesses are pretty accurate; **file** gets directories and special files right (special files were described in Chapter 7, "The Root of the Matter: Files and Directories") and does fairly well on the rest. It sometimes misses on which "flavor" a particular file is.

The following screen shot shows the contents of a directory; the output from the **ls -aF** command shows you which files are directories (bin), and which are programs (clear, grep, and ipxtli.com); the rest are just regular files. Below the **ls** listing are **file**'s guesses about each program. You'll notice that **file** is always right about whether a file is a directory, a program, or a text (or data) file. **file** then goes on to try and guess what flavor each file is. For example, it says that clear is not just a program (which is all **ls -aF** said) but it's commands text. And it says that hello.c isn't just a regular file but it's c program text. (It's up to you to know that "commands text" is a program and "program text" is not; **file**'s not very kind, that way.)

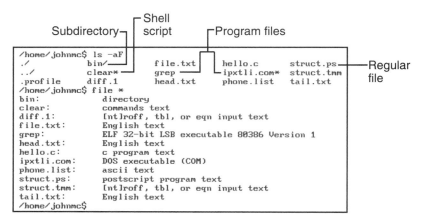

*The **file** program tells what three file types are and provides more information about what kind of file the others might be.*

Each version of **file** has different descriptions for the types of files it knows. The version of **file** in the figure really only knows five kinds of files: command files, data files, directories, text, and program files (though it may know many flavors of each kind).

➤ A *command file* is some kind of program. If the description says executable, the file is a binary program file; most programs are this type. If **file** says command text, the file is a text program file. (These are also called shell scripts; I discuss shell scripts in Chapter 18, "The Shell Game.")

➤ A *data file* is a binary file. Sometimes **file** can tell you the program that uses the file; sometimes it can't.

➤ You already know that a *directory* is a file that holds other files.

➤ A *text file* is a file that contains text. **file** recognizes text well, but its guesses about the kind of text file are sometimes wrong. For instance, there's not really any difference between the files head.txt and phone.list listed in the figure, but head.txt is described as English text while phone.list is described as ASCII text.

➤ *Input* text is meant to be processed by another program; **file** tells you which program, as well as it can. The file diff.1 is processed by one of the programs **nroff**, **troff**, **tbl**, or **eqn**. Program text is a set of commands in a programming language.

ASCII One way of encoding letters and characters so a computer can use them. It's not the only way, but it's one of the most common. PCs and most UNIX systems use ASCII.

The Least You Need to Know

You don't need to be Sherlock Holmes to find the file you want somewhere on a UNIX file system. However, you do need to know either the file's name or some word in the file.

➤ If you know the file's name, use the **find** command. You must supply the directory to start looking in, the name of the file, and what to do when the file is found: **find** *startdirectory* **-name** *filename* **-print**.

➤ If you want to find the file that contains a particular word or phrase, use the **grep** command. You must supply the pattern of letters you're looking for (if it contains a space, put it in double quotes) and the files to be searched: **grep** *pattern file* ....

➤ **grep** is normally case-sensitive. To make **grep** ignore the case of letters, use the **-i** option.

➤ To find the differences between two text files, use the **diff** command. The arguments are the two file names: **diff** *file1 file2*.

➤ To see if two files are different, use **cmp**. **cmp** only tells you if the files are different, not how they're different, but you can use it on all kinds of files. The arguments are the two file names: **cmp** *file1 file2*.

➤ To compare the contents of two directories, use the **dircmp** command. **dircmp** tells you which files are unique to each directory and if the files with the same names are actually identical. The arguments are the two directory names: **dircmp** *dir1 dir2*.

➤ To find out what a file's type is, use the **file** command.

Matchmaker, Matchmaker (Regular Expressions)

Have you ever looked through a file for something (like a company's phone number in the Yellow Pages) and wished there was a way to do this with the computer? Psst! There is a way. UNIX has provided you with a good utility that enables you to search files for specific letters, words, numbers, phrases, and so on. This utility is called **grep**, and you have already learned a little about it. To review, **grep** is an acronym for "global regular expression printer." In this chapter, we are going to learn about the regular expression part of **grep**.

To learn how to use **grep** with regular expressions, let's build a little test file to help us along. Create the following test file by typing each line and pressing **Enter**:

```
$ cat > phonebook
Zachary      703-1993
Carolyn      205-1965
```

```
David          876-3654
Matthew        876-2765
Cameron        875-4331
Emily          297-5454
Rachel         297-5452
Keith          756-1414
J.D.           345-2365
Kathy          345-2765
Doug           275-2751
Ginger         275-3752
Megan          346-1372
(now press the Ctrl and the letter D at the same time)
$
```

Whew! We're done. Now we have something to learn with and change, without creating havoc in your co-worker's files.

What Are Regular Expressions?

A *regular expression* is basically a pattern of letters or numbers. It can be one character or a combination of characters, such as: a, ab, abc, abc123. We use regular expressions to search a file for patterns. As an example, let's find everyone in the phonebook file who has the pattern "a" in his or her name. We use **grep** in this way:

```
$ grep 'a' phonebook
Zachary        703-1993
Carolyn        205-1965
David          876-3654
Matthew        876-2765
Cameron        875-4331
Rachel         297-5452
Kathy          345-2765
Megan          346-1372
$
```

Regular expression A way to describe a pattern of letters. The simplest pattern is a word, but a regular expression can also include wild card characters that stand for other characters. All UNIX programs that search text use regular expressions. If a word or phrase is described by a regular expression, we say it matches the regular expression.

As you see, only the names containing the letter "a" are displayed.

The quotation marks around the pattern in the command aren't always necessary, but it's good to get into the habit of using them. Some of the special characters for regular expression patterns are the same as special characters for the shell, so there's the danger that the shell will get to them first. The quotation marks (single or double) turn off the "specialness" for those characters as far as the shell is concerned; they're still special for **grep**. You don't need the quotation marks if you're using regular expressions inside a program such as an editor.

Using Regular Expressions with grep

Now that you know what a regular expression is, we can expand our little example by looking for more than one character. Let's look for the combination or pattern of characters "er."

```
$ grep 'er' phonebook
Cameron        875-4331
Ginger         275-3752
$
```

You can see that only Cameron and Ginger had the pattern "er" in their names.

So, what if you want to search for a line that begins with a certain pattern or a line that ends with a certain pattern? In order to do this you have to use an *anchor*. Oh, don't worry. We're not going sailing. In regular expressions, an anchor is a place to start looking. For instance, every line has a beginning and an end. Regular expressions use the caret (^) to represent the beginning of the line and the dollar sign ($) to represent the end of the line. Let's return to our phonebook file and search for every line that begins with the letter "K."

> If you enter the search pattern '^k' to find lines in the phonebook file that started with "K," **grep** won't find any matching lines. Remember that **grep** is case-sensitive. If you want to find uppercase letters, you have to use an uppercase letter in your search pattern.

```
$ grep '^K' phonebook
Keith          756-1414
Kathy          345-2765
$
```

The ^ (caret) tells **grep** to search for the pattern at the beginning of the line. Although there may be lines in the phonebook file that contain the letter "K," **grep** only displays lines that begin with the specified pattern.

Okay, so let's try looking for lines that end with a certain pattern. Tell **grep** to look for lines that end with the pattern "65." (Note that you place the anchor for the end of the line at the end of the search pattern.)

```
$ grep '65$' phonebook
Carolyn          205-1965
Matthew          876-2765
J.D.             345-2365
Kathy            345-2765
$
```

Now that you've got the basics of using regular expressions with **grep**, let's make our search patterns a little more complicated. Say you want to look for lines in which the second letter is "e." Hmmm! Now this is more difficult. You need **grep** to understand that you don't care what the first character on the line is, but that you want the second character to be "e." As a placeholder for the first character, you use a special character that represents a single character in the pattern: the period or dot. The pattern ^.e tells **grep** to search for lines that begin with any character followed by the letter "e."

```
$ grep '^.e' phonebook
Keith            756-1414
Megan            346-1372
$
```

grep finds the names Keith and Megan in the file. In this case, the period special character stood in for both the "K" in Keith and the "M" in Megan.

If necessary, you can use more than one dot special character in a row. For example, if we entered the command **grep '^...a' phonebook**, **grep** would only find Megan. The . (period) holds the place for any character, letter, or number. Therefore, three periods in a row hold the places for three characters.

Now let's say you want to find all lines that contain the characters K, k, M, or m. For this, you use another special character: brackets [ ]. The brackets tell **grep** to search every line for each individual pattern. In the following example, **grep** finds all lines in the phonebook file that contain K, k, M, or m.

```
$ grep '[KkMm]' phonebook
Matthew        876-2765
Cameron        875-4331
Emily          297-5454
Keith          756-1414
Kathy          345-2765
Megan          346-1372
$
```

As you can see, **grep** displays all the lines that contain the letters K, k, M, or m. (Remember that UNIX is case-sensitive. So in order to find every line containing k or m, you must use both upper- and lowercase letters.) Experiment with other combinations, and you will see this is a very powerful pattern searching tool.

Now that you know how to search for a character in a certain position (with the period character) and how to search for more than one character (with the brackets), put the two together. If you wanted to find any line in phonebook with the character "o" or "i" in the second position, your command would look like this:

```
$ grep '^.[OoIi]' phonebook
Doug          275-2751
Ginger        275-3752
$
```

The caret (^) is the anchor that tells **grep** to start the search at the beginning of the line. The period (.) represents any character at the beginning of the line, and the pattern [OoIi] tells **grep** to look for "o" or "i" in the search. In response to this pattern, **grep** finds Doug's and Ginger's phone numbers.

You can also use the bracket characters to search for ranges of characters. For instance, let's search the phonebook file for any line that contains any uppercase letter A through D. To do this, use the minus sign range operator (–):

```
$ grep '[A-D]' phonebook
Carolyn        205-1965
David          876-3654
Cameron        875-4331
J.D.           345-2365
Doug           275-2751
$
```

If you wanted to include the lowercase letters a through d, you could add the pattern a-d to the brackets like this: [A-Da-d]. In our example phonebook file, **grep** would display every line in phonebook because every line contains at least one of the letters a-d in either uppercase or lowercase.

Okay, you know you can use multiple periods consecutively to represent a specific number of characters. But what if you don't know how many characters are between the beginning of the line and the letter you want? Or, what if you know a file contains two specific characters, but you don't know how many characters are between those two letters? Regular expressions use the * wild-card character to represent any number of characters. To see the * character in action, let's search for lines that contain the letter "a" followed (somewhere) by "e."

```
$ grep 'a*e' phonebook
Matthew        876-2765
Cameron        875-4331
Rachel         297-5452
Keith          756-1414
Ginger         275-3752
Megan          346-1372
$
```

Matthew, Cameron, and Rachel are all correct. But the command also displayed Keith and Ginger, which don't even have an "a," and Megan, where the "a" is after the "e"! What gives?

The * in a regular expression is slightly different from the * in a file name wild card. In a regular expression, * is a modifier: it means any number of the character it follows. And by any number, * means any number including zero. That's why Keith, Ginger, and Megan match. Each one contains an "e" that has zero "a"s before it.

The way to do what we were trying to do (an "a" followed by any characters followed by an "e") is to let the * modify a different character: the dot, which stands for any single character:

```
$ grep 'a.*e' phonebook
Matthew        876-2765
Cameron        875-4331
Rachel         297-5452
$
```

This time, the pattern only matched the lines that contain an "a" followed by an "e" and have zero or more characters in between.

This example shows you that the * wild card gives you a very powerful and effective method of searching. For example, it could be extremely useful if you needed to search for a number pattern (such as to find all ZIP codes that ended in 99).

Some Useful Miscellaneous Searches

Now that you've learned how to use regular expressions and special characters, let me show you a couple of useful searches that might come in handy.

To find blank lines in a file, use the pattern ^$, as shown here.

```
$ grep '^$' filename
```

This pattern uses the beginning of the line anchor with the end of the line anchor. Since there are no spaces or characters between the anchors, this regular expression tells **grep** to search for only blank lines.

How can I find lines with a period in them? Because regular expressions interpret a period as a placeholder for any single character, you need to distinguish that you want to find the actual period character. In regular expressions, you do this by placing a \ (backslash) in front of the character:

```
$ grep '\.$' filename
```

This example searches for every line that ends with a period. The backslash is called the escape character.

What Are the Special Characters?

You can use the following special characters in your regular expression searches.

Special Character	Function
x	Searches for that specific character anywhere in the file.
.	Represents any one character.
*	Represents any number of characters.
^	Anchors the beginning of the line.
$	Anchors the end of the line.
[*xx*]	Searches for every specified character within the brackets.
[*x–x*]	Searches for a range of specified characters.
\	Tells the search program to ignore the function of the special character and search for the literal character in the file. (This is called the escape character.)

What Utilities Use Regular Expressions?

There are a number of utilities that use regular expressions. I have listed them below. Some you have already learned about in this book; some I won't discuss at all.

grep	Global regular expression printer (see this chapter and Chapter 12)
vi	Visual Editor (see Chapter 16)
emacs	Another editor (see Chapter 17)
awk	A powerful file processing utility
PERL	A powerful file and report processing utility
more	A command that displays text on-screen (see Chapter 8)
sed	A stream editor (see Chapter 14)

The Least You Need to Know

➤ UNIX is case-sensitive. Searching for "a" and "A" are two different searches. You can combine them using the bracket characters [ ].

➤ Regular expressions provide you with a means of finding text in a file.

➤ You can use [,], ., ^, $, and *char* in any regular expression together or alone. (Please use a little logic here though: abc^ and $end do not make sense.)

➤ You can have more than one range in the brackets and you can have more then one set of brackets. For example, **grep 'F[Aa][DdZz]e'** would search for FADe, FaDe, FAde, FAZe, FaZe, and Faze.

➤ To look for an actual period, caret, or bracket in the text, you can use the backslash escape character (\).

Part III
A Textbook on Text

A lot of what you do with UNIX involves text: putting words in a file, taking words out of a file, shuffling the words that are already in the file. That's what this part of the book is about: using UNIX's tools to shuffle words in files. With a text editor, you can write and edit a hundred words in the time it takes you to find a pen that's still got ink in it.

They say that the pen is mightier than the sword. I guess that makes the text editor mightier than the food processor.

EDITING ... THE EARLY DAYS.

Chapter 14

Write Like the Prose

In This Chapter

➤ Text processing in UNIX

➤ UNIX text processing programs

➤ Text editors

➤ Changing your default editor

So far I've told you how to find text files, move and remove them, and how to change their names, but I haven't really told you how to make and edit them. Because most of what people do with a computer is writing and printing, you need to know how to put words in a file and how to change them once they're there.

Originally, all configuration and startup files on a UNIX system were created as text; you could edit them with a text editor. Even the word processing tools provided with UNIX use plain text commands instead of hidden commands. Lately, applications that use binary data files and startup files have become popular. The only way to edit these files is to use the application itself. There's nothing wrong with this; it just means you can no longer edit all configuration files using only a text editor.

In this book, I'll focus on the standard tools that come with all UNIX systems because they are also the most commonly used UNIX text editors. I will go over the fundamental differences in the UNIX text editors because these differences affect how you use the tools, but before we dive into all that, I'll tell you a little about the word processors and desktop publishing tools available on UNIX.

Text and Documents

As far as you and I are concerned, a text file is any file that contains text but no magic control characters. Some text files are meant to be read by programs (such as your shell startup files), and some are meant to be read by people (such as your mail messages). As opposed to a text file, a document is intended to be printed. Therefore, the lines are formatted, there are margins, and it has been made to look pretty.

The business of producing text files and documents and then changing them is basically done with three kinds of programs:

➤ Text editors, which put text in a file. A text editor is like a stripped-down word processor. Each UNIX system comes with at least three editors, usually more.

➤ Word processors, which provide some formatting and printing features such as pagination, WYSIWYG, and different fonts. Word processors are available for UNIX, but they're not standard equipment. You have to buy them separately.

➤ Desktop publishing, which gives you the most control over how the text looks on the page. As with word processors, desktop publishing tools are not standard equipment with UNIX. You have to buy them separately.

Most DOS word processors and desktop publishing programs provide WYSIWYG capabilities. (WYSIWYG stands for "what you see is what you get," and it's pronounced "whizzy-wig.") They show you on-screen what the document will look like when you print it. The formatting commands are hidden in the file so you never see the command itself, only the results of it. (If you've ever used the WordPerfect word processor, however, you can see both the embedded commands and the results of the command by switching between the document window and the Reveal Codes window.) You can only edit the file with the word processor that created it, but you have the advantage of being able to see what it will look like before you print it.

UNIX doesn't have a tradition of WYSIWYG among its text tools. The document tools on UNIX combine the text with the formatting commands so you always see the formatting commands on-screen, but you don't see the results of those commands. The advantage of this is that you can create a document with any editor; the disadvantage is that you have to print the file to see the results of the formatting commands you have inserted in the text.

To apply some very basic formatting to text files, you can use a text editor and the **fmt** and **pr** commands described in Chapter 9, "Printing Is Pressing." These commands will format your text so you have regular margins and your document is paginated. If you want anything more sophisticated (like italic text), you need to use a document program, such as a word processor or **troff**.

Word Processing

The most standard word processing tools supplied with UNIX are **troff** (usually pronounced "tee-roff") and **nroff**. The commands work the same, but **troff** works for laser printers, while **nroff** is meant for character displays like terminals and line printers. Your system may have an alternate version of **troff**; common ones are **ditroff** and **groff**.

Just as you put formatting commands like bold or italics in a word processor file, you put similar **troff** commands right in a **troff** text file, but while a word processor interprets the commands and shows you the results of the command (bold or italicized text), the **troff** commands appear on-screen as part of the text. The only way to see the results of the **troff** format commands is to print the document. For example, the command to switch to italic text is **\fI**, and the command to switch back to the previous font is **\fP**. So, this sentence from a **troff** file

I don't know \fIhow\fP that shortbread got on my plate.

prints as:

I don't know *how* that shortbread got on my plate.

When you want to print the file, you run the **troff** command on the file. The complete command to print a **troff** file (such as the file diet.excuses) on our system is

```
$ troff diet.excuses | dpost | lp
```

171

The **troff** command interprets all of the formatting commands and converts them into an intermediate form. The first ¦ sends that intermediate form directly to the **dpost** program, which changes it into the correct form for our PostScript printer. The last ¦ sends the PostScript file produced by **dpost** to our printer.

That's a long command to print one lousy excuse! Depending on your printer, you may use a command other than **dpost**. Most system administrators hide all of this detail in a single command. On our system, I can get the same result with the **ts** command: **ts diet.excuses** is the same as the longer command I just gave.

The details of printing a **troff** command vary from manufacturer to manufacturer. Ask your system administrator if you have an equivalent to our **ts** command.

The name **troff** stands for "typeset run-off." **troff** is the typesetting version of **nroff**. **nroff** stands for "new roff," and it was based on an older command called **roff** (which in turn was based on a command called **runoff**). To give you some idea of how old these programs are, **runoff** came before UNIX (on a different operating system).

Many systems have another word processing tool called TeX or a variant called LaTeX. (The X is actually a Greek letter, pronounced like the "ch" in the German "ach.") Like **troff** commands, the formatting commands in TeX are text commands inserted right into the file. Here's how you'd indicate italicized text in TeX:

I don't know {\it how} that shortbread got on my plate.

The {\it command turns on italicized text, and the closing } turns it off.

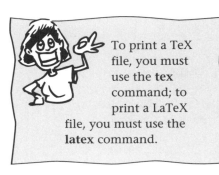

To print a TeX file, you must use the **tex** command; to print a LaTeX file, you must use the **latex** command.

Some people claim that both **troff** and TeX are sophisticated enough to produce publishing-quality pages. They're probably right, but the formatting commands in both are sufficiently complex that it takes an expert to get that kind of output.

However, if you need top quality output, there is hope. Some of the large PC word processor manufacturers have moved into the UNIX marketplace, so you may be able to get a big name word processor for your UNIX system. I know that WordPerfect has a UNIX version.

Desktop Publishing

Desktop publishing is "word-processing-plus." It gives you far more control over every aspect of the page. With a desktop publishing program, you can control where each column appears on the page, switch column widths halfway down the page, and more. Designing a page of a magazine is difficult (if not impossible) with a word processor, but it can be done easily with a desktop publishing program.

All of the desktop publishing programs I know of are WYSIWYG, including the ones for UNIX. In addition, all of the UNIX programs require that your UNIX system be running X Windows.

Surprisingly enough, UNIX has several desktop publishing programs that started on UNIX instead of being brought over from the PC. The two most popular are FrameMaker and Interleaf. (FrameMaker is also available for Windows PCs.) Both of these programs have WYSIWYG capabilities, but they require that your UNIX system be running X Windows.

Working with Text Editors in UNIX

One of the first uses for UNIX was text processing. UNIX was first used in the Bell Labs patent office for the preparation of patent application forms. Because of that and the fact that most files on a UNIX system are text files, UNIX has a lot of text processing tools.

I'm using the ugly term "text processing tools" not because the programs are like food processors, but because they manipulate text in some way. You can change things in files, add to files, and chop sections out of files. (Okay, so they are a little like food processors.)

The most basic text processing tool is a text editor. A text editor is like a stripped-down word processor: it enables you to create a text file, change it, and save it. You can print the file using the commands described in Chapter 9, "Printing Is Pressing."

Before UNIX, computer systems divided up files into different kinds: record files, supervisor files, program files, and text files (and, for all I know, nail files). A text file could never be a record file, and programmers had to know which they were going to use in their programs. Those early computers even stored the different kinds of files differently.

UNIX, on the other hand, stores all files as if they're text files. A file may not be text (a program file certainly isn't), but it's stored like a text file. That's what the gurus mean when they say that all files on UNIX are text files.

There are other programs for extracting information from text files, sorting text files, joining text files, and generally finding out about text files. You can use the **cut**, **awk**, and **sed** commands to extract text, but I won't be discussing them in this book. The **sort** command (described in Chapter 25, "Neat Stuff") sorts lines of text, and **cat** (described in Chapter 8, "Branching Out: Working with Files and Directories") enables you to join text files. An example of a command that shows you information about a text file, the **wc** (for word count) command shows you how many characters, words, and lines are in a file. You use the **wc** command in the format **wc** *filename* (or **wc** *filename filename* for multiple files) as this example shows:

```
$ wc proposal.mm attachments.mm
    222    1465    8170    proposal.mm
    151    2788   15485    attachments.mm
    373    4253   23655    total
```

The first number in the output is the number of lines: proposal.mm has 222 lines. The second number is the number of words: proposal.mm has 1,465 words. The third number is the number of characters: proposal.mm has 8,170 characters. If you only need to see one of these numbers, you can use certain options. To see just the number of lines, use **wc -l**. To see just the number of words, use **wc -w**. To see just the number of characters, use **wc -c**.

Text Editors and How They Differ

Every UNIX system provides at least three editors, sometimes more. Here's a description of the types of editors you can reasonably expect to find and how they differ. (I describe how to use each of these editors in the Chapters 15, "What's My Line (Editor, That Is)?," 16, "Viva vi!" and 17, "Circus Emacs-Imus.")

There are two important ways in which editors can differ:

➤ Do they show you the text while you're editing it?

Editors that don't show you the text while you're editing it are called *line editors*. Editors that show you a full screen of text so you can see what you're editing are called *screen editors*.

➤ Can you give commands while you're typing in new text?

Editors that don't allow you to do this are said to have two modes of behavior: *insert mode* and *command mode*. You must switch from one mode to the other depending on what you want to do. Most modern word processors allow you to enter both commands and text without switching modes.

These two distinctions are only apparent when you're changing text in previously saved text files. When you're entering new text, the text editors look much the same.

Line editors don't show you the text you're changing unless you ask them to use a print-to-screen command. (In **ed**, for example, the **p** command prints a line of text.) I know it's difficult to believe, but it's true. These editors work on text one line at a time, hence the name "line editors." Because they don't show you the line, you can't move the cursor back and forth while editing. In addition, there's no command to delete a word because the editor only deals with lines. (For DOS users, the old **edlin** editor is an example of a line editor.)

Screen editors always show you the contents of the file you're editing. When you change a word, the change shows up immediately. Because they show you a screenful of the file at a time, these editors are called screen editors. Most modern editors and all modern word processors are screen editors.

Line editor An editor that works on only one line of text at a time. It doesn't show you the line unless you ask it to. (This would be like editing with your hands in a box where you can't see what you're doing.)

Mode A way of behaving. A program has modes if commands are available only some of the time. Mode-based editors have an *insert* mode (in which you type text) and a *command* mode (in which you give commands such as to delete or change lines of text). The same command key can mean something different in each mode.

Some editors have two different ways or modes of behavior. You use one mode, called the *insert mode*, only when you're typing text. You use the other mode, called *command mode*, when you're editing existing text. With this type of editor, pressing x adds an "x" to the file if you're in insert mode, but it deletes the letter on which your cursor is resting if you're in command mode. These dual-mode editors are frustrating for both beginning and experienced users because you must always remember to change modes before switching tasks. Inevitably you will forget and be aghast at the results of what you thought was a simple text change.

Other editors (and all modern word processors) allow you to give commands while you're editing text. In this type of editor, commands are never individual letters; they have to be Control-key sequences. This eliminates the problem of having to switch between modes.

A Fistful of Editors

Here is a brief description of the editors that are on every UNIX system. Although I mention several here for your information, I will only discuss the **ed**, **emacs**, and **vi** editors in detail in this book.

ed is the standard editor on most UNIX systems, and it's also the oldest UNIX editor. It is a mode-oriented line editor. **ed** has two advantages: it's on every UNIX system, and it works tolerably well even when the system is very slow. Because it comes standard with every UNIX system, I'll tell you more about **ed** in Chapter 15, "What's My Line (Editor, That Is)?" Just the same, you don't ever want to use **ed**, because it's archaic. Trust me on this.

ex is another line editor. It's nearly a copy of **ed**, but **ex** is noteworthy because it's also part of **vi**, which is more bearable than **ed**. I'm not going to talk about **ex** separately in this book. You need to know a couple of **ex** commands to use **vi**, but I'll talk about them in Chapter 16, "Viva vi!"

vi is probably the single most commonly used editor in UNIX. Although it is at least a screen editor, it's still a mode-oriented editor, which a lot of people don't like. Yet **vi** is reasonably quick even when the system is slow, and it's very good for changing text. I find the search-and-replace feature in **vi** to be more useful than the one in **emacs**, but a lot of people disagree with me. Incidentally, some people pronounce it "vee-eye"; others say "vye."

emacs is the most "modern" of the editors. For starters, **emacs** is a screen editor. Second, it's modeless; you give commands with Control-key combinations. **emacs** has so many features built into it, it would take a book this size to describe them all. On the down side, **emacs** is not standard (though it's a rare system that doesn't have **emacs**), it requires a lot of computer power to run, and on a busy UNIX system, **emacs** can be slow. What's even worse, some of the commands do the opposite of what you'd expect. (For example, it's difficult to make the Backspace key perform the actual Backspace function instead of giving you Help.) I'll talk about the **emacs** editor in Chapter 17, "Circus Emacs-Imus."

There are a bunch of other editors modeled after **emacs** (such as **jove**, **mg**, and **microemacs**), but most of them lack some of **emacs'** more baroque features. If you know the basic **emacs** commands, you can use any of them.

So, which should you use? I don't recommend the two line editors at all. In addition, I use both **vi** and **emacs**, but I use them for different things. I use **emacs** when I'm writing new files, and I use **vi** for editing existing files. If your system has **emacs**, I recommend that you use it because it's most like a word processor. However, if you find **emacs** slow or if you discover you don't like it, try **vi**.

You might also ask your system administrator if there are any other editors installed on your system. Two common editors are **joe** (for Joe's Own Editor) and **pico**. **joe** uses the same commands as the DOS word processor, WordStar. **pico** is the editor provided with the pine electronic mail system. **pico** doesn't have as many features as any of the other editors mentioned here, but it's easy to use. Both **joe** and **pico** are freely available through the Internet.

There's one more editor I have to mention: **sed**. **sed** is a non-interactive editor. **sed** is very useful if you need to make repetitive changes to many files. All of the other editors I've mentioned are interactive: you open the file, you change the text, you save the file. With **sed**, you supply a list of commands to change the text and a list of files you want to change. **sed** does the rest of the work without you by inserting the changes into the files.

Suppose you have a number of form letters that contain your address, and then you move. With an interactive editor, you need to change the files one at a time (start the editor, open a file, change the address, save the file, go to the next file). With **sed**, you can type the command to change the address and the names of the affected files, and **sed** does the rest.

Defining Your Default Editor

Many programs that aren't editors enable you to edit text by letting you access your default editor to make your changes. For instance, let's say you need to edit a mail message before you send it, so the mail program allows you to bring up your mail message in the text editor and change it before you mail it. Some versions of the **less** command also enable you to edit a file you're reading.

When you want to edit a file in one of these programs, unless you tell your system otherwise, the editor you gain access to will probably be **ed** (though it might be **vi**). I've already told you that you don't want to use **ed**. To tell the system which editor you want to use inside other programs, you have to set your **EDITOR** environment variable (see Chapter 19, "Environ-Mental Health").

How you set your **EDITOR** environment variable depends on the kind of shell you're using. The way I show here assumes that your prompt is a dollar sign (as in the examples). If you want your default editor to be **emacs**, use this command:

```
$ export EDITOR=emacs
```

If you want your default editor to be **vi**, substitute **vi** for **emacs**. If you prefer some other editor, substitute that name in the appropriate place. To verify that the command worked, you can check the value of the **EDITOR** environment variable with the command **echo $EDITOR**.

```
$ echo $EDITOR
emacs
```

This change only lasts until you logout. If you want to change your default editor permanently, you need to add the new environment variable to your startup files (as explained under the heading "Making Changes Permanent" in Chapter 19, "Environ-Mental Health").

178

The Least You Need to Know

UNIX has many programs for creating and editing text files and for producing documents. This chapter discussed what's available on most systems.

➤ **wc** tells you how many characters, words, and lines are in a text file.

➤ To create and edit text files, you use a text editor.

➤ The **ed** and **ex** editors are mode-oriented line editors. Editing commands aren't available while you're entering text, and these editors don't show you the text as you're editing it.

➤ **vi** is the most used UNIX editor. It's a screen editor (it shows you a screenful of text at a time), but it also has modes.

➤ **emacs** is almost as popular as **vi**, and it's the editor most like a word processor.

➤ **sed** is a non-interactive editor. You use it to do repetitive editing jobs on a large number of files.

➤ For word processing, UNIX systems supply **troff**, which requires that formatting commands be put into the file as text. Also available are TeX, which is similar in principle to **troff**, and some word processors that have come to UNIX systems from PCs.

➤ Desktop publishing programs are available for UNIX but aren't standard.

179

Chapter 15

What's My Line (Editor, That Is)?

In This Chapter

➤ Starting and quitting **ed**

➤ Adding and deleting text

➤ Saving a file

➤ Searching for and replacing text

➤ Changing files

One editor has been standard on all UNIX systems since the beginning: **ed**. Not many people use **ed** anymore because it is the least user-friendly of all the UNIX text editors (see Chapter 14, "Write Like the Prose"). Although some new UNIX-like operating systems (such as Linux) don't even provide it, it's still nearly everywhere.

There are two reasons why you would want to know how to use **ed**:

➤ If you know how to use **ed**, you can edit a file on nearly any UNIX system.

➤ Other UNIX programs were influenced by how **ed** does things. **ed**'s commands for searching and replacing text were adapted for almost every other UNIX command. (The **grep** command is just one of **ed**'s commands turned into a separate program.) Understanding **ed** can help you understand those other programs.

At the very least, you want to know how to quit **ed**, in case you end up using it by accident some day.

ed is a line editor: it lets you edit text one line at a time. Instead of seeing a screen filled with text, you see only the line you're working on. When you're entering text into a file, you can backspace only to the beginning of the current line. When you're entering commands, most of the commands apply only to the current line. These restrictions make this text editor cumbersome to use, but never fear. In this chapter, I'll show you how to get around these limitations and others.

When UNIX was being developed, many of the terminals were teletypes (like typewriters with big rolls of paper attached). When you're printing on paper, you can't keep retyping the contents of the screen, partly because there is no screen, and partly because it would take too much time and paper.

That's the kind of terminal **ed** was developed for. **ed** shows you text as you type it in, but it won't show you what's already there unless you ask for it.

Editing à la Mode

Using **ed** commands takes some getting used to. In this section, I'll describe how the **ed** editor differs from modern editors and word processors, and I'll provide a list of the most common **ed** commands and examples of how to use them.

In a nutshell, the differences between **ed** and other editors include:

➤ **ed** is different from modern editors and word processors in that it has two modes: *insert mode*, in which you type new text into a file, and *command mode*, in which you give commands (you can save the file, do search-and-replace operations, change existing text, and quit). You can't give commands in insert mode, and you can't insert text in command mode.

➤ All commands in **ed** are single letters, and you must press **Enter** after you type the command. For instance, to print on-screen the line you're working on, press **p** and then **Enter**.

➤ Normally a command applies only to the current line, which is the line you worked on last (remember, **ed** works on a file one line at a time). You can tell **ed** which line (or lines) the command applies to by specifying an *address*. The address is just the line number, and it goes before the command. For example, to print line 11 to the screen instead of the current line, type the command **11p** and press **Enter**. The 11 is the address.

➤ Some commands, such as the "show line number of" command (=), only work on one line. Some commands can work on either a single line or a range of lines in a file.

> **Range** A group of consecutive lines. You can make most commands apply to a range of lines by telling **ed** the starting line and the ending line separated by a comma. To print from line 20 to line 31 of a file, give the command **20,31p**. In this case, the address 20,31 indicates that the command should start printing on line 20 and continue until it prints line 31.

Starting (and Quitting) ed

To create a new file using **ed**, simply type **ed** at the command line and press **Enter**. When **ed** starts, it shows you the cursor, which is usually a blinking line or a square (the shape of the cursor depends on your terminal).

```
$ ed
  - -
```

If you want to load a file automatically (whether it is a new file or a previously saved file), you can include the file name in your command when you start **ed**. For example, the command **ed .profile** starts **ed** with the file .profile already loaded for editing. You can only name one file on the command line. **ed** tells you how big the file is in bytes, and beneath that you see the cursor.

183

Now you're in **ed**. By default, you always start in command mode. When you want to start typing text, you have to give the command to enter text insert mode. I'll tell you how to do that in just a minute, but first let me show you how to quit **ed**.

Quitting ed

You can only quit **ed** from command mode. To quit, type **q** and press **Enter**. If the file hasn't been changed since the last time you changed it, **ed** stops and takes you back to the command prompt (which is just the cursor). If you've changed the file and haven't saved the changes, **ed** displays a question mark. This gives you an opportunity to save the file with the **w** command (see "Saving the File," later in this chapter). If you really want to quit without saving your changes, give the **q** command again:

```
q
?
q
```

Switching Modes

Switching between modes is very simple; the difficult part is remembering to do so. In command mode, **ed** will tell you immediately if you're trying to do the wrong thing by displaying a question mark.

To get to command mode from text mode, start a new line by pressing **Enter**. Then type . and press **Enter** again. The line consisting of only a period doesn't become part of the file; it switches you to command mode. Now you're ready to use any command simply by typing it and pressing **Enter**.

To get to the insert mode from the command mode, simply type the command **a** (for add or append) and press **Enter**. Now you can type new text into your file. (I'll remind you about these modes a few more times, but then, you're on your own.)

Basic Text Tasks

Here I'll show you how to insert new text into a file by starting text insert mode and how to go from text insert mode back to command mode. I'll also show you how to delete lines of text and how to move around in the file.

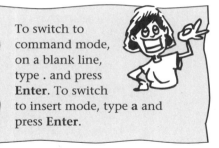

To switch to command mode, on a blank line, type **.** and press **Enter**. To switch to insert mode, type **a** and press **Enter**.

These are the basic **ed** commands. You must press Enter after each of these. All of the addresses shown are optional; if you don't supply an address, the command applies only to the current line.

Command	Function
q	Quits **ed**. You must press **q** again to quit without saving changes to a file.
w*file*	Saves (writes) the current file into a file named *file*.
e*file*	Quits current file and edits new file named *file*.
a	Enters text insertion mode, adding text after current line.
#a	Adds text; the new text starts *after* the line number #.
.	Returns to command mode. This command only works in text insert mode.
d	Deletes current line.
#d	Deletes line number #.
***start*,*end*d**	Deletes lines number *start* through *end*.
h	Gives explanation for last ? response.
.=	Prints line number of current line.
$=	Prints line number of last line in file.
p	Prints current line.
#p	Prints line number #.
***start*,*end*p**	Prints lines from *start* to *end*.

continues

185

Command	Function
/word/	Searches forward in file for *word*.
?word?	Searches backward in file for *word*.
s/old/new/	Replaces the first occurrence of *old* on this line with *new*.
*s/old/new/***g**	Replaces all occurrences of *old* on this line with *new*.
*start,end***s/old/new/**	Replaces the first occurrence of *old* on this line with *new* for the specified range of lines.
*start,end***s/old/new/g**	Replace all occurrences of *old* with *new* in these lines for the specified range of lines.
u	Undoes last change.

Inserting Text

To start inserting text, you must be in insert mode. If you've just opened **ed**, you're in the command mode. To switch to insert mode, type **a** and press **Enter** (the **a** command stands for add or append). If you don't supply an address, the **a** command starts adding text after the current line.

Here's a sample letter I'll use to demonstrate how the common **ed** commands work. I've put in line numbers to make references easier; you don't have to type the numbers. **ed** doesn't wrap lines for you; you must press **Enter** at the end of each line of text. If you don't press Enter, **ed** puts all of the text on one line. You separate paragraphs with a blank line (press **Enter** again).

```
1  Dear Mr. Smith:
2
3  According to our records, you still haven't paid for
```

186

```
4  the E-Z Sweep Electronic Lawn Rake you bought in
5  September. Please arrange payment now. If you do not
6  pay the full amount, we shall be forced to call our
7  lawyers.
8
9  In case you've forgotten, you owe us $302.95.
10
11 Have a nice day.
12
13 Yours sincerely,
```

If you want to insert text into a particular part of the letter, you can give a line address and use the **a** command. The command **$a** adds text after the last line in the file. The command **0a** adds text before any other text (it's after line 0, the very beginning of the file). If you wanted to add text after line 9 you would use **9a** as your insert text mode command.

To stop adding text, start a new line by pressing **Enter**, type ., and press **Enter** again. This puts you back in command mode. (This last line containing the period isn't saved as part of the text.)

Displaying Text

To display text, use the **p** (print) command. You must first be in the command mode (press **Enter**, type ., and press **Enter** again). Now you can type **p** and press **Enter** to display your current line of text on-screen. In addition, you can use addresses with the **p** command. For example, every file has a last line, but the number varies from file to file. You don't have to know the number of lines in the file before you start; you use the dollar sign in an address to stand in for the number of the last line. Therefore, **$p** prints the last line in the file, and **1,$p** shows the entire file from line 1 to the last line ($). The following figure shows what the above letter looks like using **1,$p**.

Pressing **Enter** shows you the next consecutive line. You can read through an entire file just by pressing **Enter**.

```
1,$p
Dear Mr. Smith:

According to our records, you still haven't paid for
the E-Z Sweep Electronic Lawn Rake you bought in
September. Please arrange payment now. If you do not
pay the full amount, we shall be forced to call our
lawyers.

In case you've forgotten, you owe us $302.95.

Have a nice day.

Yours sincerely,
```

1,$p shows the text of the entire file.

Just as the $ stands for the last line in a file, a dot (.) stands for the number of the current line (the one you're working on). Thus, the command **1,.p** prints everything from line 1 to your current line on the screen.

Moving Around in the File

In a line editor, you move around in the file by changing your current line. You can go to a line just by typing the line's number. For example, type **12** to go to line 12 and view the line on-screen. The **$** command takes you to the last line in the file. (Remember that **$** as an address stands for the last line in the file.)

A lot of the commands change your current line for you. For example, if you add an address to the **p** command, when that line is printed, it becomes the current line. (In fact, the commands **12** and **12p** do exactly the same thing.) If you print more than one line, the last one printed becomes the current line.

The = command shows you the line number of its address without going there. That's not much use when you use an address like 12 (you already know it's line 12), but it's useful with some other symbols used in addresses. The address . stands for the current line. So you can show the line number of your current line with the command .=.

ed doesn't handle mistakes and bad commands very well, I'm afraid. **ed** complains to you by printing a ? symbol. When you see a ?, you know **ed** didn't understand the command or something went wrong. To get a terse explanation of the ?, use the **h** command:

```
h
no such file or
directory
--
```

In this case, **ed** balked because it couldn't find a file with the name you gave.

If you don't give the = command an address (such as . or a specific line number), it displays the line number of the last line in the file (which is the same as typing **$=**). If you use the = command by itself in regard to the earlier sample letter, = displays line **13**.

Here are a couple more examples. To go to the beginning of the file, give the line number **1**. **ed** automatically prints the new current line to the screen:

```
1
Dear Mr. Smith:
```

To go to the last line, use **$**:

```
$
Yours sincerely,
```

Deleting Text or Lines

To delete a line of text, use the **d** command. Let's say you typed the sample letter from earlier in the chapter and then realized that the closing "Have a nice day" isn't really appropriate in a letter threatening legal action. In order to delete that line, it must be the current line; move to it by typing **11** and pressing **Enter**. Then you can delete the line with the **d** command. When you print the letter to your screen again (with the **1,$p** command), you see that the closing "Have a nice day." has been deleted.

```
d
1,$p
Dear Mr. Smith:

According to our records, you still haven't paid for
the E-Z Sweep Electronic Lawn Rake you bought in
September. Please arrange payment now. If you do not
pay the full amount, we shall be forced to call our
lawyers.

In case you've forgotten, you owe us $302.95.


Yours sincerely,
```

189

Because **d** only removed the current line, there are now two blank lines before "Yours sincerely,". You'll see how to fix that after I show you how to undo a change to the file.

You can give **d** single-line addresses or ranges. For example, **12d** deletes line 12, and **2,6d** deletes lines 2 through 6.

The **d** command only deletes lines. To delete a word from a line, you have to use **s**, which is the substitute command. I'll tell you about **s** in the section "Searching for and Replacing Text," later in this chapter.

Undoing a Change

The **u** command undoes the last change you made to the text. To clarify "last change," note that it does not undo the last change if that change was a command for something like printing to screen or moving around in the file. Instead, it undoes the last change that actually altered the text, such as a **d**, **a**, or **s** command.

If you're working through this chapter sequentially, in the last section you deleted line 11 ("Have a nice day.") from the sample letter. If you use the **u** command now, it undoes that deletion. The following example shows the **u** command and the resulting letter as it was printed with the **1,$p** command.

```
u
1,$p
Dear Mr. Smith:

According to our records, you still haven't paid for
the E-Z Sweep Electronic Lawn Rake you bought in
September. Please arrange payment now. If you do not
pay the full amount, we shall be forced to call our
lawyers.

In case you've forgotten, you owe us $302.95.

Have a nice day.

Yours sincerely,
```

As you can see, the line "Have a nice day" is back. Doing **u** again undoes the undo, taking you back to where you started (the line is gone again). Try it and see.

Any command that doesn't change the text won't affect the results of the **u** command. For instance, you could save the sample letter or print it on the screen, and run **u** again, and it would still switch back and forth between deleting and adding line 11. As soon as you make another change to the text, that's the change **u** works on.

Let's say your final decision was to leave out the line "Have a nice day." Now you need to delete the extra blank line before "Yours sincerely," which is the second-to-last line in the file. Use the command **$** to tell you the line number of the last line in the file, which is 11. This tells you that you want to delete line number 10. Use the command **10d** to delete that extra blank line.

Saving a File

The **w** command saves a file. In this example, since you didn't specify a file name on the command line when you opened **ed**, **ed** doesn't know what the file's name is. The first time you save a new file, you have to tell **ed** the file's name. This is how you save the letter by the name of remittance.ltr:

```
w remittance.ltr
298
```

The 298 is the number of characters in the file. (This is not the same as the size of the file, because **ed** doesn't count the invisible end-of-line characters in this number.)

Once you've saved a file with a name, **ed** knows what the file's name is. Therefore, when you need to save it again, you only have to give the command **w**:

```
w
317
```

You can also use **w** to save the file under a new name. Go ahead and save the file as deadbeat.ltr:

```
w deadbeat.ltr
317
```

This second name doesn't change the original file name that **ed** uses when you give the **w** command alone. The next time you save changes with **w**, the new changes will be saved under the original file name remittance.ltr.

191

Searching for and Replacing Text

To search for a line of text in **ed**, you must surround it with slashes. For example, **/you/** finds the next line that contains "you" and prints it to the screen. You can repeat a forward search by typing / again; **ed** remembers the text you're looking for. If a line matches, it becomes the new current line and is printed to the screen. If you want to search backwards in the file (towards the beginning), use **?** instead of /. Type the command **?you?**. Here's what the searches look like in our example file:

```
/you/
According to our records, you still haven't paid for
/
the E-Z Sweep Electronic Lawn Rake you bought in
?
According to our records, you still haven't paid for
?Mr. Smith?
Dear Mr. Smith:
```

The / and ? commands search forward and backward (respectively) for text.

In this example, I actually did four searches, using these commands: **/you/** to find the next line containing you; **/** to repeat that search; **?** to repeat the search again, but backwards; and **Mr. Smith?** to search backwards in the file for the phrase "Mr. Smith." By the way, all of these searches are for regular expressions, not just text. Regular expressions are described in Chapter 13, "Matchmaker, Matchmaker (Regular Expressions)."

The **s** (substitute) command lets you replace one bit of text with another. To put this command to work, go to the first line in the file by typing the command **1**. To replace "Mr. Smith" with "Deadbeat," use the **s** command.

```
1
Dear Mr. Smith:
s/Mr. Smith/Deadbeat/p
Dear Deadbeat:
```

To use the **s** command, you enter the text you want replaced between the first set of slashes. Enter the text with which you want to replace it between the second set of slashes. The **p** at the end prints the line after you've changed it.

If part of the text you are searching or replacing contains a slash (/), put a backslash in front of it: \/. This tells **ed** not to interpret the / as a metacharacter. You see, **ed** uses the slashes to figure out where the old text ends and the new text begins; the backslash tells **ed** to ignore that special meaning of slash for this particular character. Slash and backslash are *metacharacters* in **ed**; for more information about metacharacters, see Chapter 13, "Matchmaker, Matchmaker (Regular Expressions)."

If you want to search for a word and delete it, use that word as the text to be replaced and nothing as the text to replace it with. For example, to delete the word "Dear" from our letter and then print the line to see the results, use this command:

```
s/Dear //p
Deadbeat:
```

When you use the **s** command to search for and replace text, only the first occurrence of the search text is replaced. If you want to replace all occurrences of that particular word, you can add a **g** to the end of the command line. For example, "Deadbeat" contains two "ea" pairs. To change them both to the letter "u," use this command:

```
$ s/ea/u/gp
Dudbut:
```

Without the **g** at the end, you'd just get "Dudbeat."

Getting a New File

If you want to edit a file other than the one you are currently in, you don't have to quit **ed** and restart it. You can load a different file for editing by using the **e** command and the name of the new file. For example, let's say you are currently in the remittance.ltr file, but now you want to open the deadbeat.ltr file (which we saved earlier in our example). To start editing the file deadbeat.ltr, get in command mode and type **e deadbeat.ltr**.

Since you haven't saved the last changes you made to the remittance.ltr file (from the exercise in the above section), you get a ? response. If you want to save this version of remittance.ltr, use the **w** command. If you don't want to save it, give the **e** command again.

After you give the **e** command, **ed** "remembers" the new file's name. So you can edit the file to your heart's content, and when you give the **w** command to save the file, **ed** writes the changes to this new file.

The Least You Need to Know

That's the **ed** survival guide. Here's hoping you never need to use it.

➤ To start **ed**, type the command **ed**. If you supply a file name, **ed** loads that file for editing. To quit **ed**, use the **q** command. If the file's been changed since the last time you saved it, you have to give the **q** command twice.

➤ To access insert mode and add text, use the **a** command. To stop adding text and get into the command mode, start a new line by pressing **Enter**, type **.**, and press **Enter** again.

➤ With almost all commands in **ed**, you can give an address at the beginning. The address can be a line number or a range of line numbers.

➤ To print a line, use the **p** command.

➤ To delete a line, use the **d** command.

➤ To substitute one bit of text for another, use the **s** command in this format: **s/*old text*/*new text***. If you add a **g** to the end of the command, **ed** replaces all occurrences of the old text with the new text. Otherwise, only the first occurrence is changed.

➤ To undo the last editing change you made, use the **u** command.

➤ To save the file, use the **w** command. You can save to a different file name by giving the new file name after the **w** command.

Chapter 16

Viva vi!

In This Chapter

➤ Starting and quitting **vi**

➤ Adding and deleting text

➤ Saving a file

➤ Searching for and replacing text

➤ Changing files

vi, pronounced "vye" or "vee-eye" (take your pick), is a screen editor. It actually shows you a screen's worth of text at a time, and the cursor shows your current position in the file. Even though **ed** is described as the standard UNIX editor, in practice the standard editor is **vi**. **vi** is available for every UNIX platform, and there are even versions produced for PCs. **vi** is an excellent editor for programmers, but it's very cryptic for the beginner.

Even if you don't intend to use **vi**, it's worth knowing the four basic movement commands (**h**, **j**, **k**, and **l**), because other UNIX commands use them.

Commanding vi

Like **ed**, **vi** is a mode-based editor. That means that not all commands are available all the time. Think of it this way: When you're dressed for a formal dinner party, you're not about to play a game of pick-up basketball; you're in formal mode. Likewise, when you're in sweats and sneakers, you're not going to a dinner party; you're in exercise mode. In the same way, **vi** has two modes: *text-insertion* mode, which you use to enter new text, and *command* (or edit) mode, which you use to give commands (such as to save files, search-and-replace, delete, and move the cursor through the file). In a nutshell, these are the idiosyncrasies of **vi**:

➤ **vi** has short commands and long commands. Short commands are usually one or two letters, such as **ZZ** (which saves a file and quits **vi**). **vi** doesn't show you short commands on the screen; it only shows you the result.

➤ Long commands are commands that start with a colon (:) or commands that take some kind of user-supplied information. You must press **Enter** at the end of these commands to tell **vi** that you've finished the command. For instance, to search forward in the file for some text, you type **/*text*** and press **Enter**. **vi** displays long commands on the bottom line of the screen so you can see what you're typing.

➤ Many of the commands that move from one screen of text to another (either forward in the file or backward in the file) are key combinations. You must press **Control** and a letter to use these. For example, **Control-F** moves you forward one screen. Although I write them here with capital letters, key combinations can use upper- or lowercase letters.

➤ One thing to remember is that even though **vi** shows you a screenful of text at a time, it deals with it one line at a time. If you're typing text and you want to backspace, you can only backspace to the beginning of the line.

vi can also behave like a line editor. (vi is called **ex** when it's behaving like a line editor.) **ex** does not put your changes on the screen. In addition, in **ex**, you can only use the **vi** commands that start with : and the search commands / and ?. **ex** is closely modeled after **ed**. (See Chapter 15, "What's My Line (Editor, That Is)?" for more information on **ed** and line editors in general.)

Starting (and Quitting) vi

To start **vi**, type **vi** at the command line. When you start **vi**, by default you start in command mode. To get to text-insertion mode, type **a** and press **Enter**. Then you can begin typing your text. To get back into command mode from text-insertion mode, press **Escape**.

If you want a particular file to load automatically when you start **vi** so you can edit it immediately, name it on the command line. For example, enter the command **vi memo** to open the file named memo for editing. (If the file memo doesn't exist, **vi** creates it the first time you save your text.) If there's not enough text to fill the screen, **vi** puts a bunch of ~ characters on the screen. That just means there's no text there (yet).

If you try to insert text while you're in command mode, or if you try to use commands while you're in text-insertion mode, **vi** rudely beeps at you. This will keep you honest (and a little frustrated) until you get the hang of it.

To start typing a memo, give the command **vi memo**. Your screen will look something like the one in the following figure.

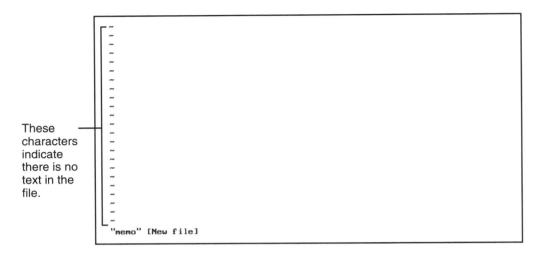

These characters indicate there is no text in the file.

```
~
~
~
~
~
~
~
~
~
~
~
~
~
~
~
~
~
~
~
~
~
~
"memo" [New file]
```

*The **vi** screen for a new file.*

On the bottom line is a message telling you the name of the file and the fact that it's a new file. If it weren't a new file, that message would tell you how many characters there were in the file.

To save your file and quit, type **ZZ**. To quit without changing your file, type **:q!** and press **Enter**.

Basic Text Commands

vi has a lot of commands. As a matter of fact, I'm still learning new ones. This chapter concentrates on the basics of **vi**, so this is a bare-bones list of **vi** commands:

Command	Function
a	Changes to text-insertion mode and adds text after the cursor.
A	Changes to text-insertion mode and adds text at end of the current line.
i	Changes to text-insertion mode and adds text before the cursor.
I	Changes to text-insertion mode and adds text at the beginning of the line.

198

Command	Function
o	Changes to text-insertion mode and adds text after the current line.
O	Changes to text-insertion mode and inserts a blank line before the current line.
Escape	Switches from text insertion mode to command mode.
#j or **#Enter**	Moves cursor down one line or # of lines.
#k	Moves cursor up one line or # of lines.
#h or **#Spacebar**	Moves cursor one character to left or # of characters.
#l or **#Backspace**	Moves cursor one character to right or # of characters.
^	Moves cursor to beginning of line.
$	Moves cursor to end of line.
#w	Moves cursor to beginning of next word or # of words ahead.
#b	Moves cursor back to beginning of previous word or # of words back.
#G	Moves cursor to line #. If you don't supply #, moves to last line in file.
Control-F	Scrolls forward one screen.
Control-B	Scrolls backward one screen.
dd	Deletes current line.
#dd	Deletes # of lines, starting with the current line.
#d*movement*	Deletes text from current cursor position to where the *movement* command goes, # of times.
x	Deletes character at cursor (same as **dl**).

continues

199

Command	Function
X	Deletes character to left of cursor (same as **dh**).
yy	Copies current line into buffer.
#ymovement	Copies into buffer text from current cursor position to where the *movement* command goes.
p	Inserts after the cursor the last text deleted or yanked (for moving text).
P	Inserts before the cursor the last text deleted or yanked (for moving text).
:w file	Saves file as *file*.
ZZ	Saves file and quits.
:q!	Quits without saving file.
:n	Goes to the next file in list given on the command line.
:n!	Goes to the next file even if you haven't saved changes to the current file.
:r file	Inserts the contents of *file* into the current file.
:e file	Edits new file named *file*.
/words	Searches forward in file for *words*.
?words	Searches backward in file for *words*.
:s/old/new	Replaces first occurrence of *old* on this line with *new*.
:s/old/new/g	Replaces all occurrences of *old* on line with *new*.
:%s/old/new	Replaces first occurrence of *old* on each line with *new*.
:%s/old/new/g	Replaces all occurrences of *old* with new.

You can put a repeat number at the beginning of **j**, **k**, **h**, **l**, **w**, **b**, and **G** to move more than one line, character, or word, as the case may be. For example, **5k** moves the cursor up 5 lines. Similarly, for the delete commands (**dd** and **d**) you can delete multiple lines or characters.

We'll use all of these commands in examples throughout the rest of this chapter.

Inserting New Text

vi has two different commands for entering text-insertion mode, depending on whether you want the text to go before or after the cursor. Because we don't have any text to start with, it doesn't matter which command we use. **a** starts inserting text immediately after the current cursor position; **i** inserts text before the cursor. For our example, type **vi memo** and press **Enter**. Then type **a** and press **Enter**. You are now in text-insertion mode. Type in this sample letter to work with throughout the chapter.

```
MEMO

Subject: It's a boy!

After about a thousand hours of labor, Elizabeth and I are
proud to announce the birth of our first child, an eight
pound boy. We didn't care which, so a boy is great.
Elizabeth is doing great, too.

We're thinking of naming the boy "Honorius James."

Free chocolate cigars in the main lunchroom.
```

Remember that you have to press **Enter** at the end of each line because **vi** doesn't automatically wrap your paragraph like word processors.

If you make a mistake and decide to backspace over it, you can only backspace as far as the beginning of the line. To change the previous line, you have to go into command mode, move up one line using the **k** command, delete the old text (with the **d** command), and then get back into text-insertion mode (by using the **a** or **i** command) to insert new text.

To stop entering text and go back to command mode, press the **Escape** key. If you press the **Escape** key more than once, it has no extra effect; you remain in command mode.

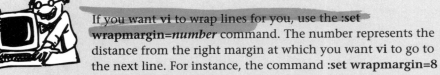

If you want **vi** to wrap lines for you, use the **:set wrapmargin=***number* command. The number represents the distance from the right margin at which you want **vi** to go to the next line. For instance, the command **:set wrapmargin=8** makes **vi** insert a line break whenever a word you type comes within 8 characters of the edge of the screen. To set this command every time you run **vi**, put the line **set wrapmargin=8** in a file named .exrc in your home directory. (.exrc is the **vi** startup file. **vi** runs the commands in .exrc every time it starts.)

Moving Around the File

Now that you have some text, you can move the cursor around. The following table summarizes the movement commands:

Command	Function
j	Moves cursor down one line.
k	Moves cursor up one line.
h	Moves cursor one character to left.
l	Moves cursor one character to right.
^ or 0	Moves cursor to beginning of line.
$	Moves cursor to end of line.
Shift-G	Moves cursor to the end of the file.
Ctrl-F	Moves the cursor forward one screenful.
Ctrl-B	Moves the cursor backward one screenful.

Plus, on most systems, the arrow keys and page down button work as well.

Cursor movement commands are all short, so you don't have to press Enter. If you press Enter anyway (out of habit, perhaps), the cursor goes down an extra line because in command mode, Enter does the same thing as the **j** command. As I tell you about these commands, try using them in our memo file.

To move the cursor to a specific line, use *linenumber*G. For instance, **1G** moves the cursor to the first line in the file, **6G** moves to the sixth line, and so on. If you don't give a line number, **G** goes to the last line in the file. (That way, you don't need to know how many lines are in the file to go to the last line.)

To find out what line the cursor is currently on, use the command **Control-G**. vi displays information about the current file at the bottom of the screen: `"memos" line 12 of 12 --100%--`.

If you find these movement commands difficult to remember, think about how the letters j and k look on a line of text. The letter j dips *down* below the line, while k sticks *up* above the other letters. And note that on the keyboard, h is to the *left* of j and k, and l is to the *right*.

To move the cursor to the beginning of the line, use ^. To go to the end of the line, use the **$** command. Because **vi** works on text one line at a time, you can't move the cursor left or right past the end of the line. The cursor stops there; it doesn't go on to the next line. To go to the next line, use **j** or **k**.

You can also move the cursor one word at a time. **w** moves to the beginning of the next word, and **b** moves back to the beginning of the previous word.

If you're reading or skimming through a file, you'll probably want to move forward and backward a screen at a time. Press **Control-F** to move forward one screen at a time, or press **Control-B** to move back one screen at a time.

Deleting and Moving Text

The command to delete a line of text is **dd**. By default, **dd** deletes the line of text the cursor is currently on. Let's try this on our example. Move the cursor to the "Free chocolate cigars" line. (It's the last line in the file; to go there, type **G**.) Now delete the line by typing **dd**.

Even though the text is gone, it's not forgotten. You can put the text you've deleted somewhere else (move it, that is) with the **p** (for put) command. Move the cursor to the third line, the "Subject" line, by typing the command **3G**. Enter **p**, and the "Free chocolate cigars" line appears after the "Subject" line. The file now looks like this:

```
MEMO

Subject: It's a boy!
Free chocolate cigars in the main lunchroom.

After about a thousand hours of labor, Elizabeth and I are
proud to announce the birth of our first child, an eight
pound boy. We didn't care which, so a boy is great.
Elizabeth is doing great, too.

We're thinking of naming the boy "Honorius James."

~
~
~
~
~
~
~
~
~
~
~
~
```

The dd command deletes a line; the p command "puts" whatever you last deleted into the file.

The **p** command doesn't empty the storage space; you can put as many copies of the line as you want back into your file. The deleted line is stored inside **vi** until you delete something else; then the new deleted text replaces this deleted text.

By combining the **vi** commands, you can make just about any editing change. In our sample memo, let's move up the blank line at the end of the file so that it's between the "Subject" line and the "Free chocolate cigars" line. To do so, go to the last (blank) line by typing the command **G**, enter **dd** to delete it, enter **3G** to go back up to the "Subject" line, and press **p**. (If you use the **P** command instead of **p**, the text is inserted before the cursor. In this case, if you had used **P** the blank line would have been inserted before the "Subject" line.)

If you want to delete more than one line at a time, you can specify the number of consecutive lines you want to delete before the **dd** command. For example, **5dd** deletes the current line and the four lines after it.

You can also combine **d** with the cursor movement commands to delete different amounts of text. For example, you could combine **d** with the **w** command (which moves to the beginning of the next word). The combined command **dw** deletes from the cursor to the beginning of the next word. Similarly, **dl** deletes the character on which the cursor rests (it deletes from the current cursor position to one character to the right).

In our sample memo, let's combine the **d** and **w** commands to delete the name "Honorius James." Move the cursor to the "H" at the beginning of "Honorius James" and type **dw**. "Honorius" and the space after it disappear. Instead of using **dw** again to remove "James," enter **5dl**. Here's what the memo looks like now:

```
MEMO

Subject: It's a boy!

Free chocolate cigars in the main lunchroom.

After about a thousand hours of labor, Elizabeth and I are
proud to announce the birth of our first child, an eight
pound boy. We didn't care which, so a boy is great.
Elizabeth is doing great, too.

We're thinking of naming the boy "."
~
~
~
~
~
~
~
~
~
~
~
"memos" 12 lines, 311 characters
```

*The command **dw** deletes from the cursor to the beginning of the next word.*

Now let's insert some text *before* the cursor. Instead of using **a** to switch to text-insertion mode, use the **i** command (to add text before the cursor). Then type the name **Chris**. When you've finished typing the name, press **Escape** to leave text-insertion mode and go back to command mode.

Now the file looks like this:

```
MEMO

Subject: It's a boy!

Free chocolate cigars in the main lunchroom.

After about a thousand hours of labor, Elizabeth and I are
proud to announce the birth of our first child, an eight
pound boy. We didn't care which, so a boy is great.
Elizabeth is doing great, too.

We're thinking of naming the boy "Chris."
```

205

Sometimes you don't want to move text; you want to copy it. You could do that by deleting a line with **dd** and using **p** twice (once to put it back where it was, and once to put it in the new location). The creators of **vi**—lazy little programmers that they were—thought that was one command too many and created another command for copying: **yy**. Instead of deleting text like **dd** does, the **yy** command just copies the text into the same storage space that **dd** uses.

You use the **yy** command exactly as you do the **dd** command. For example, the command **5yy** stores a copy of the current line and the following four lines. Use the **p** or **P** command to put the copied text back into the document.

Saving a File

To save the file, use the command **:w** and press **Enter**. Since you gave the file a name (memo) on the command line when you started **vi**, **vi** already knows that the file's name is memo. At the bottom of the screen, **vi** tells you how big the file is: `"memo" 14 lines, 316 characters`.

If you have not provided a file name when you type **:w**, **vi** prints a message at the bottom of the screen telling you it needs a file name. To give a new file a name or to save an existing file under another name, supply the name after the **:w** command.

If you want to change the name of the file after you've already saved it once, you can simply enter the new file name at the **:w** command. For example, you could rename the memo file birth by typing **:w birth** and pressing **Enter**.

When you save a file under a new name, it doesn't change the file that **vi** is currently working with (in our case, the memo file). Even if you save the message as birth and then make changes to the file on-screen, the next **:w** command saves the file as memo again. (You must use the **:e** command to edit the file under the new name. See "Editing a Different File" later in this chapter.)

If you want to save and quit, enter **ZZ**. (You don't have to press Enter.)

Searching for and Replacing Text

vi has two commands for searching for text: / and **?**. The / command searches forward through the file, and **?** searches backward through the file. When **vi** finds the text you're searching for, the cursor moves to the line containing the word or words. (If the word isn't in the file, the cursor doesn't move.)

Let's try this out. To search for the line containing "Subject:" type /**Subject:** and press **Enter**. You can find the next occurrence of "Subject:" by using the commands / and **?** without text; they simply repeat the last search forward or backward (respectively) in the file. The text you're searching for is actually a regular expression, as described in Chapter 13, "Matchmaker, Matchmaker (Regular Expressions)."

vi has two extra regular expression characters that can be very useful: \< matches the beginning of a word, and \> matches the end of a word. Normally, if you searched for the word "to," you'd also find "tooth" and "pesto" and "stout." Although you could avoid having to search through those by adding a space on either side of the word "to" and putting it all within quotes (such as " to "), **vi** wouldn't find it if it came at the beginning or end of a line. In **vi**, you can search for \<**to**\> to find only the word "to."

To search and replace a word on a line, use the **:s** command (for substitute). You have to tell the **:s** command both the text you want to search for (the *old text*) and the text with which you want to replace it (the *new text*) separated by slashes. For example, let's change the baby's sex on the "Subject" line of our memo. To do so, type **:s/boy/girl/** and press **Enter**. The subject line now reads:

```
Subject: It's a girl!
```

To change the baby's sex throughout the file, put a **%** between the : and the **s**. (Here, the % sign is a short form that means "the current file.") Type **:%s/boy/girl/** and press **Enter**. The file now looks like this:

> If you wanted to search for and delete text, you wouldn't put anything between the second and third slashes.

```
MEMO

Subject: It's a girl!

Free chocolate cigars in the main lunchroom.

After about a thousand hours of labor, Elizabeth and I are
proud to announce the birth of our first child, an eight
pound girl. We didn't care which, so a boy is great.
Elizabeth is doing great, too.

We're thinking of naming the girl "Chris."
```

 If **vi** stops printing your changes on the screen and presents a colon on the bottom line of the screen, you've told it to behave like a line editor (the **Q** command does this). To get back to regular **vi** mode, give the command **vi** and press **Enter**.

There's only one problem: the second occurrence of boy on line 9 didn't change! That's because the **:s** command only changes the first match it finds on each line. To make **:s** change all of the matches on the line, you have to add a **g** (for global) at the end of the command. If you type **:%s/boy/girl/g** and then press Enter, all occurrences are changed.

If you don't like the changes you've made, you can undo the most recent change by pressing **u**. (The **u** command undoes the last editing change you made.) If you press **u** twice, you can undo the undo command.

Save this version of the file by typing **:w** and pressing **Enter**.

Editing a Different File

While you are working on a file in **vi**, you may decide you need to open another file to do some work. To edit a different file, use the command **:e** followed by the file's name. For example, if you wanted to start editing the file named obituary instead of our memo file, you'd type **:e obituary** and press **Enter**.

If you have made changes to the memo file that you haven't saved, **vi** complains. You can either save the memo file first, or you can force **vi** to switch files by putting an exclamation mark after the **e** like this: **:e! obituary**. However, if you use the !, you lose all of your unsaved changes in the memo file.

208

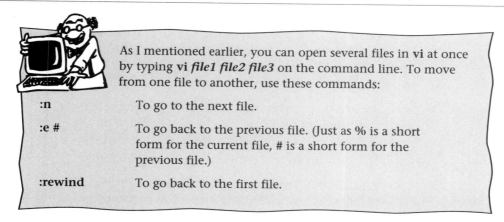

As I mentioned earlier, you can open several files in **vi** at once by typing **vi** *file1 file2 file3* on the command line. To move from one file to another, use these commands:

:n	To go to the next file.
:e #	To go back to the previous file. (Just as **%** is a short form for the current file, **#** is a short form for the previous file.)
:rewind	To go back to the first file.

While you're editing one file, you may want to include the contents of another file. The command to read in another file is **:r** *file*. For example, some of the documents I write contain nearly identical text with only minor changes from document to document. I use the **:r** command to include that boilerplate text (the text that's identical) into my current file, and then I edit it. However, the boilerplate file isn't affected by these changes because I've inserted a copy of it into my file.

Recently, I was editing a file named cm_intro, and I wanted to include information about our product line, which is in the file product_descriptions. The command I used to include a copy of product_descriptions in cm_intro was **:r product_descriptions**. Once cm_intro contained the appropriate text from product_descriptions, I edited it to insert references to the product I was currently writing about.

The Least You Need to Know

➤ To start **vi**, type the command **vi**. If you want **vi** to automatically open a file, add the file name to the command line. You can give as many file names as you want.

➤ **vi** is a mode editor, which means it has two modes: text-insertion mode and command mode. To start adding text right after the cursor, use the **a** command. To start adding text before the cursor, use the **i** command. To stop adding text and go back to command mode, press **Escape**.

➤ To save the file without quitting, use the command **:w** and press **Enter**. To save the file and quit, either type **:wq** and press **Enter** or type **ZZ**. To quit the file without saving, type **:q!** and press **Enter**.

➤ You can use the commands **j** and **k** to move the cursor down one line and up one line, respectively. The commands **h** and **l** move the cursor one character to the left and one character to the right, respectively.

➤ You can cut and paste text with the **dd** command (which deletes the current line) and the **p** command (which puts whatever you've just deleted after the cursor).

➤ You can perform a search with the **/*text*** command, and you can search and replace with the **:s/*old text*/ *new text*/** command.

Circus Emacs-Imus

The second-most popular editor in UNIX is **emacs**. Discussions of which is better, **vi** or **emacs**, always remind me of ten-year-old boys trying to decide who's better, Batman or Superman. They've each got their good points and their bad points.

For you and I, what's important is that both **vi** and **emacs** are text editors: they let you write text, save files, and edit files. For sheer power, however, I'd have to say that **emacs** is Superman in this argument (and I think Superman is better than Batman).

emacs is a screen editor that lets you edit more than one file at a time. And (unlike **vi**) it even lets you see both files on-screen! **emacs** is modeless: you can give commands while you're typing text without switching from an insert mode to a command mode—see Chapter 15, "What's My Line (Editor, That Is)?." All the commands are Control key combinations or combinations of the Escape key followed by a command. **emacs** has so many features and commands that it needs both the Control key and the Escape key.

It's a Floor Wax and a Dessert Topping!

emacs has more features than a dusk-to-dawn drive-in theater. You can read electronic mail or Usenet news in **emacs**, or even run programs inside **emacs**. Heck, **emacs** even contains an entire programming language, so you can write programs in **emacs**.

Actually, you don't need most of those features, so I'm not going to tell you about them. This chapter is about basic editing with **emacs**. If you want more, **emacs** includes a tutorial, which I will tell you how to access. **emacs** also has an extensive help section, but (like all UNIX help systems) it's so difficult that you feel like you have to walk around the world to get across the street.

Richard Stallman, the man primarily responsible for **emacs**, says that **emacs** isn't an editor, it's a work environment. He claims that if you keep entering and exiting **emacs**, you're using it wrong. In Stallman's view, you start **emacs** when you login, and you stay there and do everything you need to do until you exit UNIX.

Well maybe his claims are true, and maybe doing all your work in **emacs** is what you like to do. But for me, **emacs** is an *editor*, for goodness' sake. It's a tool. The fact that I can use it to program in Lisp (assuming I *want* to learn how to program in Lisp) is irrelevant to what I do. So don't let yourself be bullied by the **emacs** geeks. Edit with it. If you like the extra features, use them, but don't be forced into it.

Modestly Modeless

In **emacs**, you can give commands while you're typing text. A program such as this, in which all commands are available at all times, is called a *modeless* program: it has no modes. For more information on editors and modes, see Chapters 14, "Write Like the Prose," 15, "What's My Line (Editor, That Is)?," and 16, "Viva vi!."

There are three ways to give commands in **emacs**: Control-key combinations, Escape key commands (which are also called Meta commands), and typed (or "extended") commands. In addition, there are combinations of these; some commands require the Escape key and a Control-key combination. (Although I show them as capital letters here, they don't have to be capital letters in the commands. In fact, in the **emacs** documentation, they're shown as lowercase.)

➤ *Control-key* commands are key combinations in which you press the Control key and some other letter key or combination of letter keys. In the **emacs** documentation, these are described with a "C-" prefix. For example, **Control-X Control-S** (C-x C-s in the **emacs** documentation) is the command to save a file. To enter this command, you hold down the **Control** key, press the **X** key, and then (while still holding down Control) press the **S** key.

➤ *Meta commands* require you to press the Escape key and then the letter key. In the **emacs** documentation, these are described with an "M-" prefix (for "meta"). For example, **Escape->** (**M->** in the **emacs** documentation) is the command to move the cursor to the end of the file. You press **Escape** and then you press the > key. (You do have to press **Shift** to get the > key—otherwise it would be Escape, which isn't a command.)

Why call them "Meta" commands? **emacs** was developed using terminals that had a key called "Meta" that worked just liked the Control key; you held down Meta and you held down the key. (Those terminals also had a Control key.) As **emacs** was used on terminals that didn't have a Meta key, a substitute had to be found: the Escape key. Most terminals nowadays have Escape, and very few have Meta.

Because of the way the Escape key works, you press **Escape** and then the key. If your terminal doesn't have an Escape key or a Meta key, some other key is used to replace Meta; it may be the Alt key. Check with other users on your system to see; the **emacs** documentation may also help.

➤ *Extended commands* are commands that aren't available as either Control or Meta key combinations. These tend to be commands that aren't used very often. To use these commands, you have to access the command buffer by pressing **Escape-X** (**M-X**), and then you have to type the name of the command into the command buffer. (The X stands for eXtended command.)

In fact, you can do *everything* in **emacs** through extended commands (if you want to)—all of the other commands are just shortcuts for these commands.

> **emacs** does have modes, but they only affect some commands (none of which I talk about). For instance, there's a mode for text, a mode for each programming language you might use, another for mail, and so on. One mode you can get from text mode is auto-fill-mode. In auto-fill-mode, **emacs** automatically inserts line breaks whenever a line is more than 72 characters long (this is like the word wrap feature in a word processor) so that you don't have to press Enter at the end of every line.

Some commands require input: maybe you need to enter a new file name, for example. For these commands, the cursor automatically moves down to the command buffer and moves back to the text buffer after you press Enter. (We'll talk about these buffers in the next section.)

Starting (and Quitting) emacs

To start **emacs**, type **emacs** at the command line and press **Enter**. **emacs** may take a few moments to start because it's a very big program. Here's what **emacs** looks like when you start up:

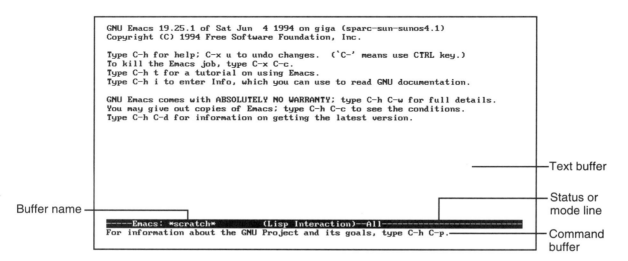

*The **emacs** screen.*

When you start **emacs**, it presents a little advertising message about the GNU project. As soon as you start typing, this message goes away. If you want to eliminate the message permanently, ask your local **emacs** guru to set up your .emacs file so the message doesn't appear.

Every file you edit in **emacs** is said to be in a *buffer*, a temporary storage area in **emacs**. When you open a file in **emacs**, it is stored in a buffer until you close that file buffer. The screen is divided into several buffer windows. You can load new files into **emacs** throughout your session, and a new buffer is automatically created. When you "kill" a buffer, the file the buffer contained is closed.

In the previous figure, the big window is your *text buffer*—where you edit files. You can have more than one text buffer showing at once. (I'll show you how to do that later in this chapter.) If you're on an X-Terminal and using X Windows (see Chapter 6, "Surviving Window Pains" for a description of X), your version of **emacs** will probably appear in its own window.

At the bottom of each text buffer is a *status line* (also called the mode line). The status line shows you the name of the file in the buffer and other information. At the very bottom of the screen is the *command buffer*. When you need to type in commands or command information, it goes into this buffer.

The *status line* shows the name of the current buffer (usually `*scratch*` unless you named a file on the command line) and the name of the current mode. The mode is usually `Fundamental` (although on our system at work it's `Lisp Interaction`; I don't know who set that). In either case, it won't seriously affect writing and editing files.

If you want, you can name the file or files you want to edit when you start **emacs**. For example, if you want to work on the three files letter, memo, and anvils.text, you would type **emacs letter memo anvils.text**. **emacs** loads the files letter, memo, and anvils.text into three buffers (which have the same names as the files). The files you name don't have to exist; **emacs** will create them for you.

When you want to quit **emacs**, use the command **Control-X Control-C** (hold down the **Control** key, press X, and then C). If you haven't saved the changes to any file you have open, **emacs** asks you if you want to save the file. It presents a question like this for each file that's been changed but not saved:

```
Save file /home/johnmc/anvils.text? (y, n, !, ., q, C-r or C-h).
```

215

 You hit the Backspace key thinking it would delete letters, and now you're getting help when you don't need it (except to get out of Help!). To get out of Help press **Control-G**. To do what Backspace *ought* to do (delete letters), use the **Delete** key.

To save the changes to the file, press **y**. Press **n** to close the buffer without saving changes. To save all the changed files that are currently open, press **!**. Press **.** to save this file but none of the remaining ones. To quit without saving any of the files, press **Q**. If you press **q**, **emacs** asks you again if you want to quit, with this message:

```
Modified buffers exist; exit anyway? (yes or no).
```

This time you have to type **yes** and press **Enter** to quit.

The **Control-R** command displays the file in question, so you can look at it and decide if you really want to save the changes. The **Control-H** command shows you a help message explaining each of these options.

Learning the Basic emacs Commands

Entering text in **emacs** is pretty simple: you just type. Type the following text, and remember that you have to press **Enter** at the end of each line. Press **Enter** twice to create a blank line to separate paragraphs.

```
MEMO TO ANVIL SALES STAFF

Sales of our anvils have dropped sixteen percent in the
last year. Unlike other industries, we showed almost
no increase in sales over the Christmas season. People
are no longer giving anvils as gifts. Our last
marketing survey showed that anvils are generally
regarded as old-fashioned or as specialty items.

I'd like everyone to consider alternate uses for
anvils. I want some way to market anvils to Mr. and
Mrs. America and all the little Americans.

Let's put an anvil in every home!

Maxwell S. Hammer,
President
```

If you make a typing mistake, remember to use the Delete key to backspace and delete the error instead of trying to use the Backspace key. If you backspace past the beginning of a line, **emacs** continues to the previous line.

If you want **emacs** to break lines for you as you type (like a word processor's word wrap), you need to enter the auto-fill-mode. To do this, press **Escape-X**, type **auto-fill-mode** in the command buffer, and press **Enter**. You can type spaces instead of the - characters when entering the command; **emacs** turns them into hyphens.

Saving a File

The command to save the current buffer is **C-X C-S** (**Control-X Control-S**). If you issue this command but the file doesn't have a name yet, **emacs** asks for one down in the command buffer. Type the name and press **Enter**.

Moving Around the File

When you finished typing the earlier memo, the cursor was on the line below "President." Experiment with these commands, which move the cursor around your file:

Press	To
Control-P	Move the cursor to the previous line.
Control-N	Move the cursor to the next line down.
Control-B	Move the cursor one character back (to the left).
Control-F	Move the cursor one character forward (to the right).
Control-E	Move the cursor to the end of the line.
Control-A	Move the cursor to the beginning of the line.
Escape-<	Move the cursor to the beginning of the file.
Escape->	Move the cursor to the end of the file.

continues

Press	To
Control-V	Move forward by one screen.
Escape-V	Move backward by one screen.
Escape-F	Move forward by one word.
Escape-B	Move backward by one word.

You may or may not be able to use the arrow keys to move around in the file; it depends on the type of terminal you have.

There are two things you need to note here. First, if you move the cursor past the end of the file, **emacs** automatically adds more lines to the file. And second, when you back up one character past the beginning of the line, the cursor moves to the last space in the previous line. (Amazing, isn't it?)

Deleting Text

To delete the character at the cursor's current position, press **Control-D** (for delete). You can't use the Delete key because Delete is busy playing the part of Backspace.

Let's practice deleting some text in our memo. Move the cursor to the "S" in "Maxwell S. Hammer" and press **Control-D**. The "S" appears to have been deleted. However, it was actually put into a temporary storage place called the "kill buffer." Go ahead and delete the period that's left between "Maxwell" and "Hammer."

You can *undo* a change with the undo command, **Control-U**. Press **Control-X U** now, and you'll notice that only the period reappears in the memo. Press **Control-X U** a second time, and the "S" also reappears. **emacs** keeps a record of about the last hundred changes you've made to your file in the kill buffer, and it can undo them all. It's a pretty powerful feature and can be a lifesaver at times.

You can also delete larger chunks of text. To do so, use any of these methods:

➤ To delete from the cursor to the end of the line, press **Control-K**.

➤ To delete from the cursor to the end of the current word, press **Escape-D**.

218

➤ If you want to delete a region of text, place the cursor at the beginning of the text you want to delete. You need to *mark* where the region starts by pressing **Control-Space**; then move the cursor to the end of the region and delete the text with the command **Control-W**. (**Control-D** deletes only one character at a time.) **emacs** doesn't highlight the marked text. (If you are using an X Windows terminal, you can use the mouse to mark a region of text, and then it *will* be highlighted.) You can have only one section of text marked at any time.

You just deleted a whole chunk of text that should've stayed. You can bring back the text you just deleted by "yanking" it from the buffer. Just press **Control-Y**. Press **Control-Y** again to get a second copy of the text. (**Control-Y** only brings back the last text you deleted.)

Moving and Copying Text

Now you're going to learn how to move and copy text from one place to another in your file. In fact, you can use these commands to move and copy text between files in buffers, once you know how to move from one buffer to another.

As an example, let's swap the first and second paragraphs in the sample memo. To do so, you need to mark the first paragraph. Move the cursor to the beginning of the first paragraph (the cursor should be resting on the "S" in "Sales") and press **Control-Space** to start marking the area. Then move the cursor to the beginning of the second paragraph (the cursor should be resting on the "I" in "I'd"). Press **Control-W**, and the entire first paragraph disappears. Now move the cursor to the "L" in "Let's." Press **Control-Y** to bring back the text. (This whole process is equivalent to a cut and paste procedure in a word processing program.)

If you only want to copy text into the kill buffer (you don't want it removed from its original position), mark the region as if you were going to delete it, and press **Escape-W** instead of **Control-W**. A copy of the marked text is placed in the kill buffer, but the original text stays where it was. Then move the cursor to the position where you want the copy inserted and press **Control-Y** to place a copy of the text. (This whole process is equivalent to a copy and paste procedure in a word processing program.)

Searching for and Replacing Text

There are not very many commands that you need to know to search and replace text in your file, but learning them will save you a lot of time. These search and replace commands always require additional input from you, so once you press the command key sequence, the cursor will jump to the command buffer and await your input, which is either a word or phrase (whatever you want to search or replace). Study the commands in this table first, and then we'll practice using them in our sample memo.

Press	To
Control-S	Search forward for a word or line of text.
Control-R	Search backward for a word or line of text.
Escape-%	Search and replace text between the current cursor position and the end of the file.

 You pressed a command sequence, but now you've changed your mind. How do you get the cursor out of the command buffer? **Control-G** is the "cancel" command; it kills any command that still needs input from you. (Note, however, that you can't use **Control-G** to stop a Save File command, since it doesn't need input from you after you hit the keys.)

To search forward for a word or line of text, use the **Control-S** command. For example, let's search for the first occurrence of the word "anvil" in our memo. Move the cursor to the beginning of the sample memo (press **Escape-<**) and press **Control-S**. In the command buffer, **emacs** asks for the text you want to find. Type in **anvil** and press **Enter**. (By default, **emacs** ignores whether a letter is uppercase or lowercase.) **emacs** finds and highlights the word "ANVIL" in the first line.

To search backward for a word or line of text, use the **Control-R** command. This works the same as **Control-S**, but it searches in the opposite direction. To search for the word "anvil" in our memo, move the cursor to the end of the file (press **Escape->**) and press **Control-R**. In the command buffer, **emacs** asks for the text you want to find. Type in **anvil** and press **Enter**. **emacs** finds and highlights the word "anvil" in the last line of the memo (before the president's name).

To search and replace text between the current cursor position and the end of the file, use **Escape-%**. **emacs** asks you for the text you want to search for, and then for the text with which you want to replace it.

To try this out, let's replace the word "anvil" in our memo with "Davy Crockett Hat." Go to the beginning of the memo (press **Escape-<**) and press **Escape-%**. In the command buffer, the prompt Search for: appears. Type in **anvil** and press **Enter**. After you press Enter, the prompt Replace: appears beside the search text. Type in **Davy Crockett Hat** and press **Enter**. **emacs** searches for the first occurrence of "anvil" and asks if you want to change it:

Query replacing anvil with Davy Crockett Hat? (? for help).

At this point, you have three options:

➤ To replace the word "anvil," press **y**.

➤ To keep the original word, press **n**.

➤ To replace all occurrences of the word "anvil" without further prompting, press **!**.

By default, the search-and-replace function is case-insensitive and does not use regular expressions. If you want **emacs** to pay attention to the case of letters in search-and-replace procedures, and if you want to use regular expressions, ask your local **emacs** guru to configure your .emacs file (which is located in your home directory).

Loading a New File

In the course of your work, you may want to open a new file for editing. To do this, press **Control-X Control-F**. **emacs** prompts you for the name of the new file, as shown in the following figure. (Note that **emacs** automatically puts it in the directory you were in when you started **emacs**.) Type in the new file name and press **Enter**.

221

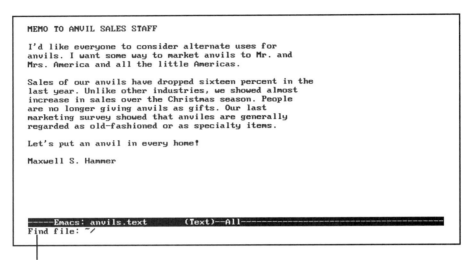

Prompt for new file name

*When you use the **Control-X Control-F** command to load a new file, **emacs** prompts for the file's name.*

When you're entering the **Control-X Control-F** command, if you forget to hold down Control for the F, you'll reset your line width to 1, which is awful if you're using auto-fill-mode. Here's the command to fix it: **Control-U 72 Control-X F**. This sets your line width back to 72 characters (the normal value).

Each file is in its own buffer, whether you named them on the command line or loaded them later with **Control-X Control-F**. The new file takes up the full window you were using, and the window with the old file is hidden.

To see the list of buffers currently in emacs, use the command **Control-X Control-B**. **emacs** displays another buffer, the buffer list, which shows you the list of buffers for the files you currently have open (see the following figure).

Currently selected buffer

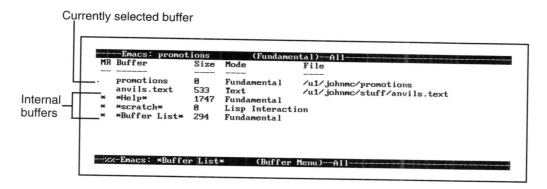

Internal
buffers

The command **Control-X Control-B** *shows you a list of buffers.*

The name of a buffer is usually the same as the name of the file it holds. The . in the first column indicates the buffer that's currently selected. Some of the buffers listed (such as *scratch* and *Buffer List*) are always there; **emacs** uses them.

You can use the normal up and down movement commands to select a different buffer. To enter one of those buffers, select it and press **f**. To move to another buffer, press **Control-X B**, and then type in the buffer's name (the file name).

Incidentally, if you want to close the buffer (and file) you're currently in, the command is **Control-X K**. If you've changed the file, **emacs** asks if you want to save the contents of the buffer to a file. This figure shows the buffer called promotions, in which I changed the contents before giving the command to close.

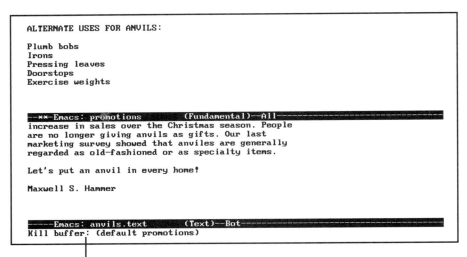

```
ALTERNATE USES FOR ANVILS:

Plumb bobs
Irons
Pressing leaves
Doorstops
Exercise weights



--**-Emacs: promotions      (Fundamental)--All----------------
increase in sales over the Christmas season. People
are no longer giving anvils as gifts. Our last
marketing survey showed that anvils are generally
regarded as old-fashioned or as specialty items.

Let's put an anvil in every home!

Maxwell S. Hammer



-----Emacs: anvils.text       (Text)--Bot------------------
Kill buffer: (default promotions)
```

Prompt for confirmation (y to kill, n to keep)

*The command **Control-X K** closes (kills) your current buffer.*

Doing Windows in emacs

When I started using **emacs**, I had a terrible time with the windows. New ones were always appearing, and when I used the help command (**Control-H**), I could never seem to find the command to get back to having only one window on the screen. You use the commands in the following table to display and move between windows in **emacs**:

Press	To
Control-X 1	Close extra windows, leaving you with one.
Control-X 2	Open a new window.
Control-X O	Move between open windows.
Control-X 0 (zero)	In X Windows, to remove the current "frame."

To turn one window into two, press **Control-X 2**. This is useful when you want to look at two files at once. When you split the window into two, both windows "look into" the same buffer. If you want each window to contain a different file, you have to display a new buffer in one of them, using **Control-X B** or **Control-X F**. Once you have two windows open, you can switch back and forth between them with **Control-X O**. (That's the letter "o," for "other.")

If you only want one window on your screen, press **Control-X 1**. The window currently containing the cursor "grows" to fill the screen and hides the other windows. None of these commands closes files; all of the buffers are still there, you're just changing how **emacs** displays them.

If you're using the latest version of **emacs** on an X Windows terminal (I described X Windows in Chapter 6, "Surviving Window Pains"), there are two types of windows. There are the subdivisions in **emacs**, which I've called *windows* for this chapter, and there are X Windows windows, which **emacs** calls *frames* (because they were using the word "window" to mean something else). On X Windows, **emacs** displays a new frame instead of splitting the current window into two. I find it very annoying.

If you're in the main (original) **emacs** frame, you can get rid of all extra frames with the command **Control-X 0** (that's the number zero). If the cursor is in a secondary frame and you just want to remove that frame, use the command **Control-X 50** (that's the number zero again).

Help in emacs

To get help in **emacs**, press either **Control-H** or the **Backspace** key. The first window you see is a list of the types of help you can get. Press one of the letters to select the particular kind of help you want. If you press Backspace while you're in Help, **emacs** gives you another Help screen.

```
-----Emacs: *scratch*        (Text)--All--------------------------
You have typed C-h, the help character.  Type a Help option:
(Use C-v or M-v to scroll through this text.
Type q to exit the Help command.)

a   command-apropos.  Give a substring, and see a list of commands
        (functions interactively callable) that contain
        that substring.  See also the  apropos  command.
b   describe-bindings.  Display table of all key bindings.
c   describe-key-briefly.  Type a command key sequence;
        it prints the function name that sequence runs.
f   describe-function.  Type a function name and get documentation of it.
-**-Emacs: *Help*          (Fundamental)--Top----------------------
Type one of the options listed or Space to scroll: -
```

*This is the help screen for **emacs**, which you get when you press **Backspace** or **Control-H**.*

Why is Backspace the help key? Because the Backspace key sends the signal Control-H, and H stands for help. Richard Stallman, who built it this way, once won an award for being a genius—yet he forgot that most of us don't know or care what signal the Backspace key sends.

Here are the forms of Help that I find useful:

a (apropos) Searches for commands whose long names contain a particular word. (This is similar to the **apropos** command I described in Chapter 5, "Won't You Please Help Me?".) As I said earlier, the Control and meta commands are all shortcuts for the common extended commands. For example, **Control-R** (the backward search command) is the shortcut for the extended command **isearch-backward**. When you do an **apropos** help, **apropos** prompts you for a word and then displays all of the extended commands that contain that word. This figure shows the results of an apropos search for the word "search." The command I typed was **C-H A search Enter**:

```
MEMO TO ANVIL SALES STAFF

I'd like everyone to consider alternate uses for
anvils. I want some way to market anvils to Mr. and
Mrs. America and all the little Americas.

Sales of our anvils have dropped sixteen percent in the
last year. Unlike other industries, we showed almost
increase in sales over the Christmas season. People
are no longer giving anvils as gifts. Our last
------Emacs: anvils.text       (Text)--Top----------------------
isearch-*-char              (not bound to any keys)
  Function: Handle * and ? specially in regexps.
isearch-abort               (not bound to any keys)
  Function: Abort incremental search mode if searching is successful, signallin\
g quit.
isearch-backward            C-r
  Function: Do incremental search backward.
isearch-backward-regexp     ESC C-r
  Function: Do incremental search backward for regular expression.
isearch-complete            (not bound to any keys)
  Function: Complete the search string from the strings on the search ring.
------Emacs: *Help*          (Fundamental)--Top------------------
Type C-x 1 to remove help window.  M-C-v to scroll the help.
```

*The **apropos** help command lists all extended commands containing a word.*

You can scroll down this list by using the command **Escape-Control-V**, or you can switch the cursor into the help window (with **Control-O**) and use the regular movement commands to move.

h (help)   Gives you help about using the Help system.

i (info)   Puts you into the **emacs** documentation system. This system is not like the regular UNIX manual section; it's specific to **emacs**. Many people swear by it, but I mostly swear at it. I find it too technical and too oriented to the programmer's way of thinking, but it's the only up-to-date information on **emacs**, so you might have to use it some day.

t (tutorial)   Starts a tutorial on **emacs**. If you discover you like **emacs**, you might want to work through this tutorial.

Commands at a Glance

Press	To
Ctrl-X Ctrl-C	Quit **emacs**.
Ctrl-H or **Backspace**	Get help.
Ctrl-N	Move cursor down one line.
Ctrl-P	Move cursor up one line.
Ctrl-A	Move cursor to beginning of line.
Ctrl-E	Move cursor to end of line.
Escape-<	Move cursor to beginning of file.
Escape->	Move cursor to end of file.
Ctrl-X Ctrl-S	Save file.
Ctrl-X Ctrl-F	Load new file for editing.
Ctrl-X Control-B	Show list of buffers.
Ctrl-X *filename***Enter**	Switch to buffer *filename*.
Ctrl-X K	Kill current buffer.
Ctrl-S*text***Enter**	Search forward for text.
Ctrl-R*text***Enter**	Search backward for text.
Ctrl-X 2	Split current window into two windows.
Ctrl-X 1	Make current window the only one.

continues

Press	To
Ctrl-X 0	Remove all other frames (in X Windows **emacs**).
Ctrl-X 50	Remove current frame (in X Windows **emacs**).
Escape-%*old*Enter *new*Enter	Start search forward and replace.
Space or **y**	Replace current instance of *old*.
Delete or **n**	Skip replacement of current instance of *old*.
!	Replace all occurrences of *old* with *new*.

The Least You Need to Know

➤ To start **emacs**, type the command **emacs** on the command line. You can name any number of files on the command line as well, and each of them will open in its own buffer.

➤ To quit **emacs**, press **Control-X Control-C**. If you have buffers that have been changed but not saved, **emacs** asks if you want to save them.

➤ The commands **Control-N** and **Control-P** move the cursor down and up one line, respectively. The commands **Control-F** and **Control-B** move the cursor forward and backward one character, respectively.

➤ Press **Control-D** to delete the character at the cursor position. Press **Delete** to delete the character to the left of the cursor.

➤ To delete a block of text, mark the beginning of the block by pressing **Control-Space**, move the cursor to the end of the block, and press **Control-W**.

➤ To search forward for text, use **Control-S**. To search backward (in reverse) for text, use **Control-R**. To search and replace *old text* with *new text*, use the **Escape-%** command.

Part IV
Mastering the Mysteries

Now that you know the password and the secret handshake, I can tell you that which was hidden before. What's the secret of your shell? How can you save your environment? How do you network if all you've got is a keyboard? Does electronic mail contain bills?

This part tells you about customizing your UNIX environment, using electronic mail and the Internet, and a few of your system administrator's secrets.

Chapter 18

The Shell Game

> **In This Chapter**
>
> ➤ What a shell is and what it does for you
>
> ➤ What are the three main shells, and which do you have?
>
> ➤ Making a shell run a command every time you login
>
> ➤ Changing your shell

All through this book I refer to your "shell" and, more specifically, to the Korn shell. Although I briefly explained shells in Chapter 2, "Operating on Systems," it's time to talk about them a bit more.

The shell acts like a go-between for you and the operating system's kernel. (The kernel is the part of the operating system that stays in the computer's memory; it's a program.) The shell turns your commands into instructions for the operating system; the operating system turns those into instructions for the computer's hardware. It's the shell that puts you in the driver's seat of your UNIX system.

In fact, that's not a bad way to think about it. Imagine that the shell is the dashboard controls in your car (the operating system is the engine and transmission). There are some controls you just have to have, such as a brake pedal, a steering wheel, or a speedometer. Some controls in a car are just conveniences, such as power mirrors.

All UNIX shells must be able to run other programs according to your commands. Some features of shells are just conveniences, like the ability to move programs into the background (discussed in Chapter 20, "A Little Background Music"). Each shell organizes these features (essential and non-essential) slightly differently, in the same way that every car's dashboard is slightly different. In this manner, a UNIX shell gives UNIX some of its "personality."

Why does UNIX have several shells? Because it can, basically. Whenever a programmer didn't like the official UNIX shell, he or she wrote a new shell program. Some of these new shells, like the C-Shell, caught on and became part of the standard UNIX package.

The shell is the program you use while you're logged in. When you type commands, you're typing them into your shell. When you exit, you're really exiting your shell. Your shell is just a program that's really good at running other programs.

Because you spend almost all your UNIX time using your shell, it's important that you're comfortable with it. Being comfortable with your shell is the difference between being able to use UNIX and giving up. (I don't insist you *like* your shell; that may be asking too much.) Most people stick with the shell they learn first, but you can change if you want to. When I started my current job, I switched shells because it was required.

In this book, I've chosen to describe the Korn shell. I chose the Korn shell because it's a standard shell. It's available with most UNIX systems and has more features than the Bourne shell. (The Bourne shell is the standard shell like **ed** is the standard editor: most people don't use it.) The Korn shell is also the shell described in the POSIX standard for computer user tools, so the Korn shell is used on systems besides UNIX systems. (I explained POSIX in Chapter 2, "Operating on Systems.")

Kernels and Shells

In terms of the operating system "being" somewhere, you could say it's in the kernel, which is the program part of the operating system. So what does your shell do? Your shell is a go-between; it sits between you and the kernel.

Your shell runs programs for you. It takes the commands you type and translates them into requests to the operating system: "Please run this program with these options and arguments." It also keeps track of some housekeeping information for you. It knows where your home directory is, for example, what your login name is, what the name of your terminal is, and what type of terminal it is. (Your shell stores a lot of this housekeeping information in the *environment*; I'll discuss the environment in the next chapter.)

Kernel   The part of the operating system that's active in your computer's memory. It's the part that gets files for other programs, checks permissions on files, and starts programs when asked to.

Shell   The program that you use to interact with a computer, including running other programs. The shell program gives you access to the features of the computer system and is written specially for that operating system. The shell programs for UNIX run programs for you, create pipes, and handle input and output redirection.

If you've used DOS, you may be saying to yourself, "Well, even DOS is more sensible than that!" In fact, it's not. What most people think of as "DOS" is just a shell program called **command.com**. Some companies sell other shell programs for DOS machines. You can even get DOS shells that make your DOS computer look like UNIX shells, within the limits of the operating system.

When you enter a command, the shell translates it into two parts: the command and the instructions for the command (the arguments). Then it tells the kernel: "Run this command, and use these instructions."

The **echo** command is useful for figuring out what the shell is saying to the kernel. If you've put together some kind of command that's not doing quite what you want, you can use the **echo** command to figure out how the shell is interpreting your command. Just put **echo** in front of the command to see what the shell is *really* saying to the kernel.

Commands and Shells

The shell runs commands for you. Any command that's a separate program (that is not built into the shell) will run the same no matter which shell you're using. For example, when you want to print something, the print command always works the same.

Some commands are built into the shell, which means they're part of the shell and may change from shell program to shell program. For instance, the **exit** command is really a built-in shell command. When you type **exit**, that tells your shell to quit, and UNIX knows you're done with that session. Some shells use the built-in command **logout** instead of **exit**. There are three kinds of commands built into the shell:

➤ *Common* commands start a little faster if they're part of the shell.

➤ *Customization* commands enable you to customize your shell.

➤ *Programming* commands make up the shell programming language.

cd is one of the common commands built into the Korn shell. The only difference between the separate **cd** program and the **cd** command that's built into the Korn shell is that the Korn shell doesn't have to look for the built-in command. Because of this, the built-in **cd** command runs a little bit faster.

If you switch shells, you won't notice any difference in the common commands that were built-in solely to improve speed (such as **cd**). These commands are the same from shell to shell. However, the customization and programming commands will change. You'll learn more about customization and programming commands in Chapter 19, "Environ-Mental Health."

Kinds of Shells

The first shell program, which is the standard one, was written by S. R. Bourne at Bell Labs. Not surprisingly, it's called the Bourne shell, and the program is called **sh**. Unfortunately, the Bourne shell isn't very good for users. It doesn't provide any of the useful shortcuts available in shells that came later.

When the boys and girls at Berkeley produced the Berkeley Software Distribution (BSD), they wrote a new shell that incorporated some neat ideas and was a joy to use. The new shell was called the C-shell (or **csh**) because its programming language was modeled after the C programming language. Unfortunately, the C-shell didn't handle Bourne shell scripts very well.

Next, AT&T produced the Korn shell, or **ksh.** (Can you guess the last name of the principal designer?) The Korn shell combines most of the neat features from the C-shell with the Bourne shell. It looks a lot like the Bourne shell but is nicer to use.

However, users were unhappy again because they had to pay AT&T extra money to get the Korn shell. So a bunch of programmers, called the Free Software Foundation, got together and wrote the Bourne-Again shell (or **bash**). **bash** is a different combination of the Bourne shell's programming style and the C-shell's neat features, and it's free.

The people who liked the C-shell and just wanted it to handle shell scripts better still wanted a shell that looked like the C-shell. So they wrote **tcsh**, which added command and file name completion and fixed many of the C-shell's problems.

All this talk of shells comes down to this: There are shells that have a lot in common with the Bourne shell, and there are shells that have a lot in common with the C-shell. The question is, which one do you have? And which one do you want?

FSF The Free Software Foundation was founded by Richard Stallman. Members of the FSF believe that software should be free. However, they don't mean free in the you-don't-have-to-pay-me-for-it sense, but free in the I-have-to-give-you-the-source-code-if-you-ask-for-it sense. They can still charge you for it. (In reality, the FSF only charges for producing the copy, but they don't stop anyone else from charging for it.) Once you have the source code, you can make whatever changes to the program you want—if you're a programmer.

File name completion The shell's capability to guess what file name you're typing after you've typed the first few letters. (This could be very useful if you use file names like abracadabra and xylophone.)

Identifying Shells

You only need to know which kind of shell you have if you're going to alter the shell startup files or your environment variables, change your prompt, run programs in the background, or write shell scripts. If you don't plan to do any of these things, don't worry about which kind of shell you have.

The first clue to determining which shell you have is your prompt. If your prompt contains a dollar sign ($), you've probably got one of the Bourne-style shells. If your prompt contains a percent sign (%), you've probably got one of the C-style shells. (I say *probably* because anyone can change the prompt. If someone else set up your account for you, he might have changed it. But it's not likely.)

To find out which shell you have, here's a quick and dirty works-ninety-per-cent-of-the-time method. Type **echo $SHELL**. You'll see something like this:

```
$ echo $SHELL
/bin/ksh
```

If you don't get any response, you've got the C-shell.

Another way to find out which shell you have is with the **finger** command (which may not exist on your system). **finger** tells you about users on the system and includes information about the user's shell. For example, when I type **finger** with my own login name on our system, this is what I get. As you can see, I use the Korn shell, and my home directory is /home/johnmc.

```
$ finger johnmc
Login name: johnmc         In real life: John McMullen
Directory: /home/johnmc    Shell: /home/ksh
On since Sep 22 20:29:57 on ttyrd from mks-ts1
No unread mail
No Plan.
```

Here is a list of the different shells in alphabetical order, with a brief description of some of their best features.

bash   The Bourne-Again shell has many of the same features as the Korn shell, but you don't have to pay the same people for it. If this is the shell you've got, you're probably working on a UNIX variation such as LINUX.

236

csh   The C-shell has job control (good) and aliases-with-arguments (also good). Check to see if you can change to **tcsh**, since there are still known bugs in the C-shell. Better to be safe than sorry.

ksh   The Korn shell has job control (good) and aliases-without-arguments (not as good). You might be happy with it, but you might want to try one of the C-shells.

sh   If you have the Bourne shell, think about changing. It doesn't have job control or aliases, and both of these are useful features.

tcsh   The Tenex C-shell has file- and command-completion (which were taken from an operating system named Tenex). If you think you'll use this feature, try **tcsh** instead of **csh**. If you think you're going to write shell scripts, definitely use this instead of the C-shell.

Job control   The capability to run a job in the background without using any special commands. Running a job in the background enables you to go ahead and give other commands without having to wait for the background job to finish.

Alias   Another name for a command. If you frequently use one option with a command (such as **ls -F**), you can create an alias for that command. For example, if you make *lf* an alias for **ls -F**, anytime you type **lf**, the system turns it into **ls -F**.

Shell Startup Files

When you login, the **login** command starts your shell for you after you type your password. The first thing your shell does is look in your home directory for a *startup file*. A shell startup file contains instructions you want run every time you start your shell program. Different shells use different startup files. The Bourne shell and the Korn shell use .profile and .environ. The .profile file contains commands to be run, and .environ normally contains customization commands such as environment variables. The C-shell uses files called .cshrc and .login. The Bourne-Again shell uses a file named .bashrc.

Startup file A file containing commands that are run when a program starts up. Startup files are a way to customize your commands. Because of this, startup files are also called *configuration files*. In UNIX, these commands are in a file that's usually found in your home directory, and their names uusally start with a dot and end with "rc" (which stands for "run command").

You should put any commands you want run every time you login into your shell startup file. Here are some commands that are often in the startup file:

alias Defines a new name for a command. For instance, to print the PostScript files created by Word for DOS on my UNIX system, you must print the file postscrp.ini first, so I have an alias that makes the command "wpr" (for Word print) the same as "lpr postscrp.ini".

biff y Turns on the program that notifies you when electronic mail arrives for you. See Chapter 22, "Send Me a Letter," for more information about **biff**.

calendar Reminds you of appointments or deadlines for today and tomorrow. I discuss **calendar** in Chapter 25, "Neat Stuff."

export In Bourne-style shells, **export** defines an environment variable. I discuss **export** in Chapter 19, "Environ-Mental Health."

fortune Displays a quip or a clever saying. I discuss **fortune** in Chapter 25, "Neat Stuff."

function Defines a shell function. A function is a set of commands you want to run together, so functions are like small shell scripts. Unfortunately, there's not enough room in this book to discuss functions. (Maybe in the next book.)

set -o vi or **set -o emacs** In the Korn shell, this turns on command-line editing. This command lets you edit previous commands using the editing commands of **vi** (**set -o vi**) or of **emacs** (**set -o emacs**). This command isn't available in other shells.

stty erase ^H Defines the key on your keyboard which acts as the Backspace key. (On some UNIX systems, the Delete key acts as the Backspace key.) Other **stty** commands may be used to change which keys are significant to UNIX, as I described in Chapter 10, "When It Goes Wrong."

Shell startup files often contain other customization commands. The most common kind of customization is the setting of environment variables, such as your prompt, your terminal type, or where to search for programs. Commands to set environment variables are also discussed in Chapter 19, "Environ-Mental Health."

Depending upon the shell you are using, you may have more than one startup file in your home directory (as does the Korn shell). Usually one startup file contains commands to run (like **stty**), and the other sets environment variables for the shell. This makes it easier to change commands without accidentally changing environment variables, and vice versa.

You can also tell a shell to run certain commands every time you quit your session. The C-shell has an *exit file* (like a startup file) containing commands that run each time you exit UNIX. For the C-shell, the exit file is called .logout. For the Bourne and Korn shells, you have to use the **trap** command (which is a bit too technical for this book).

Trading Shells

If you don't like your current shell, you can try another one. For instance, you might want to switch to the Korn shell so you can make full use of the examples in this book.

There are really two reasons for switching shells. The first time I switched shells was because the person who answered all of my questions used a different shell than I did and I wanted to be able to use his shortcuts. Later I switched again because I wanted to use a specific feature I'd been told about that wasn't available in my shell. Those are the basic reasons for switching shells.

If you decide to change shells, be very careful because you can lose any customizations you've made to your startup files. If you haven't made any of the customization changes described in Chapter 19, "Environ-Mental Health," you don't need to worry.

However, you can only switch to a shell your system has. Which shells does your system have? You can view a list of acceptable or permitted shells in the /etc/shells file. To see the list, enter the command **more /etc/shells**. If no list appears, your system administrator doesn't allow users to change shells. Hassle him or her about it.

Most UNIX systems have a command that allows users to change their shells. **chsh**, for change shell, asks you to type in the name of the new shell (as it appears in /etc/shells), and then it asks you to type in your password (to prove you're really you). So a session in which you change your shell might look something like this:

```
% chsh
Change shell from /bin/csh:
New shell: /bin/ksh
Password:
```

The shell change doesn't take effect immediately; you have to log-out and log back in. That's because **chsh** doesn't change the shell you're currently using; it changes the information about you in the system—specifically, it changes the name of the shell you use when you login. The next time you login, UNIX gets the name of the new shell, but in the meantime, you're stuck with the one you've got.

On large networks, the change in shells may not take effect for a day, even if you logout and log back in. That's because some networks only update that user information once a day. On networks like this, **chsh** only places a request for a change in the user information.

The **chsh** command is sometimes given other names. On some systems, for example, it is **passwd -s**, and network systems sometimes call it **ypchsh** instead. All three of these work the same way and do the same thing. If you don't have **chsh**, **passwd -s**, or **ypchsh**, you can't change your shell yourself. Ask your system administrator to change it for you.

Shell Scripts

If you have a set of commands you run often, you can put them in a file and run the file like a program (instead of having to run the individual commands time and time again). Much like an actor follows a script, your shell will take the commands from the file as if you had typed them. Thus, these files are called *shell scripts*. A shell startup file like .profile is a shell script; it contains commands for the shell to run.

A shell script can be as simple as a couple of commands you always run together, or it can be a complete program. Many of the commands our system administrator uses are actually shell scripts. For example, the command I use for printing word processor files is actually a shell script.

I have a half-dozen shell scripts that I wrote and use. For instance, when I change to a new directory, I nearly always run **ls** to see what's in the directory. I have a little shell script I use instead of **cd** which does these two commands; I call it **cl**. When I type **cl** *directory*, the shell script runs **cd** *directory*, and then it does an **ls**.

> **Shell script** A file containing a set of commands the shell runs. Like a script, it's a set of instructions. A shell script can be as simple as a long command you don't like to re-type, or it can be thousands of lines long. Many of a system administrator's special programs are really shell scripts. To run a shell script, either make it executable (give it execute permission) or give the file name as an argument to the shell, such as **ksh** *myscript*.

I also use a shell script to replace a long command line or a command that works in a slightly different way on another machine. For instance, I have three different shell scripts on different machines; each is named tprint. Each script prints **troff** files; the **troff** command is slightly different on each machine. I wrote those three shell scripts so that I don't have to remember which UNIX system I'm on and how you print a **troff** file on that system. All I have to remember is tprint.

There are two ways to run a shell script. The first way is the command **sh** *scriptname*. (Use the name of your shell instead of **sh**—**csh** or **ksh**.) The second way is to turn the shell script into a program by giving it *execute* permission. Use the **chmod** program I described in Chapter 11, "More About Files (Some Useful Tips and Tricks)" to give a file execute permission.

Customizing Your Shell

Since you spend so much time using your shell, you want to be comfortable in it. Going back to the car image, you want to adjust the seat and make sure the mirrors are correctly positioned.

Customization involves creating new commands or new names for old commands and turning on the features you like. Some of the startup commands I mentioned earlier are really customization commands. Changing your prompt is a common customization; a lot of people like to have the current directory in the command-line prompt. (I'll discuss changing your prompt in Chapter 19, "Environ-Mental Health.")

You can personalize how you work by using convenient features built into different shells. Almost all of a shell's convenience features involve that step of translating the command. Most of the differences between shells lie in how you customize them.

Here are some of the customization commands that you can use in the Korn shell. There are commands to do the same things in other shells, but they have different names.

alias Creates a new name for a command.

export Creates an environment variable (see Chapter 19, "Environ-Mental Health" for more information about environment variables).

set Turns some of the Korn shell's options on and off.

unalias Removes an alias for a command.

The Least You Need to Know

Your shell is your "office" in UNIX. Being comfortable with your shell improves your productivity with UNIX.

➤ The shell is the program you use to communicate with UNIX. There are two major types of shells: Bourne-style shells and C-style shells. More recent shells try to combine the best features of the Bourne shell and the C-shell.

➤ You can find out which shell you're using by looking at the prompt ($ indicates Bourne shells; % indicates C-shells) or by using the commands **echo $SHELL** or **finger** *yourloginname*.

➤ The first thing your shell does when you start a UNIX session is run all of the commands in your shell startup file. You should put any commands you want run whenever you log into your shell startup file.

➤ For the Korn shell, the startup files are .profile (which contains commands to be run) and .environ (which contains customization commands such as environment variables).

➤ Use the **chsh**, **passwd -s**, or **ypcsh** commands to change to a different shell. If you don't have these commands, ask your system administrator to change your shell.

Chapter 19

Environ-Mental Health

In This Chapter

➤ What is your environment?

➤ How UNIX finds a program

➤ Setting your prompt

➤ Configuring your terminal

➤ Other useful environment variables

When you walk into your home after a long day at work, there are things (variables) about the environment inside your home that you will change to make yourself comfortable. You may turn on some lights or turn some off, turn up the heat, close the curtains, rearrange some furniture, or turn on the television—all in an attempt to make yourself comfortable with your surroundings so you can relax and, well, feel at home. Similarly, there are variables in our UNIX shell that we can change to make our work more efficient and make us more comfortable within our UNIX environment.

It's Everywhere!

In the real world, the environment is everything surrounding you. In UNIX, the environment is a list of names (variables) and values that are available to all your programs. Programs check the values of these variables and use the values to determine how the programs will behave. These variables are called *environment variables*. When you are first given an account on UNIX, these environment variables are usually set to a default value (which means they have been preset) by the system administrator. These values are what the system administrator believes will be the most useful to most of the people using UNIX most of the time. Although you may never need to change anything about your environment, chances are you probably will.

Environment variable A piece of information (like your home directory) that is given to all of your programs. Many programs check environment variables for some kinds of information. This is how all the programs that look in your home directory for startup information know where your directory is. Using an environment variable instead of a command option enables you to give the same information to all your programs without retyping it over and over.

There are other uses for environment variables besides changing how a program or a command behaves. For example, you might use an environment variable to eliminate your need for typing in the same options every time you use a particular program. Environment variables are the mechanism UNIX uses for automatically controlling a program's behavior without using options.

In addition, environment variables tell programs where to look for other UNIX programs, what kind of terminal you're using, where your home directory is, and which printer you like to use. For example, the **TERM** variable names the kind of terminal you have. Any program that writes on the screen checks this so it knows what your terminal can do, and how it does it. Can your terminal present underlines? Bold letters? Pictures? The program can figure that out by knowing what kind of terminal you have.

Listing Your Environment Variables

You've already got some environment variables set. You've got **LOGNAME** (your login name), **HOME** (your home directory), **PATH** (the directories that hold programs), and **TERM** (the kind of terminal you're using). You may have more. If you want to see your environment variables, use the **env** command. You'll get a long list, so you may want to pipe it through **more**, as shown in the following figure.

```
/home/johnmc$ env | more
_=/usr/bin/env
HZ=100
CODEPAGE=pc437
PATH=/usr/bin:/usr/ucb:/usr/X/bin:/home/johnmc/bin
XNLSPATH=/usr/X/lib/nls/elsXsi/US
COUNTRY=1
XGUI=OPEN_LOOK
LOGNAME=johnmc
MAIL=/var/mail/johnmc
TERMCAP=/etc/termcap
XWINHOME=/usr/X
XKEYBOARD=US
DESKTOPDIR=/home/johnmc
CONSEM=no
DISPLAY=xjohnmc:0.0
SHELL=/usr/bin/ksh
TIMEOUT=0
HOME=/home/johnmc
DT=yes
LD_LIBRARY_PATH=:/usr/X/lib
TERM=xterm
PWD=/home/johnmc
--More--
```

*The **env** command shows you what's in your environment.*

If you use a C-shell, use the **printenv** command instead of **env**.

As you can see, I've got a lot of environment variables. Most of them were put there by my system administrator when he created my account or by programs I use.

You can view the value of a particular variable by using the **echo** command (don't forget to put a dollar sign before the name of the value). This example shows the result of using **echo** to see the value of your **PATH** variable (yours will probably be slightly different). The **PATH** variable contains the list of places where the shell looks for programs when you give a command.

```
$ echo $PATH
/usr/bin:/usr/bin/X11:/usr/local/bin:
```

In this case, the **PATH** variable contains the names of three directories (separated by colons): /bin, /usr/bin, and /usr/local/bin. When you type a command (say, **lp contents**) to print the file contents, your shell looks for the **lp** program in these three directories, in the order they're given here. I'll have more to say about the **PATH** variable later in the chapter.

Setting an Environment Variable

When you give an environment variable a value, you are setting it. To set an environment variable, use the **export** command: type **export**, the name of the environment variable, an equals sign, and the value of the environment variable. Don't put any spaces around the equals sign. For example, the **lp** command checks the value of the **LPDEST** environment variable to find the name of the printer you want to print with. Here I'm setting it so that when I print, I use the printer named *printer1*.

```
$ export LPDEST=printer1
```

(On BSD systems, the **lpr** command is used instead of **lp**—**lpr** looks for an environment variable named **PRINTER** instead of **LPDEST**. If your system has both commands, you can probably use either variable.)

If the value you're giving an environment variable contains spaces, put the entire value in quotation marks, as in `$ export PAGER="more -s"`. (The **man** command uses the value of **PAGER** as the command to run whenever output would go off the screen.)

If you're using the C-Shell, use the command **setenv** to set environment variables. Instead of using an equals sign, use a space between the variable's name and its value: **setenv PRINTER** *printer1*.

Unsetting a Variable

There may come a time when you want to get rid of an environment variable you've set. Let's say, for example, that today you want to use the default printer instead of the printer you established with the **LPDEST** environment variable.

If you make a mistake when setting a value, just set it again. The new value replaces the old value.

Unsetting the variable gets rid of it entirely so your program reverts to using the default value established by the creators of UNIX or (perhaps) your system administrator. To do this, you use the **unset** command and the variable name. So to remove the variable **LPDEST**, you would use the command shown in the following figure.

```
/home/johnmc$ export LPDEST=printer1
/home/johnmc$ echo $LPDEST
printer1
/home/johnmc$ unset LPDEST
/home/johnmc$ echo $LPDEST

/home/johnmc$ █
```

*Here I set the **LPDEST** to Printer1, then I unset it.*

Finding Programs ($PATH)

All commands are programs. As I mentioned in Chapter 18, "The Shell Game," when you give a command, your shell program finds that command and then runs it. How does your shell find the command?

The same way you find a pen when you need one—the shell has a list of likely places to look. Just as you look in your purse or pocket, then in your desk, then in that mug by the phone, your shell has a list of places to look for command programs. Your shell's list is stored in an environment variable named **PATH**. The list is a list of directories, separated by colons. Here's my **PATH**, as shown by the **echo** command:

```
$ echo $PATH
/usr/bin:/usr/ucb:/usr/X/bin:/home/johnmc/bin
```

When I type a command, my shell looks in each of those directories for the command. When I type **lp**, my shell looks for the program file /usr/binlp; if the file is there, my shell runs it. If the file isn't there, my shell looks for lp in the next directory in the list (/usr/ucb), and so on until it either finds the program or runs out of places to look. The **PATH** is like a roadmap, as shown in the following figure.

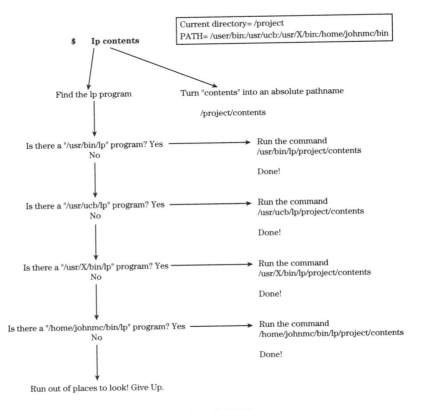

*How the shell finds a program using **PATH**.*

Without that list of places to look, I'd have to know the exact location of every program I wanted to run. Every time I wanted to run the **lp** command, I'd have to type **/usr/bin/lp** instead of just **lp**. As you can see, the **PATH** environment variable saves you a lot of typing. **PATH** also means you don't have to know which directories your system administrator uses to store programs.

When you type a command (such as **lp**), your shell goes looking for the **lp** program and uses your PATH to determine where to find it.

For example, if your shell was looking for the **lp** program in the **PATH** shown above, the shell would first look in the /bin/lp directory for **lp**. If it couldn't find **lp** there, the shell would look for it in the /usr/bin/lp directory. If the shell still couldn't find **lp**, it would tell you command not found (because those are the only two directories that contain programs).

Sometimes there are two versions of the same program on your system. For instance, our UnixWare system has two versions of **man**—/usr/bin/man and /usr/ucb/man. The /usr/ucb/man version has the **-k** option I discussed in Chapter 5, "Won't You Please Help Me?," but the /usr/bin/man version doesn't. Since the shell takes the first **man** program it finds, I always use /usr/bin/man instead of /usr/ucb/man. If I wanted to use the **-k** option, I'd have to use the command **/usr/ucb/man**. And if I *always* wanted to use the version of **man** in /usr/ucb instead of the version in /usr/bin, I would change my **PATH** so the shell looked in /usr/ucb before it looked in /usr/bin.

You can restore your startup values if you've accidentally changed or unset an important environment variable. (If you've unset your **PATH**, you can't run any programs!) You can get your environment variable settings from your shell startup file with the . command. In the Korn shell, the command to restore your environment from the .profile file is **. .profile**. If your environment variables are stored in the file .environ, the command to use is **. .environ**. If you're using the C-Shell, the . command is called **source**. In the C-Shell, you would give the command **source .cshrc** or **source .login** (depending upon which file contains your environment variable settings).

If you want a quick way to add another directory to the beginning or end of your current **PATH**, include the **$PATH** variable (which contains your existing path) as part of the command for adding the additional directory. For instance, suppose you want to make a directory to hold your own programs—mine is called /home/johnmc/bin. (Use the **mkdir** command to create the directory. See Chapter 7, "The Root of the Matter: Files and Directories" to learn about **mkdir**.) You need to add the name of this directory (/home/johnmc/bin) to your **PATH**. This command adds it to the end of your **PATH**: **export PATH=$PATH:/home/johnmc/bin** (see the following figure).

To make this change permanent, you should put this line in your startup file, after any existing commands that set the **PATH**.

```
/home/johnmc$ echo $PATH
/usr/bin:/usr/ucb:/usr/X/bin
/home/johnmc$ export PATH=$PATH:/home/johnmc/bin
/home/johnmc$ echo $PATH
/usr/bin:/usr/ucb:/usr/X/bin:/home/johnmc/bin
/home/johnmc$ █
```

How to create a /bin and add it to your path.

Prompting Your Prompt

One of your shell's variables is your prompt (named **PS1**). You can change your prompt to include any information you want. Some people change the prompt to include helpful information, such as the date or the current directory. Others include something playful, such as "Howdy, Partner! What can I do for you? $".

Only the Korn shell and the Bourne shell use the variable **PS1** for the prompt; the C-Shell uses the variable **prompt**. To change the value of your prompt in the C-Shell, use the command **set prompt=*"your prompt here"***.

It's quite easy to change your prompt in the Korn shell: you simply change the value of **PS1**. So if you want your command prompt to read "Your wish is my command, master$ ", type **PS1="Your wish is my command, master$ "**. Normally, you include a $ (or a %) at the end of the prompt to remind you that it's the end of the prompt. You need the double quotes to include the spaces in the prompt. I always add an extra space after the $ because I find it easier to read the screen that way.

In the Korn shell, single quotes and double quotes can make a big difference in your prompt. In the prompt example, single quotes around **PWD** let the prompt take on a new value when you change directories. If you use double quotes, the prompt is set to the value of the directory you were in when you typed the command. In UNIX jargon, the single quotes "delay interpretation" of the variable, but double quotes do not.

Suppose you hate typing **pwd** all the time to find out where you are. All you have to do is set your **PS1** environment variable to always include your current working directory in the prompt. How do you do that?

Well, with the Korn shell, it's quite easy. The shell variable **PWD** holds the value of the current working directory. The only tricky thing is that you have to use single quotes, such as:

```
$ PS1='$PWD$ '
/home/johnmc$
```

Getting Your $TERM Straight

TERM is the environment variable that describes what type of terminal you have. You don't need to change it unless you change terminals or you're seeing junk like `"^[[^7mNAME^[[^4m"` on the screen. If your terminal is acting up, your **TERM** variable may be set to the wrong value. The solution is to change the value of your **TERM** variable to indicate a new terminal type.

UNIX systems keep a big list of terminal types and what each terminal can do. For instance, on System V systems, this list is called "terminfo." When a program needs to write to your terminal, it checks the value of your **TERM** variable and then checks the terminfo list to see how it should create underlines, make bold letters, and so forth for your particular terminal type.

Unfortunately, I can't tell you what kind of terminal you have. I can tell you that if you have a mouse attached, it's probably an X-terminal, so you should try the setting **TERM=xterm**. However, if you need a definite right answer about your terminal type, ask your system administrator.

If you're using a PC to login to a UNIX system, your situation is a little more complicated. Some UNIX systems have a terminal type named "pc", but most don't. Instead, when you run a program on your PC to connect to the UNIX system, the program acts like some other

251

kind of terminal—this is called *terminal emulation*. The documentation that came with your PC program tells you what kinds of terminals it can emulate. Once you know what kind of terminal the PC program is pretending to be, you tell the UNIX system. For instance, if your PC program says it does "vt100 emulation," you would set your **TERM** variable for a vt100 terminal: **export TERM=vt100**.

Making Changes Permanent

When you change or set an environment variable, that change lasts only until you change it again or until you quit your UNIX session. If you want to make the change permanent, you have to put the command in your startup file. (I described startup files briefly in Chapter 18, "The Shell Game.") Use one of the editors described in Chapters 14 through 17 to change your startup file.

Before you go changing your startup file, make a copy of it with the command **cp .profile .profile.old**. That way, if you make a mistake with the changes, you can go back to your old startup file easily by typing **mv .profile.old .profile**.

For the Korn shell, it's traditional to put almost all of your environment variable settings in the .environ file in your home directory. You could put them in .profile if you wanted, but most people just put them in .environ so they're almost all in one place. If you only have a .profile file, add new environment variables to that file. If you have both .profile and .environ, add new environment variables to .environ. If your **PATH** is set in .profile and everything else is set in .environ, change the **PATH** in .profile and keep it there.

Here's part of a .profile file that sets some environment variables:

```
PS1='$PWD$ '
export PATH=/usr/local/bin:$PATH:.
export TERM=vt102
export EDITOR=/usr/local/bin/emacs
```

The first line of this .profile file sets the prompt so that it always shows the current working directory. The second line adds /usr/local/bin to the beginning of the **PATH** and the current directory to the end of the **PATH**. The third line sets the terminal type to what's called VT102. The fourth line declares that the user wants to use **emacs** as the editor when inside other programs.

If you have an environment variable called **ENV** or **ENVIRON** set in your .profile file, leave it there; don't move it into the .environ file. The **ENVIRON** variable is what tells your shell to look in the .environ file for more instructions. If it's not there, all environment variables have to be set in .profile or they will be overlooked.

The Most Common Environment Variables

There are about a dozen important environment variables that you should know about. Some you'll probably want to set, some you'll only need to set once in awhile, and others you shouldn't set—but you should know they exist.

The first category includes environment variables you'll probably want to set, such as the following variables:

PATH   This is a list of directories which contain programs. If you don't have anything set for this variable, you'll have to type in the full path name for every program you want to run.

LPDEST   This tells the shell which printer to use. If you don't set this, the shell will always use the system's default printer (which may be fine). See Chapter 9, "Printing Is Pressing" for more about printing.

EDITOR and **VISUAL**   These are your number one and two choices of editors to use when you're inside other programs. You should change these, because the number one choice is usually **ed**, and you don't want to use **ed** to edit files. However, you may not want to use **vi** either, which is usually the number two choice. You can find out about your choices of editors in Part III, "A Textbook on Text."

PS1 or **prompt**   One of these variables contains your *prompt*, the message your shell prints to indicate it's waiting for a command. If you use the Korn shell or the Bourne shell, your prompt is stored in **PS1**; if you use the C-Shell, your prompt is stored in **prompt**. (These aren't actually environment variables; they're just variables.)

The second category contains environment variables you may need to change once in awhile, but you don't need to set them most of the time. The following variables fall into this category:

TERM   This tells the shell the kind of terminal you have (I talk about this later in this chapter). You only need to change this variable if you change terminals.

PAGER   This is the command that **man** runs if a man page is longer than one screenful. You almost never need to change this variable.

TZ   This tells the shell which time zone you're in. Your system administrator should take care of setting this variable.

LINES   This tells how many lines of text your display can handle. You should only need this if **TERM** doesn't work right for you. The UNIX commands **more** and **less** use this variable.

COLUMNS   This indicates how many characters can appear across your display. Like **LINES**, you should only need this if **TERM** doesn't work right for you.

The last category contains variables that you don't need to change but that you'll see in a listing of environment variables and should know exist. (In fact, changing them can cause problems.)

HOME   Your home directory. A lot of programs use this so they know where to look for startup files.

LOGNAME   Your login name.

MAILDIR   The directory where your mail is stored. The **mailx** program uses this variable.

The Least You Need to Know

This chapter taught you about the environment in which your UNIX programs work. Your environment is different from everyone else's. Some of it is predefined by your system or your system administrator, but you can change any part of your environment. Changing your environment changes how some of your commands work. The environment is just a way to pass control information to programs that need it, without typing options for every command.

➤ An environment variable provides you with a way to make information known to a lot of programs without using option flags.

➤ The environment variable is a single word, usually all in capital letters, such as **HOME**. If you want to refer to the value of the environment variable, put a dollar sign in front: **$HOME**.

➤ In the Korn shell, you set any environment variable with the command **export** *VARIABLE=value*. You unset it with the command **unset** *VARIABLE*.

➤ Your most important environment variable is the **PATH** variable. It tells your shell where to look for programs. Your path is a list of directory names separated by colons.

➤ Your **TERM** environment variable describes the type of terminal you have.

➤ To set new environment variables automatically every time you login, put them in your startup file.

A Little Background Music

One really useful thing about UNIX is its capability to run two (or more) programs at once. When you type a command on the command line, you normally have to wait until the command has finished before you can type the next command. The reason you have to wait for this command to complete itself before you run the next command is because it is executing in the foreground. If you've asked the computer to do something time-consuming (like find all the *.txt files on the system or sort a very big file), you might not want to wait until the computer's finished before you type your next command. You can get around this by running the first program in the *background*.

Back-to-Background

A background process (or job) is like background music and background action in a movie. It happens, but you don't have to pay attention to it. A program running in the foreground is just the opposite: you *have* to pay attention to it, and you have to type commands in order for the program to complete its task.

The best programs to run in the background are ones that don't write to the screen and don't ask you to type any commands. The **sort**, **find**, and **lp** commands are good examples of programs you can run in the background. Interactive programs (programs that require you to enter information in order for them to complete a task) are not good candidates for running in the background. For example, you wouldn't normally run the **ls** command or an editor in the background.

Running a Command in the Background

Suppose you need to sort a large file named humongous-list, and you want to save the sorted file to a file named sorted-file. The command is simple: **sort -o sorted-file humongous-list**. If humongous-list is really big, the command may take awhile to complete. Of course, you don't want to sit around waiting on it; you want to go on with your work and type other commands. To resolve your dilemma, you can tell the shell to run the **sort** command in the background by putting an ampersand (&) after the command. Your command should now look like this:

```
$ sort -o sorted-file humongous-list &
[1]     3178
$
```

3178 is the process identification number (PID) of the file. (I described process identification numbers in Chapter 10, "When It Goes Wrong.") The [1] is the *job number*: this is background job number one.

While this program is running in the background, you can do other things. When the background program finally finishes, it waits until you press Enter to get a command prompt in your foreground task. Then it prints a message on-screen like this :

```
[1] - Done sort -o sorted-file humongous-list &
$
```

Make It Stop! (Interrupting a Background Command)

There will come a time when you need to stop a background job. Maybe you told the **sort** command to sort the wrong list, or maybe you need to make one more change to a file before it prints. Whatever the reason, it will happen—it's inevitable.

You can't stop a background job with Control-C. You have to use the **kill** command (which I described in Chapter 10, "When It Goes Wrong") if you want to stop a program while it is in the background. The basic steps to kill a process (from Chapter 10) apply here:

1. Find the job's process ID number (3178 in our previous example). You may remember it from running the command, or it may still be on the screen, or you might need to use **ps** to find it.

2. Starting with a "gentle" kill, try to kill the command using the process ID number (**kill 3178** in our example).

3. If that doesn't work, move up to the more severe **kill** commands (**kill -1 3178** or, as a last resort, **kill -9 3178**).

Some systems let you substitute **%*job-id*** for the process number. For instance, to kill background job 1 on one of these systems, you could give the command **kill %1**. Some versions of the Korn shell and some versions of the C-Shell allow this.

Often you can kill a background process by bringing it to the foreground with **fg** and then using **Control-C** to kill it. I describe using **fg** later in this chapter, under the heading "Moving a Command to the Foreground."

All of your jobs are killed when you exit UNIX, even the jobs you have running in the background. If you want a background job to keep running even after you exit, put the word **nohup** at the beginning of the command line, like this: **nohup lp really-big-file &**.

Other Background Options

You can string several commands together and run them in the background just as you can in the foreground. For example, say you have a file called autobiography that you need to format (**fmt**), set page breaks in (**pr**), and then print (**lp**). (This is your bestselling novel, and you want it to look good when you ship it to the publishers.) The command to do all this is **fmt autobiography ¦ pr ¦ lp**.

If you put the ampersand after a piped command—pipes are described in Chapter 11, "More About Files (Some Useful Tips and Tricks)"—the entire command structure runs in the background. Thus, the following command formats the file autobiography, paginates it, sends it to your default printer—all in the background:

```
$ fmt autobiography ¦ pr ¦ lp &
[2]        3212
$
```

Now suppose you want a list of all of the files in the /bin directory (which is a big directory). This directory listing can take awhile to print on-screen, and you have other work you need to get done on the system. Run the directory listing using the **ls** command, but tell your shell to save the contents of the directory listing in a file instead of printing it to the screen. You can enter the command > **/binlist** and then check the contents of the file later. Here's the syntax for doing such a task:

```
$ ls /bin > ~/binlist &
[3]        3521
$
```

This saves the output of **ls /bin** in the file binlist in your home directory. (The & goes after all file redirection instructions.)

Another thing you might find useful is the capability to run a command in the background and have UNIX store any error messages in another file that you can check out later. To explain this concept better, let me give you a possible scenario.

As you work in UNIX more and more, you'll probably begin using the **find** command to find lost files (as described in Chapter 12, "The Search Is On"). Some of these searches may turn out to be quite time-consuming, especially if you haven't a clue where you put your beloved file or if you're looking for a number of files. During this search, **find** might come across some files that it can't open (because you do not have permission to read these directories). You can find out which directories **find** can't open by having it print an error listing of those directories as part of the results of its search. So, you want a command that saves both the search output and the error output, and you want to run all these commands in the background so you can continue with your other work.

For example, what if you want to find all the files in the system with names that end in .txt. Let's say you want to save the output of the search to a file called filelist; you want to save the list of directories that the **find** command can't open (and any other errors that may occur in this search) in a file called errorlist. The following command takes care of all of this:

```
$ find / -name "*.txt" -print > filelist 2> errorlist &
[4] 3501
$
```

Did you follow all that?

Moving a Command to the Background

After starting a command, you might discover that it's taking a long time and decide you should have run it in the background. The capability to control such things is called *job control*, and it's part of your shell (see Chapter 18, "The Shell Game"). Most modern shells have job control.

Before you can move a currently executing command from foreground to background, you must first "suspend" the command. You do this with the **Control-Z** command on most systems. Then you need to restart the command in the background, which you do with the **bg** command.

For example, suppose you are checking the spelling in your autobiography with the **spell** command and saving the output of **spell** in the file misspelled.txt (**spell autobio > misspelled.txt**). In the middle of the process, you decide you want to move the command to the background. Suspend it by pressing **Control-Z**, and then move it into the background. Here's what it looked like on my system after I pressed Control-Z:

```
[5] - Stopped (SIGSTP) spell autobio > misspelled.txt
$ bg
[5]      4277
$
```

261

Control-Z is actually the control character for the suspend signal. If Control-Z doesn't work for you, either you've got a shell that doesn't understand background jobs, or suspend is assigned to some other control character. To see what that other control character is on your terminal, run **stty -a** and check for the control character associated with **susp**. You can use **stty** to set the control character, as described in Chapter 10, "When It Goes Wrong."

Finding Out What Background Jobs You Have Running

The **jobs** command tells you what commands you have running in the background. Here's an example of **jobs** output for the jobs I've put into the background throughout this chapter.

```
$ jobs
[1]    Running    sort -o sorted-file humongous-list &
[2]    Running    fmt autobiography ¦ pr ¦ lp &
[3]    Done       ls /bin > ~/binlist
[4]  - Running    find / -name "*.txt" -print > filelist 2> errorlist &
[5]  + Running    spell autobio > misspelled.txt
```

Most of these commands are still running, but job 3 has finished. The + beside job 5 indicates that job 5 is the default job for **fg** (foreground); the default job is usually the job that you put in the background last, and it will have the highest job number. If you use the **fg** command (see the next section) without specifying the job, this is the one **fg** will work on. The - indicates that job 4 will be the default job after job 5. (If you use the **fg** command twice, it moves job 5 into the foreground first, and then it moves job 4 into the foreground after that.)

The **ps** command (described in Chapter 10) lists all the commands you have running in both the foreground and background, but it doesn't specifically tell you which are running in the foreground and which are running in the background. Here's what the **ps** command output looks like for the session in this chapter:

```
$ ps

   PID TTY      TIME COMD
  2962 pts002   0:00 ksh
  3178 pts002   1:12 sort
  3212 pts002   0:59 fmt
  3501 pts002   0:15 find
  4277 pts002   0:04 spell
  4624 pts002   0:00 ps
```

Some versions of **ps** show you more of the actual command line you typed and not just the program's name.

Some older UNIX shell programs don't "know" about jobs or job numbers. The & still runs commands in the background, but the shell doesn't give you a job number—just the process id number. If you have a shell program that doesn't know about jobs, you can't use Control-Z to suspend a job, and you can't use the **jobs** command to see what background jobs you're running. The only solution is to switch to another shell program; see Chapter 18, "The Shell Game," for instructions on how to switch.

Moving a Command to the Foreground

The **fg** command moves a background job into the foreground. You might want to do this if you changed your mind about running the job in the background. You tell **fg** which command to bring to the foreground by using the command **fg %***job id*. If you don't tell **fg** which job you want brought to the foreground, **fg** uses the default job, as shown by the **jobs** command. (This is normally the job you put in the background last.) **fg** only works on jobs that are still running.

Suppose you wanted to bring the **sort** command to the foreground. For instance, in the **jobs** listing in the previous section, the **sort** command was job id 1. You could bring it to the foreground with the command **fg %1**. The % is necessary to identify it as a job id number.

Running a Command Later

There may be times when you want to run a large job during a time when the computer is not being used so heavily by others. Running large programs during off-peak hours keeps your job from taking so long to complete and prevents the system from slowing down for the other users. The **at** command lets you run a job at a certain time (that's where the name comes from).

You need permission to run **at**. If **at** tells you that you're not authorized, ask your system administrator to add you to the list of people who can use **at**.

The **at** command schedules a job or jobs to run in the background at a specified time. For instance, in our office, we use the **runoff** command to print a manual; it takes quite awhile to run and slows the system down considerably. (If the system is busy, **runoff** may not finish for hours.) Therefore, I often print a manual late at night so I can review it the next day. (Your system won't have **runoff**; we wrote it ourselves.)

When the **at** command runs, it runs in the directory from which you typed it. If the **at** command produces output or if there are any error messages, **at** mails them to you via UNIX e-mail. (See Chapter 22, "Send Me a Letter," for a description of electronic mail.)

To use **at**, give the time (either 24-hour clock time or the standard time with am or pm attached) and press **Enter**. Type in the command (or commands) you want to run, press **Enter**, and then press **Control-D**. For example, the following listing shows you how to run the big **sort** command at 11:00 P.M.

```
$ at 2300
sort -o sorted-file humongous-list
<Control-D>
job 784701000.a at Sat Nov 12 23:00:00 1994
```

In this case, the job is number 784701000.a.

You can include more than one command in an **at** command. Instead of pressing **Control-D**, type another command and end it with **Enter**. You can enter as many commands as you want this way, and the entire sequence of commands will start at the time you specified.

at is quite flexible about how you can enter the time: instead of 2300, I could have written 23:00, 23, 11pm, or 11:00pm. **at** also recognizes the times "noon" and "midnight." (Even though it gives you the scheduled time to the second, **at** only accepts times specified to the minute.)

If you want, you can include the date. The command **at 3:40 Friday** runs the job at 3:40 Friday morning. You can use a day of the week or the month and day. (For month and day, use the first three letters of each: Fri Jan 23.) You can even put a date, such as Jan 23 or May 15, after the **at** command.

If you need to get information about jobs you've scheduled with the **at** command or you need to cancel a scheduled job, you can use the **-l** and **-r** options. **at -l** shows the list of jobs you have scheduled, including the job id numbers. (You need the job id number in order to cancel a job.) Use the command **at -r *job id*** to cancel the job with number *job id*.

Why So Slow?

A fact of life on UNIX is that every command you run slows down the system just a little bit because the system must juggle more programs. This applies to all programs in the foreground and the background. On a lot of systems, programs running in the background are automatically given a slightly lower priority than programs running in the foreground. After all, you're not immediately interested in the program's result or you wouldn't be running it in the background.

Processes that are given reduced priority are referred to as "niced" because the **nice** command is used to reduce a command's priority. Background jobs are usually given a reduced priority (they are niced) by UNIX. For instance, every other command you're running may get 1/500th of a second of attention every second while a background job only gets 1/1000th of a second every second.

With the **nice** command, you can reduce a command's priority. (Note, however, that only the system administrator can increase a command's priority.) To nice a command, simply put **nice** at the very beginning of the command. For instance, to nice the command **lp autobiography**, enter the command as **nice lp autobiography**.

The Least You Need to Know

➤ To run a command in the background, type **&** after the command.

➤ Each command running in the background has a job id number, which you can use to refer to the command in the **fg** and **kill** commands.

➤ To move a command that's already running in the foreground into the background, suspend it with **Control-Z**, and then restart it in the background with **bg**.

➤ To see which jobs you have running in the background, use the **jobs** command.

➤ To bring a background job to the foreground, type **fg** [*job-id*]. If you don't supply a job id number, **fg** brings the default job (usually the job you put in the background last) to the foreground.

➤ To kill a job in the background, use either **kill** *process-id* (if you remember the process id) or **kill** *%job-id*.

➤ You can keep a command from being stopped when you exit UNIX by putting the **nohup** command in front of it.

➤ You can run commands at some later time with the **at** command, like this: **at 2130**. Type the commands one to a line. To end the list of the commands, press **Control-D**.

Chapter 21

Everybody's Talkin'

In This Chapter

➤ What a computer network is

➤ How UNIX machines trade files and information

➤ Transferring files between computers

➤ Logging into another computer

➤ Exchanging files between DOS and UNIX computers

This chapter is about computer networks and sharing files between computers. Well, that's what computer networks are about, really: sharing files between computers. A computer network is a group of computers that share applications, files, programs, and other resources (such as printers). Each computer in a network is often called a *site* or *host* and has a *hostname* or *sitename*. The host you're logged into is called your *local host*; any other host (such as another computer on the network) is *remote*. (Site implies that there's some geographical distance between the computers, but that's not a hard-and-fast rule.)

Communications Between Systems

One advantage of UNIX is its built-in networking capability. If you have a clever system administrator, you can have more than a dozen computers on the network and never know that you're sharing files between them. Computers on a network may share files so intimately that, while you are logged onto your local host, you can actually use a program on another computer.

You are probably not on a network (at least not on my network) if you have to copy a file onto a magnetic tape or a floppy disk and carry it to me so that I can use it.

You may be on a network and not know it. One of the main features of UNIX is its capability to join file systems. (A file system is made up of all the files and directories on a computer and the gritty technical details of how UNIX stores them.) A system administrator may decide to make a directory and all of its contents available to other computers on the network. (This directory can be large, like the root directory, or it can be small.) Other computers on the network can accept the offered directory and put it in one of their own directories, joining the file systems of the two computers.

Once that's done, the fact that the files and directories are on another computer is invisible to you, the user. All of the regular UNIX file commands (**cp**, **mv**, and so on) and the programs work just as if the files were on your system. You may never know that the files are "really" on another computer.

NFS (Network File System) and RFS (Remote File System) are examples of file systems that can be joined between two computers.

File Transfer—Paying Attention to Protocol

The earliest method of trading or transferring files between two UNIX systems was over phone lines. In order to exchange files between computers, the files had to be in some uniform format which could be recognized by both computers so files would not become jumbled and unreadable during the transfer process. This uniform format is called a communication protocol, and UUCP (which stands for Unix-to-Unix **cp**) was the first communication protocol available for this. When you wanted to send or get a file, you requested it, and the system fetched it for you the next time it phoned the other machine. Because UUCP works in batches, it's called a "batch" networking protocol.

UUCP works well, but when you say "networking," most people think of a continuous connection between two computers. (Actually, I think of exchanging business cards, but that may just be me.) UUCP connections are intermittent. In the early 1980s, the BSD versions of UNIX came with a communications protocol called TCP/IP (Transmission Control Protocol/ Internet Protocol). TCP/IP is not a batch protocol; the computers stay connected and can exchange information continuously.

Because TCP/IP was found to be a pretty reliable way of sending messages between computers, people started building programs to take advantage of it. The most common of these is FTP for File Transfer Protocol.

Like many file transfer programs, FTP distinguishes between transferring *text* and transferring *binary* files. If you transfer a binary file (such as a program) as text, you'll probably ruin it. The reason is that various operating systems store text files differently than they store binary files. Most file transfer programs fix up text files so they're in the format the receiving system expects. This involves adding or subtracting characters, which scrambles a program or other binary file.

> **Protocol** An agreed upon set of messages and message formats that enable computers to exchange information. Some common protocols are UUCP, FTP, Kermit (file transfer), and TCP/IP (networking).
>
> **UUCP** A protocol for exchanging files, usually over the phone lines. UUCP stands for UNIX-to-UNIX **cp** (although some claim the CP stands for "Copy Program"). A lot of electronic mail is exchanged using the UUCP protocol. UUCP is batch-oriented: you must request the file transfer and then wait until the next time the two computers "talk" to each other to get the file.

> What's the difference between, say, Ethernet and TCP/IP, or FTP and UUCP? We have to go back to the layers of a UNIX system to explain this. Think of computer communication as a bunch of layers. (Computer scientists can leave the room for a moment; I'm simplifying here.)
>
> At the bottom layer, the computers have to be physically connected to each other (by a phone line, Ethernet cable, or something else). Some of the "higher" layers work specifically with one kind of hardware connection,

269

others try to work with more than one kind. Ethernet is a hardware connection; so is a phone line. (Ethernet can carry a *lot* more information than a phone line, though.)

At the next layer up, we already know the computers are connected so they can send signals to each other, but the computers have to agree on what form the signals are going to take. For instance, will they be long or short signals? We'll call this connection a communications protocol. Technically, UUCP and TCP/IP are communications protocols.

At the next layer, the computers have to agree on what the signals *are*. When one computer sends the signal HS, does that mean "Hello, Start" or "Hang up, Stupid"? This includes the signals that mean "Send a file" or "Run this program." We'll call this layer of agreement the transfer protocol. FTP and Kermit are transfer protocols. Some types of transfer protocols are sophisticated enough that you can run a network with them (although they're not fundamentally different from the other transfer protocols). When we're talking about transfer protocols that include signals for all of the things a network needs, we'll call it a network protocol. NFS and RFS are network protocols.

File Transfer via UUCP and FTP

The two file transfer programs I'm going to discuss here are **uucp** (which uses the UUCP file transfer protocol) and **ftp** (which uses the FTP file transfer protocol). I'm discussing them not because it's easy to remember which protocols they use (as if we really care), but because these two programs represent the two important types of UNIX computer connections: UUCP and Internet-style connections.

UUCP connections are usually over standard phone lines and are common on small systems. All UNIX systems come with some version of the UUCP programs. If you want to send a file to a computer, and your computer's connection to that computer is via UUCP, you'll need to use the **uucp** program.

Internet-style connections are usually over Ethernet lines or special high-speed phone lines. If you want to exchange files with a computer that's connected to yours through an Internet-style connection, use the **ftp** command.

Not every UNIX system has Internet-style connections to other computers. Even if you do have an Internet-style connection, it may not be to the Internet. For example, until recently my office's network of computers were connected to each other through an Internet-style connection, but they weren't connected to the Internet. I could use **ftp** to copy files from one of our computers to another, but not to any computers outside the company. If you can use the **ftp** program, you should; it's usually much faster and more convenient than UUCP.

Using UUCP: Transferring Files in Batches

UUCP is a *batch* method of copying files from one computer to another; it works on binary files as well as text files. You can only exchange files between computers that have a UUCP connection.

The most important feature of a UUCP connection is that it's not always there. Sometimes the two computers are not connected at all. Typically, one computer phones another, and while the two computers are "talking" to each other, they exchange files via the UUCP protocol. Because of the occasional nature of this connection, each computer stores file transfer requests for the other computers it calls.

Suppose you're logged into a computer named blackstone and you want to send a file to a computer named houdini. You make your request using the **uucp** command, and the file transfer request is recorded. The next time blackstone talks to houdini, all of the requests for file transfers between those two computers are carried out in a big batch. That's why UUCP is called a batch method.

You use the **uucp** command in much the same way you use **cp**, except that you must name the computer the files are on, in this format: **uucp** *fromsite!file tosite!file*. The ! character separates the site name from the file name. (If you don't name a site, **uucp** assumes the file is on your machine.) For example, the file /usr/project/membership on houdini is houdini!/usr/project/membership.

Theoretically, you could copy a file from any directory to any directory, but for security reasons, almost all UUCP sites use a special directory to store files to be transferred. This directory is called the "public UUCP directory," and its name is /usr/spool/uucppublic. To send a file, you may need to copy it to /usr/spool/uucppublic before you give the **uucp** command. You should transfer files to or from /usr/spool/uucppublic or one of its subdirectories. (If you have special permissions to send files to a different directory, your system administrator will tell you.)

Of course, you don't want to type /usr/spool/uucppublic all the time, but that's okay. **uucp** understands that !~/ refers to /usr/spool/uucppublic. Let's say you're on blackstone in the UUCP public directory. To copy the file receipts from the current directory to the UUCP public directory on houdini, use this command:

```
$ uucp receipts houdini!~/
```

Likewise, to get the file blaster.exe from the directory /usr/spool/uucppublic/dos on the system called henning to your public uucp directory, use this command:

```
$ uucp henning!~/dos/blaster.exe !~/
```

(Because you didn't name a site, !~/ is on your system. If you'd typed ~/ instead of !~/, the destination directory would have been interpreted as your home directory.) Because the file transfer requests are stored until the next connection is made, the file transfer may not happen for an hour, a day, or longer, depending on how often the two machines talk.

One last thing you may be wondering: how do you find out which machines you have UUCP connections to? Use the command **uuname**; it lists all of the sites your computer talks to.

```
$ uuname
houdini
randi
henning
wilson
cardini
penn
teller
gibson
```

The list isn't sorted in any way. This computer has UUCP connections to eight other systems. From this computer, you can use **uucp** to exchange files with any of these eight computers.

If you want to see the name of the computer you're logged into, use the command **uuname -l**:

```
$ uuname -l
blackstone
```

FTP: Interactive File Transfer

Another file transfer program is FTP. Unlike **uucp**, the **ftp** program is interactive: you login to the remote site using **ftp**, do your file transfers, and then exit. Suppose you're on a computer named pinball, and you want to exchange files with a computer named flipper.

Normally, after the **ftp** command, you name the site to which you want to connect. For example, if I want to connect to a remote computer named flipper, I would type **ftp flipper**. (You have to know the site name to connect to it.) When the login prompt appears, login with your login name and password for that site.

The following list summarizes the most common commands you will use during your file transfer sessions using FTP:

➤ To look around the remote system, use **ls** and **cd** (just like on a regular UNIX system).

➤ To get one *text* file, type **get** *filename*. To send one text file, type **put** *filename*.

Usually, you need an account on the remote site to use **ftp** to transfer files. However, some sites have anonymous ftp, where anyone can get files. You login with the login name "anonymous" and use your e-mail address as your password. You can get a lot of interesting files through anonymous ftp. To find out about FTP sites that offer anonymous ftp, you can use the programs **archie** and **gopher**, described in Chapter 23, "Internet Interests."

Always use **ftp** to connect to some other machine. Oddly enough, you *can* use **ftp** to login to the machine you're currently on (for instance, on flipper, you **ftp** to flipper), but you can't exchange files, so there's really no point to it.

➤ To transfer a *binary* file, give the command **binary** to tell **ftp** that all subsequent file transfers contain binary files. Then use **get** *filename* and **put** *filename*.

➤ To break the connection and exit **ftp**, use the command **bye**.

Here's an example. In this case, I was sending from my machine (named giga) to a machine named flipper. I had an account on flipper, so I was sending the file desktop.xwd from my current directory on giga to my home directory on flipper. Starting from giga, the session looked like this:

```
$ ftp flipper
Connected to flipper.
220 flipper FTP server (UNIX(r) System V Release 4.2) ready.
Name (flipper:johnmc):
331 Password required for johnmc.
Password: (type in password here)
230 User johnmc logged in.
ftp> binary
200 Type set to I.
ftp> put desktop.xwd
200 PORT command successful.
150 Opening BINARY mode data connection for desktop.xwd.
226 Transfer complete.
local: desktop.xwd remote: desktop.xwd
51599 bytes sent in 0.14 seconds (3.6e+02 Kbytes/s)
ftp> bye
221 Goodbye.
```

Logging In from Home

If you have a PC at home, you may want to use that PC to login to the UNIX system where you work. When you do this, your PC will behave just like a terminal at the office: you'll login to your regular account and work on your UNIX account just as if you were using a character-based terminal at the office. (Although there are programs that will let you use your PC as an X-Terminal, they're rather specialized, and you're not likely to be using them at this stage in your UNIX career.)

For you to use your PC as a UNIX terminal, both your PC and your UNIX machine must have a modem attached (the modem plugs into the phone line). In addition, there are several things you'll need to know about your UNIX system before you get home and spend hours in frustration because you forgot to ask one little thing. Check with your system administrator about the following concerns:

➤ Is there a modem attached to the UNIX system that you can call into? (If not, you can't login.) What's the phone number?

➤ What are the terminal settings? (Normally they're 8-N-1; check your terminal emulator documentation for your PC to see how to set this.)

➤ Are there extra logins and extra security passwords that you need to know about? (If there's a security password, you have to give it before you login.)

You'll also need a terminal-emulator program for your PC. There are many available; one comes with Windows. Although the following information is true for most terminal-emulator programs, your terminal program might do things differently, so read the instructions. You need to know:

➤ How to dial a phone number using the program. If all else fails, you can usually type **ATDT** and the number and press **Enter**. (Use **ATDP** if you don't have touch-tone phone service.)

➤ What kind of terminal your program acts like. If you have a choice, start with a VT100 or VT102 terminal, since almost all UNIX systems can use that terminal type.

➤ How to transfer files (if you want to do that). The UNIX commands are described later in this chapter, in the section "The UNIX-DOS Shuttle: Trading Files."

> **Modem** A device that enables a computer to communicate over a phone line to another computer. A modem converts computer signals into audible tones that can be sent over the phone line, and then converts those tones back into computer signals. Modems can be inside your computer (internal) or outside (external). A modem's *baud rate* is an approximate measure of how much information the modem can send per second; higher is better.

Once you've got all the necessary information, you're ready to try it out. To login from home, follow these steps:

1. Turn on the modem and the PC (if you need to) and start your terminal-emulator program. Use the terminal program to call the phone number of the UNIX system.

2. When the message CONNECT shows up on-screen (and you hear a two-tone squeal), your PC has reached the remote UNIX system. Wait a moment. You may have to press **Enter** at this point.

3. Now you'll get a prompt. If your UNIX system doesn't have a security password, it will be the `login:` prompt, and you can login normally. Once you're logged in, you may have to reset your terminal type. See Chapter 19, "Environ-Mental Health," to see how to do this.

4. If your UNIX system has a security password for phone logins, you'll see a message like `Port password` or `Awaiting authorization`. Type in the security password. This may take you to the `login:` prompt, or you may get another prompt.

5. If it's `login:`, just login normally.

6. If your system has a network, you're probably at yet another prompt. Now you have to tell the system *which* computer you want to log into. The exact command depends on your system, but it's probably either **rlogin** or **telnet**. Both commands are used to log into a machine over a network. You use them the same way: give the command followed by the name of the system you want to log into. For example, suppose you work on a machine named pinball at work; that's the machine you have an account on. Type **rlogin pinball**. The system responds with the `login:` prompt you know. Login as usual, and then give your password.

   The procedure is the same if you have to use **telnet**. Give the command **telnet pinball**. The system responds with the `login:` prompt, and you login as usual. Then you give your password in response to the `password:` prompt.

Now, you're logged into your account just as if you were actually in the office instead of at home. To quit your session:

1. Give the **exit** command, just as you would normally.

2. Following the instructions for your PC terminal-emulator program, hang up the connection.

The UNIX-DOS Shuttle: Trading Files

People who have PCs, but who also work with UNIX systems, are always trying to figure out how to move files back and forth between DOS and UNIX systems. After all, not many UNIX systems have floppy drives!

If you have a desktop UNIX system, it probably does have a floppy drive. Your system documentation will tell you how to copy files to and from floppy diskettes.

If your PC is in the office, it may be *attached* to the network via NFS. In this case, you can use the PC to copy files back and forth between the PC and the UNIX machine using the DOS **copy** command. For example, I have a PC by my desk that is linked by NFS to the UNIX file system. The PC thinks my home directory on the UNIX system is its drive g:. If I want to see the contents of my UNIX home directory from the PC, I type **dir g:*.***. To copy the file phone.lst from my home directory to the floppy disk in drive a:, I use the DOS command **copy g:\phone.lst a:\phone.lst**. Any files on the UNIX system whose names are too long for DOS or contain characters that aren't valid in DOS are automatically "translated" to some other name. This new name is the name I have to use from the PC.

Almost all programs for connecting PCs to UNIX machines over NFS connect the PC to the UNIX file system, but don't connect the UNIX system to the PC's file system. This means you have to do all the file copying from the PC, using the DOS commands.

The two things to remember when copying files using PCs and NFS are:

➤ On almost all systems, you copy files using the PC, so you need to use the PC commands.

➤ You have to remember the differences between file names on the two systems. UNIX file names that contain capital letters or that are too long must be "translated" into new names for DOS.

If you've logged in using the technique I described in the last section, "Logging In from Home," you may want to transfer files between the UNIX system and your DOS machine while you're logged in. To do this, you must know what your terminal-emulator program's send-file and receive-file commands are. For the sake of demonstration, I'll assume that the send command in your terminal-emulator program is Alt-S and the receive command is Alt-R. (Because terminal-emulator programs vary greatly, you should check your documentation before trying this.)

The basic procedure is simple: once you've logged into your UNIX account using your PC, you start the UNIX command to send or receive files. Then you give your PC its command to receive or send files. Most PC programs won't let you do anything else on your PC until the files are transferred.

Both your UNIX command and your PC program must agree on the file transfer protocol they're going to use. Protocols found on both PCs and UNIX systems include Zmodem and Kermit. I'll show you the Zmodem programs here, since they're more common.

Let's say you want to copy all the .txt files in your current (UNIX) directory to your PC. I'll assume you've already logged into the UNIX machine from your DOS machine. On the UNIX machine, type this command:

```
$ sz *.txt
```

sz is the "send Zmodem" command, and *.txt is the list of files you want to send to the PC. Now press the "receive-files" command for your terminal-emulator program: Alt-R in my example. The UNIX system sends the files to your PC. Most terminal programs put an indicator of some kind on the screen to let you see how the file transfer is progressing. When it goes away, the files are transferred, and you get your UNIX command prompt back.

Now let's say you want to send the file yearend.doc from your PC to the UNIX system at work. Again, I'm assuming you've already logged into the UNIX system. At the UNIX command prompt, type the command:

```
$ rz
```

Then give the command to your terminal program to send the file yearend.doc using Zmodem. In this example, it's Alt-S, and the terminal program asks you for the name of the program to send. This time your PC sends the file to the UNIX system.

The Least You Need to Know

➤ A computer network is a group of computers that share information, including files. Each computer in a network has a name, called the hostname or sitename. The host you're logged into is called your local host; any other host is remote.

➤ The NFS and RFS file systems let UNIX computers share files by making it look as though all of the files from all of the computers are on one huge file system.

➤ You can use a PC with a terminal-emulation program as a terminal. With a modem, you can log into a UNIX machine from home.

➤ UUCP is a batch method of copying files from one computer to another. You use **uucp** much like you use **cp**, except that you must name the computer the files are on, like this: **uucp** *fromsite!file tosite!file*. The ! character is used to separate the site name from the file name.

➤ Most file transfer programs distinguish between transferring text files and transferring binary files. Never send binary files as text files; they'll be ruined.

➤ FTP is an interactive method of transferring files. You type **ftp** *sitename* and then use the **put** and **get** commands to send and receive files.

➤ Kermit is a program used to transfer files between computers. It's available on almost all UNIX systems and many PC terminal-emulation programs.

Chapter 22

Send Me a Letter

In This Chapter

➤ Ways to send messages

➤ Sending electronic mail

➤ Reading electronic mail

➤ Saving and printing electronic mail

If you believe what *Newsweek* and *Time* are telling us, electronic mail and the Internet are changing how we live. I can attest to that. I've used electronic mail to get articles from the Netherlands and Ireland that I couldn't have gotten any other way.

Electronic mail is like regular paper mail, except that it travels through the wires. You type a message and send it off, and in a little while, it appears at the destination. Of course, like any other social activity, you can overindulge in e-mail. According to the *Wall Street Journal* (6/22/94), the chairman of Computer Associates shuts down the company's e-mail system for five hours a day so that everyone can get their real work done. (Maybe we should rename it "electronic water cooler.")

Messages, Chats, and Mail

UNIX provides four ways to send a message to someone: **write**, **wall**, **talk**, and electronic mail.

➤ **write** sends a short message to one other user. The messages are short (a few lines at most) and can't be ignored because they pop up on-screen. The user gets the message only if he or she is logged in.

➤ **wall** is a version of **write** that sends a short message to all users currently on the system. These messages are short and can't be ignored because they pop up on-screen. Anybody who isn't logged in doesn't get the message.

➤ **talk** is interactive; it's like talking to someone on the phone (except you're both typing). Your screen splits in two, and each of you types in what you want to say. If the other person isn't logged in at that moment, he or she doesn't get the message.

➤ **Electronic mail** waits for the recipient to read it. It's also the only kind of electronic message that you can send across different networks.

To send a message of any kind, you need to know the recipient's *address*. Like a street address, the address consists of the person's login name and the name of the machine his account is on. (If the two of you are on the same machine, you can leave off the machine part of the address.) Addresses have different forms, depending on what kind of mail program you're using and how they connect. The most common address form is Internet addressing: *loginname@hostname*. For instance, my e-mail address is **johnmc@anansi.UUCP**. To break that down, my login is **johnmc**, and the computer I work on is called **anansi.UUCP**. (The .UUCP indicates that I only have a UUCP connection.)

Your system may use this kind of address: **anansi!johnmc**, in which case the site name comes first. In this kind of address, there can be more than one site name, such as **uunet!mks!anansi!johnmc**. That's because the software that uses the ! addressing isn't quite as sophisticated as the Internet addressing software, and you might have to name every computer through which the mail has to travel.

Write, Wall, and Talk

The quickest way to send a message to someone is to **write** her. You give the command **write** *address* and press **Enter**. If the person to whom you're writing isn't logged in, **write** will tell you so and quit. If she is logged in, she gets a line like Message from *yourname@yourhost* and the time and date, and you get a prompt like this:

```
msg>
```

Type in your message, pressing **Enter** at the end of each line. As you type your message, it appears on the other person's screen. When you're finished with your message, press **Enter** to start a new line and then press **Control-D**.

With **write**, you can only write to one user at a time. If you need to write to *everybody*, use **wall** (which stands for "write all"). **wall** is usually used for important messages such as, "I'm shutting down the system in five minutes. Log off!" If the super-user (that's the system administrator or someone designated by the system administrator) uses **wall**, you'll get the message even if you've turned message reception off with **mesg n**.

One problem with both **talk** and **wall** is that some programs (especially editors) redraw the screen, "erasing" the message you sent. So if the person you're sending to is using an editor, he may catch a glimpse of the message but never be able to read it.

If you want to "converse" with another user, you're better off using the **talk** program. (Two people can **write** each other simultaneously, but this leads to messy screens.) To **talk** with someone, type **talk** and the person's address.

For example, if you want to talk with Lee (another user on the system), type the command **talk lee** and press **Enter**. First, **talk** requests that Lee give a **talk** command with your name. (If Lee has turned off messages with **mesg n**, he won't get your request.) If Lee gives a matching **talk** command, your screen splits into two windows, one for your messages and one for Lee's. Now you type messages normally. The following figure shows a **talk** screen. To end your half of the connection, press **Enter** to start a new line and then press **Control-D**.

```
[Connection established]
Morning.
Where did you put the files I need for my presentation?
Do I need to know anything special to print them off?
I thought you were going to do them up in troff for me.



_____

Morning back
/usr/projects/lee/overheads.

Nope. They're just plain text.

Didn't have time.
```

*This is a **talk** screen.*

If you don't want to receive messages from **write**, **wall**, or **talk**, enter the command **mesg n**. If you want to receive messages, type the command **mesg y**. To see whether or not you are set to receive messages right now, just type the command **mesg**.

Electronic Mail

The most common of these methods of exchanging information is electronic mail. Electronic mail has several advantages over **write** and **talk**. First, your mail messages wait for you. If you're not logged in, the mail message waits until you login and read mail. Second, you can save mail messages. Third, mail travels farther; if your UNIX system has a connection to other networks, you can send mail around the world. Fourth, while you can only **talk** or **write** to one person at a time, you can send the same mail message by electronic mail to many people at once by supplying more than one address.

Electronic mail is very similar to postal mail. For example, consider this process. You write an electronic mail message and send it, and your mail programs give it to another computer to deliver. That computer may give it to another computer. If your message is going to a small computer far away, it may be passed to half a dozen or more computers before it arrives at its destination.

There are a lot of different electronic mail programs on UNIX. Every system has either **mail** or **mailx** (often both). There are many more: **elm** and **pine**, for example, are two of the easiest mail programs to use, but they are not available on all UNIX systems. (As I mentioned in Chapter 17, "Circus Emacs-Imus," you can even send and read mail with **emacs**!)

With older mail programs, there were limitations: the messages couldn't be too big (the limit was 64 kilobytes, or about 11,000 words), and messages could only contain text. Newer programs have no problem with message length, but it's still difficult to send binary files (like spreadsheets and programs). However, more and more mail programs are incorporating ways to handle binary files because they're so important for multimedia displays. You should be careful about sending binary files. (I'll talk about sending binary files later in this chapter.)

Since **mailx** is the mail program that's been made part of a standard recently, I'll discuss **mailx** in the remainder of this chapter. (**mail** is nearly identical, but doesn't have as many features as **mailx**.)

Sending Mail

As with **write**, you send mail with **mailx** by supplying the address of the recipient (or recipients) and then typing the message. You end the message by starting a new line and pressing **Control-D**.

Try sending yourself a message. Type the command **mailx** and your login name, and then press **Enter**. **mailx** asks you what the subject of the mail message is. (Most versions of **mail** don't ask for a subject.) You don't have to supply a subject, but for our example, type **Marriage Proposal** for the subject and press **Enter**.

When you're typing the message, you have to press **Enter** at the end of each line. If you make a mistake, backspace over it. You can backspace only to the beginning of a line; you can't use Backspace to go back to any earlier lines. Type the following text into your example message:

```
I love you truly, madly, deeply. I can't live without you;
you are my sun, my moon, my diet cola. Please say you'll
make me the happiest person in the world and marry me.

If the answer is no, then could you introduce me to
your friend Chris in accounting?
```

To end and send the message, make sure you're at the start of a new line and press **Control-D**. That's it. In a moment, your mail will arrive at its destination.

285

Using Commands While Sending Mail

There are some commands you can give to **mailx** while you're composing a mail message. These writing-mail commands *always* start on a new line, and *always* start with a tilde (~) character. (You won't see the tilde until you type the second character in the command.)

If you've reset your **EDITOR** environment variable to name some editor other than **ed** (as I suggested in Chapter 14, "Write Like the Prose"), the command ~e uses the editor you named instead of **ed**.

The two most important commands are the one to display the message you've typed so far, and the one to let you edit the file. To display your message so far, press **Enter** (unless you're already at the beginning of a line), and then type ~p. **mailx** prints the entire message to the screen. To edit the message so far, press **Enter** to begin a new line, and then type ~v if you want to edit with **vi**, or ~e if you want to edit with **ed**. **vi** is described in Chapter 16, "Viva vi!," and **ed** is described in Chapter 15, "What's My Line (Editor, That Is)?"

When you save the message and quit the editor, you are returned to **mailx**. There you can either add more to the message or quit with Control-D.

Sending a File

If you want to mail someone a text file (instead of composing your message on the fly), you can do it all from the command line using file redirection and the **-s** option (which lets you specify the subject line). Suppose I had written the message in our example as a text file called proposal, and I wanted to mail it to sandy. Here's what I'd type:

```
$ mailx -s"Marriage Proposal" sandy < proposal
```

The **-s** flag is one of the options in **mailx** that *doesn't* have a space between the flag and its argument. If there's a space in the subject (as there usually is), you need to put the whole thing in quotes. The **<** **proposal** part of the command is the file redirection, which I discussed in Chapter 11, "More About Files (Some Useful Tips and Tricks)." It tells **mailx** to redirect the output of the text file proposal as the input of the mail message file sandy.

Sending a Binary File

If you want to send a *binary file*, you have to turn it into a text file first with the **uuencode** program. (As you might guess, **uudecode** turns it back into a binary file.) You give **uuencode** two arguments: the name of the file, and the name you want it to have when the person at the other end decodes it. (Usually they're the same name.) So, if you want to send the word processor file chapter23.doc to melanie, first you convert it to text, and then you mail the text:

```
$ uuencode chapter23.doc chap23.doc > chap23.uue
$ mailx -s"chapter 23" melanie < chap23.uue
```

Uuencoded files have a distinctive look: they're almost all capital letters, and almost all the lines are the same length. For example, the first two lines of chap23.uue look something like this:

```
begin 644 chap23.doc
M,;X    "K           #R   2     " 3  #2345 X
```

There are two commands here: the first encodes the file chapter23.doc as text, and the second mails it. In the first command, **uuencode** is the command, chapter23.doc is the name of the file you want to turn into text, and chap23.doc is the name you want it to have after it's decoded. The first name has to be the file's "real" name; the second is the name that the decoded file will have. (You might want to give them different names if you were going to decode it in the same directory as the original, and you wanted to keep them separate.) The last part of the command, > chap23.uue, saves the result of the **uuencode** command in a temporary file named chap23.uue.

In the second command, you're mailing the temporary file < chap23.uue to melanie. The **-s"chapter 23"** gives the mail message the subject, "chapter 23."

Although this example uses a temporary file named chap23.uue, you don't actually need to create a temporary file. You can use a pipe instead. (In this example, I've left out the **-s** for space reasons.) Using a pipe, you combine the two earlier commands into this one shorter command that does the same thing:

287

```
$ uuencode chap23.doc chap23.doc ¦ mailx melanie
```

In either case, when Melanie gets the mail message sent with this command, she has to save it as a separate file (maybe named fromyou) and run the program **uudecode** on it to turn it back into a binary file. Her command looks like this:

```
$ uudecode fromyou
```

uudecode reads fromyou and creates a file called chap23.doc in the current directory. (It automatically gives the file the name you gave as the second argument to **uuencode**.)

Reading Mail

To read mail, type **mailx** without any addresses. If you don't have any mail waiting, **mailx** will tell you so and quit. If you do have mail, **mailx** presents a summary of the mail messages you have waiting (some versions of **mail** do this; others go straight to your first message).

The following figure shows a **mailx** summary screen. Each line represents a mail message. It gives a reference number for each message, the sender's login name, the date and size of the message, and the message's subject. The > points to the current message (the message you're working with).

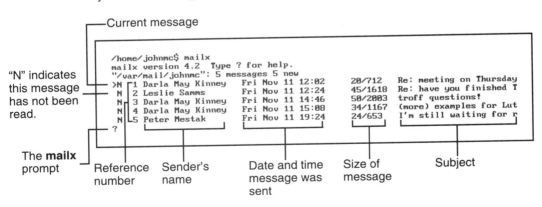

*This is a summary of the messages waiting in **mailx**.*

To read the first message (the one with > beside it), press **Enter**. You can read through all your mail sequentially just by pressing **Enter**.

This figure shows the first message that appeared when I pressed Enter at the **mailx** prompt in the previous figure.

```
        From dmk Fri Nov 11 12:02:30 1994
        Received: by anansi (MKS UUCP); Fri, 11 Nov 94 14:00:48 UTC
        Received: from cat.mks.com by mouse.mks.com (4.1/CAT-1.2)
                id AA28672; Fri, 11 Nov 94 12:02:30 EST
        Message-Id: <9411111702.AA28672@cat.mks.com>
        To: John McMullen <johnmc>
        Cc: victor
Header ─ Subject: Re: meeting on Thursday
        In-Reply-To: Your message of "Wed, 09 Nov 1994 15:30:25 EST."
                <9411092030.AA08010@cat.mks.com>
        Date: Fri, 11 Nov 1994 12:02:29 -0500
        From: Darla May Kinney <dmk>
        Status: R
        Content-Length: 226

        I'm not sure we should be meeting on Thursday.  Charlie's out of town
        and I'm caught up in an executive's meeting until about two,
Body ── and they usually make me grouchy.  Best next time is Monday at ten.
        Can it wait that long?

        D.


        ?
```

A typical mail message.

The stuff at the top of the message is called the *header*. It's mostly information for the mail program: who sent the mail, when they sent it, and how. The two important lines for you are the "From:" line, which (obviously) tells you who sent the message, and the "Subject:" line, which tells you the subject of the message. The rest of the message (what you really want to read) is called the *body* of the message.

Once you move on to another message, if you want to reread a message, you'll have to give the reference number. Unless you have other mail messages, it's 1. Enter the command **p 1 at the mailx prompt**, **?**.

To quit mail, give the command **q**, and all of the mail you've read is saved in your home directory in a file called mbox. Any mail you haven't read is kept until you read mail again.

A long message may just stream off the screen, leaving you wondering what the first paragraphs were. You can fix this by typing **set crt=24** at the ? prompt. This tells **mailx** that any messages longer than 24 lines should be sent through **more** so you can read them. Your startup file for **mailx** is called .mailrc in your home directory. If you put a line that says **set crt=24** in .mailrc, **mailx** runs the **set crt=24** command every time it starts up.

289

biff Notifies You of Mail

How do you know you have mail waiting to be read? You may be told when you login that you have mail messages waiting (see Chapter 3, "In the Beginning Was the Word: login" for an example of this). However, that doesn't help you if you received the message after you logged in.

Mail programs notify you of new mail that arrives while you're reading your other mail. But you can't spend all day in your mail program; when would you get anything accomplished? You could start your mail program every twenty minutes, just to see, but UNIX provides an alternative.

The alternative is a program called **biff**. You turn on **biff**, and it checks your mailbox for you every minute. If a mail message arrives, **biff** notifies you by beeping your terminal and displaying a few lines of the message on the screen. This figure shows a **biff** notification:

```
/home/lee$
New mail for lee@houdini has arrived:
____
Date: Sat, 17 Dec 94 14:32:39 EST
From: johnmc (John McMullen)
To: lee
Subject: Change meeting time?

Lee —

...more...
```

*This is how **biff** notifies you of a new mail message.*

In this case, there's a message from johnmc with the subject, "Changing Our Meeting?" **biff** also shows the first few lines of the message so you can decide if you want to interrupt what you're doing to read the message. You can usually clear the **biff** message off the screen by pressing **Control-L**.

A lot of UNIX books tell you that **biff** was named after a dog who used to bark at the mailman. However, just recently the authors of **biff** have 'fessed up: Biff the dog never barked at the mailman; they just wanted to name a program after him, so they made up that story.

To turn **biff** notification on, type the command **biff y** (for "yes"). To turn **biff** notification off, type the command **biff n** (for "no"). And for those days when you just want to be sure that **biff** is working because you haven't received that important message yet, the command **biff** without any argument at all tells you whether notification is on or not. On my system, **biff** gives you a response like this when **biff** notification is on:

```
$ biff
is y
```

biff can be very useful—and it can be very annoying. When I'm expecting an important message, I'm glad to have **biff** turned on, but when I'm deeply involved in editing something, it bugs me if **biff** scribbles on my screen.

If you use X Windows, there's an alternative to **biff** called **xbiff**. **xbiff** puts a little window on your screen that contains a picture of a mailbox or an inbox on a desk. Here are two examples:

With no mail waiting   With mail waiting

*The **xbiff** program also shows you whether you have mail; you can only use it with X Windows.*

When you receive mail, the terminal beeps and the picture changes color. The picture may also change, too. After you've read the mail message (or messages), the picture changes back to the "no mail" image.

Both **biff** and **xbiff** are programs you put in your startup files so they're turned on whenever you login. (See Chapter 18, "The Shell Game" for more about your shell startup files.) To turn on **biff**, include this line in your shell startup file (.profile or .login):

```
biff y
```

To turn on **xbiff**, include this line in your X Windows startup file (usually .xsession):

```
xbiff &
```

See Chapter 6, "Surviving Window Pains," for more information about X Windows and the .xsession startup file.

Commands to Use While Reading Mail

There are a few commands you can use to make reading your messages in the **mailx** program easier and more convenient. These are called (wonder of wonders) mail-reading commands. I'll talk about the four most common commands here.

When you're in the **mailx** program, you'll see the **mailx** command prompt, ?, at the bottom of the screen. When you see the question mark, you can give a **mailx** mail-reading command. (You must press **Enter** after a mail-reading command.)

When you give a mail-reading command it is applied to the current message (the one with the > next to it) unless you specify otherwise. If the command takes an argument (like the **save** and the **pipe** commands do), the argument comes after the list of messages. For example, **s 1 3 from.darla** saves messages 1 and 3 in the file from.darla.

If you want to know more **mailx** commands, type **?** and press **Enter**. You will see a summary of the most common **mailx** commands.

Viewing Header Lines

If you have so many messages that even the summary can't fit on one screen, you can move forward and backward in the list of headers by pressing z+ and z–.

Displaying Mail

Although you can read the current message just by pressing **Enter**, that restricts you to reading your mail in sequence. If you want to read a particular message, you can use the **p** command. (**p** stands for print, although in this case it means printing to the screen, not printing to a printer.)

If you want to print a message other than the current one, you can specify that by adding the message's reference number. For example, if you type **p 4**, message 4 is printed to the screen. (If there is no message 4, **mailx** gives you an error message.) You can specify more than one message to print by adding the reference numbers for all the messages you want to print, leaving a space between numbers (such as **p 2 3 5**).

There's no special command for printing a mail message. You could save the message as a file and print it like any other text file. (See Chapter 9, "Printing Is Pressing.")

If you want to send a mail message to a command (like the **lp** command), you can use the pipe command (¦). So to print, you could type ¦, the reference numbers (if any), and the command, like this: ¦ **2 3 6 lp**. You can also use this trick to decode encoded files without saving them first (¦ **uudecode**).

Deleting Mail

To delete messages, type **d** and the reference number of the messages you want to delete. For example, the command **d 2 4** deletes messages 2 and 4.

You should use **d** to clear out any unwanted messages before you quit **mailx**, because any message you delete isn't saved in mbox. The mbox file can get quite big if you arbitrarily save all the messages you get. You may want to be picky about which files you save in it.

You can read old mail messages you have stored by using the **-f** *mailfile* option with **mailx**. For example, to reread old mail stored in the mbox file, start **mailx** in your home directory by typing **mailx -f mbox**. With this and the delete command **d**, you can reduce your mbox file to a reasonable size when it gets huge. If you're not in the same directory as the file, you can read it by using the complete path name; **mailx -f ~/mbox** will read your mbox file no matter what your current directory is. You can use the **-f** *mailfile* option to read any file that is a saved mail message, whether it is mbox or another file.

Saving Mail

When you quit a mail session, all of the mail you've read goes into a file in your home directory called mbox. You may want to save a message in a particular file, though. To do this, use the **s** (save) command. Messages you save with **s** are not saved in mbox. Unless you supply an absolute path name, the file is saved in the current directory.

For example, if I want to save message 3 to a file called from.darla, I type **s 3 from.darla**. If the file from.darla doesn't exist, it is created. If the file from.darla already exists, message 3 is added to it.

Replying to Mail

Undoubtedly, you'll want to reply to a message sometime. To reply to the current message, use the **r** command. When you use **r**, **mailx** puts you into mail-sending mode and provides an address and subject line for you. Write the message and send it as I described earlier in the chapter.

The **r** command sends the reply to the author of the original message and everyone else who got a copy (including you). If you only want to send a reply to the author of the original message, use the **R** command instead. The only difference between the two commands is who the reply is addressed to.

When you're replying to mail from a mail-reading session, **mailx** lets you include the message to which you're replying. The command ~**m** includes the current message (indented by a bit) in the reply message you're writing. (If you use ~**e** or ~**v**, you can even delete lines you don't want to include.)

Suppose you've just received this message:

```
Need help right away. What's the correct way to spell that word
from Mary Poppins:
supercalifragilisticexpialadocious
or
supercalifragilisticexpialidocious
```

(Hey, I get this kind of mail.) Rather than retype the entire word, you want to reply and include the (correct) line of the original message.

When you've finished reading the message, you're back at the ? prompt. Since you only want to send the reply to the sender, type **R** and press **Enter** to reply. **mailx** displays the To: and Subject: lines:

```
To: verna
Subject: Re: How do you spell...?
```

Notice that **mailx** automatically inserted "Re:" at the beginning of the subject.

Now you're in mail-sending mode. Type whatever salutation you like (or none at all; e-mail can be very informal) and start a new line, giving the command ~m. **mailx** gives you a response like this:

```
~m
Interpolating: 1
(continue)
```

It could be any number instead of 1; that's just the number of the message you're inserting. Here's an example of what it looks like when you display it with ~**p**:

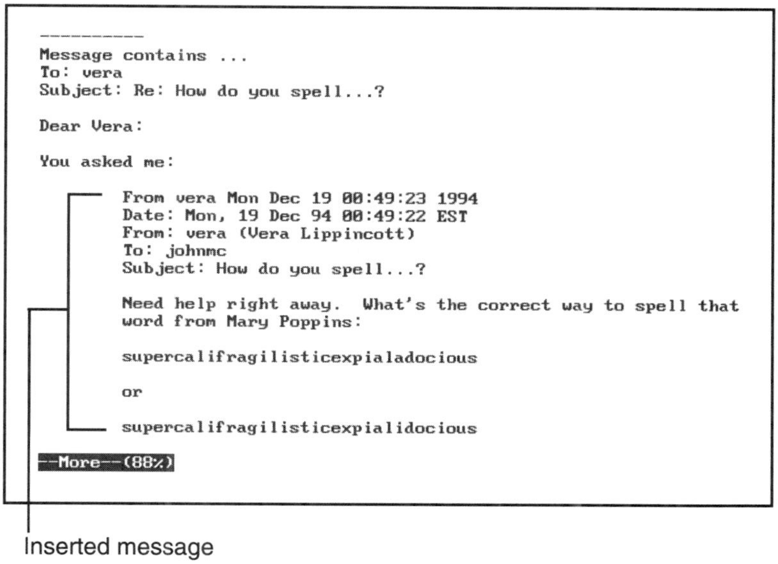

Inserted message

The ~m command inserts a mail message indented by one tab character.

295

Now you can type the rest of your message. In this case, you probably want to use the ~**e** or ~**v** command so you can edit the message so far and remove the wrong version of the word. (As I recall, the first version is correct.)

Once you quit the editor, you're back in mail-sending mode again. To send the message, start a new line and press **Control-D**.

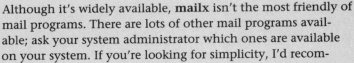
Although it's widely available, **mailx** isn't the most friendly of mail programs. There are lots of other mail programs available; ask your system administrator which ones are available on your system. If you're looking for simplicity, I'd recommend **pine**. **elm** and **mh** are also quite popular, and most people find them easier than **mailx**.

Finding an Address

Normally, you won't have any problem finding someone's address. If you want someone to send you e-mail, you give him your e-mail address; the easiest way to find an e-mail address for someone else is to ask the person. If you can't ask him, there are other ways to find the address.

➤ If you have mail from this person, you can get the address from the message header. It's on the "From:" line.

➤ Usenet news offers several methods for tracking down a person's e-mail address. See the monthly posting in **news.answers** called "Finding someone's e-mail address." (Usenet news is explained in Chapter 23, "Internet Interests.")

➤ Some companies are now publishing directories of e-mail addresses. They get these addresses from Usenet news postings. (I'm in there, for instance.)

➤ If you know the person's real name and the name of their UNIX machine, you can ask the person in charge of mail on that person's system. The person in charge of mail always has the login name of postmaster. You can send a (polite) message to the postmaster stating that you're trying to get in touch with so-and-so, and could he or she please supply you with the correct login name? Use this as a last resort, since most postmasters are overworked (and grumpy) system administrators.

The Least You Need to Know

➤ To send a brief message to someone who is logged in, give the command **write** *loginname* and type the message. To end the message, start a new line and press **Control-D**.

➤ The command **mesg n** keeps you from receiving **write** and **talk** messages; **mesg y** enables you to receive them again.

➤ To send a message, give the command **mailx** *address* ..., type until you come to the end of the message, start a new line, and press **Control-D**.

➤ An address for someone on your UNIX system is her login name. An Internet address looks like this: *name@host* (although there are other formats).

➤ To read your mail, type **mailx**. Press **Enter** to read each message in turn. To quit reading mail, give the **q** command; the mail you've read is saved in the file mbox in your home directory.

➤ To save the current message, give the command **s** and a file name. To delete it, give the command **d**. Saved and deleted messages aren't saved in mbox.

➤ To reply to the current message, use the **r** command. **mailx** puts you into mail-send mode.

➤ To print the current message, use ¦ **lp**.

Chapter 23

Internet Interests

In This Chapter

➤ What the Internet is

➤ Internet resources

➤ Usenet news

You've probably heard of the information superhighway (also called the infobahn). And you're probably sick of all the hype that surrounds it. So what is the Internet, anyway? And what does it mean to you?

I can't hope to describe the entire Internet in this chapter, but I can give you some idea of what's out there. Whether you use the Internet is up to you.

A Really Big Network

A network is a group of computers that share information. An *internetwork* is a network of networks. It's slightly different from one big network, because each of the smaller networks keeps its own identity: this network is still university computers, and that network is still all UNIX machines, and that other one is government offices. Each network joins to one (or more) of the other networks. A machine that connects two networks is called a *gateway*, because it's a doorway between networks.

Internet The set of computer networks joined using the TCP/IP protocol that remained after ARPANET was shut down. Internet includes a number of government and educational networks (including the National Science Foundation's NSFnet and two networks of NASA's) as well as some commercial and business networks.

When people talk about "the" Internet, they usually mean one particular internetwork. In the late 1960s, the U.S. Department of Defense commissioned research into computer networks that could survive being partially destroyed in the event of a nuclear attack. The result was a network called ARPANET to which people soon attached other networks using the (then new) TCP/IP protocol. This network of networks survived when the original network (ARPANET) was shut down. (After all, that's what it was designed to do: keep working even though part of it was gone.)

All networks, and the Internet in particular, are about sharing information. All of these computers can share files in different ways. Even though all of this information superhighway talk is about sharing files, there are such diverse ways to do this that you don't even notice the files any more. So don't think of it as just files. A phone call is information; so is a movie, or a song, or a basketball score. You can access all of these, or their equivalents, through the Internet.

There are two parts to the Internet: the information part and the social part. When you're talking about programs you can use to explore the Internet, you should know whether you're talking about the information aspect or the social aspect of Internet. If you're just concerned with getting files, you're dealing with the information aspect of the Internet. If you're exchanging messages with someone, it's social. (Of course, you can ask someone for information, so they do overlap.)

The Big Public Library

The best way to think of the information part of the Internet is as the largest public library in the world. All of the programs you hear about for "surfing" the Internet are programs that help you find files—and then get them once you've found them.

For instance, a lot of computers on the Internet maintain file archives, repositories of interesting files. If you want software or currency exchange rates or the index to the Library of Congress or even pictures of cartoon characters, it's in a file somewhere out there. But how do you find those files? If you know the name of the computer, you can use **ftp** to get them (I described **ftp** in Chapter 21, "Everybody's Talkin'"). But if all you know is a little bit about the name or about the topic of the file, you might never find what you're looking for.

One of the programs that was developed to solve this problem is called **archie** (short for "archive," it has nothing to do with the comic book character). On a regular basis, usually about once a month, **archie** makes a list of everything that's available in every FTP site it knows about.

When you want to find a file somewhere out there, you give **archie** some information about the file (usually some part of its name, if it's a program), and **archie** gives you the name of the site or sites where you can get the file. There are ways to use **archie** by e-mail if you need to. In addition, there are other programs that do the same job in a slightly different way.

archie does have one limitation: you can't browse. You have to know what you're looking for. If you think you've found the right file, you have to FTP it to your computer and look at it to be sure. If you want to browse the different sites in the Internet, use **gopher**. **gopher** provides a menu system that makes it easy to find topics of interest and lets you browse the files you find before copying them to your system.

And, if you can imagine, there's even a program that does for **gopher** what **archie** does for FTP sites: it keeps a catalog of what's out there. Because it's a counterpart to **archie**, it is named **veronica** (this name did come from the comic book character—or rather from her relationship with archie). **veronica** can be a great way to explore the Internet.

The Ways of the Net

One of the Internet's information services is WAIS (the Wide Area Information Server) pronounced "ways." The server itself is a program running on an Internet computer. Other programs, called WAIS clients, call it up and ask it questions for you. The actual questions are words and phrases in a language relatively close to English. The server tries to find documents that use those words and phrases, and if it does, it passes them back to you through the client program. Once you've found one you're interested in, you can ask for other documents that are related.

In order for WAIS to catalog information about a particular topic, someone has to have set up a server on the topic. There are a number of them, including ones dedicated to Usenet and the Internet, recipes, books, movies, U.S. Government programs, and the world fact book. Fortunately, there is a WAIS server that maintains a directory of WAIS servers: directory-of-servers.src. You can query this server for information on other servers.

The newsgroup comp.infosystems.wais also discusses the WAIS systems. For instructions on using your WAIS server, refer to the documentation.

What a Tangled Web We Weave

A group of physicists and programmers in Switzerland had the idea of treating the entire Internet as if it were one big computer. If a document on an Internet computer in Boston refers to a picture file on an Internet computer in Liverpool, England, why should you have to know how to connect to Liverpool? Why not have Internet follow these connections for you, as if the Internet were a big complex web?

They call this view of the Internet the World Wide Web, and there are programs to follow these connections for you. The most popular of these programs is called Mosaic. Mosaic "pieces together" files from around the world to make it look as if you're reading one big document. The files can be pictures, text, animation, or sound. Mosaic is available for UNIX, Windows, and Macintosh computers (and possibly more).

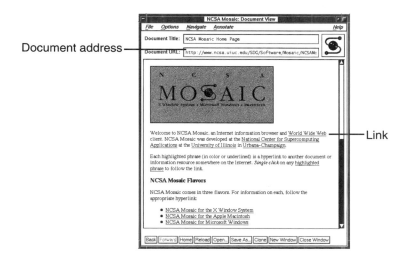

Document address —

Link

An example of a Mosaic screen. Click on an italicized word to get information about the topic.

The nicest feature of Mosaic and other World Wide Web programs is that they know how to run **ftp**, **gopher**, **veronica**, WAIS and other programs for you. They handle that part automatically. Why should you have to keep all those programs straight? In fact, you don't have to. Mosaic does it for you.

Social Networking

There's also a social part to the Internet. Some of it is social in the same way that electronic mail is social: you can exchange messages through mail or through Usenet news. Some is more immediate and interactive. For instance, IRC (Internet Relay Chat) is like a perpetual conference call (except everyone is typing).

Almost all of this socializing is handled through written messages, but don't imagine it's less "real" than meeting people in person or talking to them over the phone. A fellow in my office just got married to a woman he met through electronic mail over the Internet.

I've Got a Little List

The most accessible form of socializing on the Internet is by using electronic mail. This is just e-mail, but it connects many different computers and users. Even the President has an e-mail address on the Internet.

One way to "ease into" the Internet is to subscribe to a mailing list, a group of people who exchange messages on a specific topic. There are mailing lists on almost every conceivable topic. A list of mailing lists is posted regularly to the newsgroup news.answers. (See later in this chapter for a discussion of news.)

Incidentally, even if you don't have full Internet access, you can often use e-mail to get access to some of these services. For instance, as of the time of this writing, there's e-mail access to a WAIS server. You can get information by sending a mail message to waismail@quake.think.com; the entire message should consist of the word **help**. In the same way, there are mailservers that give you access to **archie** and **ftp**. Rather than list them here (when such a list would quickly become obsolete), I suggest you look in the newsgroup news.newusers.answers; one of the regular postings there will give you pointers to these services. (You'll also find the information in news.answers, but there are many more postings in that group, so the information is harder to find.)

Tell Me About Telnet

Telnet enables you to log into another computer and run programs on it. This means that if your computer doesn't have the program **irc** for you to try Internet Relay Chat, you can use the **telnet** program to log into a computer that does.

The **telnet** program provides you with a way to get the login: prompt on a machine that's far away. You need to tell **telnet** the name or address of the machine you want to log onto. For instance, suppose you want the longitude and latitude of a U.S. city. It just so happens that the University of Michigan provides that service, using information from the US Census Bureau, the US Geological Survey, and one from the US Postal Service, at the Telnet address martini.eecs.umich.edu 3000. To log into this "Geographic Name Server," your session would look like this:

```
$ telnet martini.eecs.umich.edu 3000
Trying 141.212.99.9...
Connected to martini.eecs.umich.edu.
Escape character is '^]'.
# Geographic Name Server, Copyright 1992 Regents of the University
of Michigan.
# Version 8/19/92.  Use "help" or "?" for assistance, "info" for
hints.
.
```

In this case, you want to log into the machine martini.eecs. umich.edu, port 3000. Not all telnet addresses have a port number after them, but some do. The line `Trying 141.212.99.9` tells you the numeric form of the machine's address. The next line tells you that you've connected and provides the merest smidgen of help.

In this case, there's no login name or password. (If there was, it would be listed with the telnet address.)

Once you've logged in, you must work according to the machine's rules. On this system, the help command is **?** or **help**. The . is this particular system's prompt. To find the information, type in your query, usually the name of the city or town, the state, and the ZIP code. To quit, type **exit**.

```
.
exit
Connection closed by foreign host.
$
```

The most important thing to remember about **telnet** is that you're really using a different computer. It may not even be a UNIX computer, so the rules may be different. Be careful and be considerate.

And Now the News

The easiest way to get involved in the Internet is to read Usenet news. (Usenet stands for User's Network.) I knew what news was long before I knew about the Internet. You probably also already know what a computer bulletin board is. It's a forum in which users call one computer and leave messages for all of the other callers to read (like a bulletin board). The messages may be divided by topics.

Usenet news is what you might get if you crossed an electronic bulletin board with a chain letter. Instead of users calling in to one computer to get messages, every computer with messages calls out to give away its messages to as many other computers as possible. Once started, a news message is harder to stop than a juicy rumor; it travels in much the same way. And as a user, you receive all of these messages; all you have to do is choose which ones you want to read.

Strictly speaking, Usenet is not the Internet; Usenet is the network of computers that gets news articles, and Internet is the network of computers that communicates using the TCP/IP protocol. Some Internet computers don't get news, and a lot of computers get news (and are therefore in Usenet) but aren't part of the Internet. (Most of them get their news through UUCP.) This distinction means your UNIX system doesn't have to have TCP/IP to have news. You might have news and e-mail but none of the other nifty Internet features discussed in this chapter.

There are thousands of articles every day. So many, in fact, that if your site got all of the Usenet news, you couldn't hope to read it all. You need to weed out what is uninteresting to you. And that's what newsgroups are for.

All of these messages are organized into *newsgroups*. Newsgroups are like subdirectories. At the top are about a dozen major divisions. These are subdivided as necessary, and the subdivisions are indicated with dots instead of slashes. For instance, **rec.martial-arts** is the newsgroup in **rec** (recreation) that is dedicated to martial arts. Likewise, **rec.arts.books** is the newsgroup that's dedicated to books.

There are thousands of newsgroups, especially in the **alt** (alternative) division. Whereas most newsgroups are created through a well-defined voting process that restricts the creation of newsgroups, anyone can create an alternative group. For this reason, many of them are of questionable taste. (And one of them, **alt.tasteless**, revels in it.)

When you read news, you only read news in newsgroups you have *subscribed* to. (When you start news for the first time, you're subscribed to all newsgroups. That's time-consuming.) You can *unsubscribe* from a newsgroup and resubscribe later.

The messages in each newsgroup are called "articles." An article looks much like a mail message. There's a header at the beginning that describes the article's subject; who sent it, when, and to which newsgroup; and the message body itself. A set of articles on one subject in a newsgroup is called a "thread." Threads often digress and split into new discussions. There may be dozens of threads carried in one newsgroup at any time. Writer Neil Gaiman once likened Usenet to a gigantic university pub where a dozen conversations and digressions are going on simultaneously. The conversations range from the idiotic and the infantile to the deep and well-reasoned.

News has its own subculture and its own language. You'll see expressions like IMHO (In My Humble Opinion) and flame (which means to aggressively attack and abuse someone in a message). To convey emotion, many people posting articles resort to symbols like :-) or :-(. (Look at them sideways: one's a smile, and the other's a frown.)

News can be addictive. I've heard stories of university students who abandoned studying after discovering this network of news. Still, Usenet is a valuable resource of rumors and news, and it represents a lot of smart and knowledgeable people. I have used news to get the answers to questions I couldn't have begun to find answers for through normal means.

With so many people joining the news network at any time, how does anyone make sense of it? Most newsgroups post periodic messages called FAQs or Frequently-Asked-Questions documents. The FAQs are intended to reduce some of the volume from new users by answering common questions. Besides being posted in the originating newsgroup, many FAQ documents are also posted to the newsgroup news.answers. Some of the most critical documents (for new users) are posted to the newsgroup news.newusers.answers. I strongly recommend you subscribe to new.newusers.answers for at least a little while.

The most common program for reading news is **rn**. Another popular choice is **nn**. Let me introduce you to them so you can get a taste of this whole new world of news.

rn (Read News)

rn is the oldest of the news programs people still use. It looks at the list of newsgroups you're interested in and presents the articles to you, one at a time, group by group. To start it, type **rn** at the command line. To quit, press **q** as many times as necessary to get you back to the command prompt.

Before starting a newsgroup, **rn** asks you if you want to read that newsgroup with a message like this:

```
*****125 unread articles in rec.arts.books. Read now? [ynq].
```

You can press **y** (yes), **n** (no, go to next), or **q** (quit reading news). Pressing the **Spacebar** is the same as selecting the first letter in the square brackets (usually y for "yes"). If you just keep pressing the Spacebar, you'll eventually read all of your news.

When you agree to enter a newsgroup, **rn** shows you the first new article. (If the article is more than a screen long, you're reading it with **more**, so pressing the Spacebar shows the next screen.) If you don't want to read the article, press **n** and you'll skip to the next article. At the end of the article, **rn** asks what you want to do: read the next article (press **y** or **Spacebar**), skip past it (**n**), or quit this newsgroup (**q**).

Here are some commands to make your life with **rn** easier:

➤ When you start reading news, you're subscribed to all of the newsgroups. There may be hundreds or thousands. The **u** command *unsubscribes* you from the newsgroup you're looking at.

Let's say you're reading news and you get the message 417 unread articles in alt.fan.lemurs [ynq]. You don't happen to be interested in that topic, so you press **u** to unsubscribe. From now on, you will not see any articles posted to alt.fan.lemurs; for you, it's as if the newsgroup doesn't exist.

➤ The = command displays the list of articles in the current newsgroup. Every article has a number, and to read a particular article, you type the article's number.

You can press = at any time. Suppose you're reading the newsgroup rec.tv.soaps (catching up on things), and you want to know if anybody's talking about General Hospital. Press the = key, and **rn** displays a list of every unread article, its number, and title. If the list is longer than one screenful, press **Spacebar** to continue.

As soon as you give a command (like the number of an article, or **n**), **rn** goes back to displaying news articles.

➤ **k** "kills" a particular topic. All of the articles with that Subject line go away. **K** is a permanent kill: no articles with that Subject line will ever show up.

While **u** removes an entire newsgroup from your sight, **k** (or **K**) only removes the articles on a certain topic; you can still read the other articles in the newsgroup.

➤ **c** "catches up" on all the articles. This is wonderful if you've been away for a week and every newsgroup has hundreds of articles waiting for you.

Suppose you're reading news and you see the message `2028 unread articles in comp.sys.ibm.pc [ynq]`. You don't want to read over 2000 articles, and you're not certain you care about them anyway. Press **c**. **rn** responds with `Do you really want to catch up on all articles? [yn]`. If you press **y**, all of the articles are marked as read; you won't see them, but you'll still be subscribed to the group. (It's kind of like **k**, but for all articles currently in the newsgroup.)

➤ **h** accesses the help screen. The Help command only works when you have an **rn** prompt (any prompt with [ynq] in it) on the screen. I think the help screen is cryptic, but it's better than nothing.

➤ **s** saves the current article. You can supply a file name to which to save it if you want. Unless you supply a full path name, **rn** saves the article in the directory News in your home directory. If you don't supply any file name, **rn** uses one based on the name of the newsgroup. For instance, articles from rec.arts.poetry are saved in the file ~/News/Rec.arts.poetry. The first time you save an article, **rn** asks if you want to save it in mailbox format. (Mailbox format lets you read saved news articles with your mail program.) Normally you don't want to do this. Answer **n** to this prompt. If the file already exists, **rn** appends the article to it.

nn (No News Is Good News)

When you're reading **rn**, the default behavior is to read every single article. If you just sit and press **Spacebar**, you will end up reading all of the articles in the newsgroups you subscribe to. **nn** has the opposite philosophy. **nn** assumes you don't want to read *any* of those articles. If you just sit and press **Spacebar**, you will end up having read none of your news articles. With **nn**, you must choose to read a particular article, or **nn** doesn't show it to you.

You start **nn** with the command **nn** (imagine that!). For each newsgroup you've subscribed to, **nn** presents a list of the articles by author and subject. You select the articles you want to read by pressing the letter beside the article summary (rather like picking an article from the headings list in **mailx**).

When you're reading articles, press **Spacebar** to see the next screenful. Press **n** if you want to skip to the next article. Each time you press Spacebar, you go to the next screenful of article titles until you've seen all of the articles for that newsgroup. After that, the next time you press Spacebar, you get the first article you selected. If you didn't pick any, you get the list of articles for the next newsgroup.

If you want to quit the newsgroup before you've read all of the articles, press **q**. If you want to quit **nn** before you've read all of the articles, press **Q**.

Here are some other commands to make your life with **nn** easier:

➤ The **?** command gives you help for the current screen.

➤ **k** "kills" a particular topic. All of the articles with that Subject line go away. **K** is a more permanent kill: no articles with that Subject line will show up for 30 days or forever, depending on how you answer the prompt.

➤ While reading an article, use **N** to skip immediately to the next newsgroup.

➤ The **S** command saves the current article. You can supply a file name if you want; if you don't, one is provided. If you specify a full path name, that's the name used for the file; otherwise, the file is saved in the directory News in your home directory. If you don't specify any file name at all, the article is saved in a file named for the newsgroup. (For example, an article from comp.risks would be saved in the file ~/News/comp.risks.) If the file doesn't exist, **nn** creates it; if the file does exist, **nn** appends the article to the file.

➤ The = command lets you select articles according to a regular expression that matches the subject. For instance, if you wanted to see all articles relating to the Internet, you could type = **Internet** and press **Enter**. (Regular expressions are described in Chapter 13.)

If your UNIX system is part of Usenet, it has a newsreader program of some kind, but it may not be **rn** or **nn** (although they're the most common). Other newsreaders include **trn** (a newer version of **rn**) and **tin**.

I've used both **rn** and **nn**, and I prefer **nn**. It lets me read news faster. However, it has a couple of disadvantages. First, it's not as common as **rn**. Second, because of how it presents the news articles, a new article shows up sooner in **rn** than it does in **nn**.

But What's It Good for?

Is the Internet for you? That depends on your needs. I am in no sense a significant user of the Internet (heck, I had to go look up what **telnet** was just to write this chapter). But I find the Internet useful, if only for electronic mail and news.

Through news, I stay up-to-date on a number of technical issues that affect my work. In addition, there have been times I've asked a question on a newsgroup that I couldn't find an answer to anywhere else—and found the answer. To be practical, though, you should check out regular resources, such as encyclopedias and libraries, first. (Many people on Usenet are short-tempered if they think they're being taken advantage of.)

The two big advantages to using the Internet are having access to all of those files out there, and having access to programs you don't have. When you find a file (or program file) that you want, you have to transfer it to your system.

The traditional way of transferring files in the Internet has been **ftp** (which I described in Chapter 21, "Everybody's Talkin'"). To find out where the files are, you can use **archie**. (You can even use **archie** if all you have is electronic mail.) You can also fetch files with **gopher** and Mosaic.

If you don't have FTP or Internet access, don't panic! If you do have an electronic mail connection to the Internet, there are *mailservers* that will FTP a file for you and mail you the pieces, uuencoded.

(Uuencoding is described in Chapter 22, "Send Me a Letter.") And don't forget that the original purpose of **telnet** was to let researchers on different computers share their resources. Through **telnet** you can access a lot of government and congressional files and databases.

The Least You Need to Know

If this chapter has sharpened your appetite for more Internet, try reading one of the (apparently zillions) of books on the topic. I suggest *The Complete Idiot's Guide to the Internet* as a good starting place (but I may be biased).

➤ The Internet is the collection of computer networks all joined using a particular kind of connection. It's very easy for computers on the Internet to share information.

➤ It's easy to send electronic mail through the Internet.

➤ Many computers on the Internet make their archives of files available to others. The **archie**, **gopher**, **veronica**, and WAIS programs help you find (and get) the files you want on the Internet.

➤ The **telnet** program enables you to log into another computer on the Internet and use it as if you were in the same building.

➤ Recently, there's been an attempt to "hide" all of the different programs you need to search through the Internet by writing programs that treat it all as one big web. One of the most popular of these programs is called Mosaic.

➤ Many Internet computers exchange messages that are meant for a general readership. This collection of messages is called "news."

➤ You can read news using the programs **rn** and **nn**.

TEN HUUUUT!

Chapter 24

Taking Charge

In This Chapter

➤ The duties of a system administrator

➤ Adding and removing users

➤ Adding and removing groups

➤ Backing up the file system

➤ Cleaning the file system

The system administrator is the supreme authority on your UNIX system. Let me make this clear: I don't expect you to be your own system administrator by the end of this chapter. Your system administrator's job is specific to the needs of your site, your computer hardware, and the version of UNIX you use. What I intend to do is to give you some idea of what your system administrator does.

The UNIX-Omnipotent System Administrator

In some systems, the manual pages never refer to a system administrator, only to a "privileged user." Whatever the person is called, he or she can login to the super-user account, also called the root account. The super-user has access to everything in the system; no file is secret from the super-user; there's no program the super-user can't use. A system administrator is like the manager of a building, with passkeys to every room.

However, (as Spider-Man said) with great power comes great responsibility. The system administrator has four big responsibilities:

➤ *Caring for the users.* This includes creating and deleting user and group accounts and doing chores for users that require an educated hand. The system administrator is also in charge of the programs that govern printing, mail, Usenet news, and other services.

Super-user The login id of the system administrator (sometimes called the "root user.") The super-user account has special privileges: It effectively owns all files and can add, remove, or change any file or directory. The system administrator must be logged in as the super-user to add new programs to the system or to start or shut down the system. On big UNIX systems, more than one person may know the password for the super-user account, which is usually called the root password.

➤ *Maintenance.* The system administrator is responsible for doing all the little chores around the system. Some of these chores are preventative; other chores are just regular cleanup or checkups. One preventative chore is making backups, copying all files to a safe place in case the hard disk crashes or some other disaster happens. An example of a cleanup chore is making sure there's space available on the hard disks; this may involve getting rid of temporary files.

➤ *Installing new equipment and software.* Although each user can install private software, only the system administrator can install software for everyone to use. And only the system administrator is trusted with the chore of shutting down and starting the computer.

➤ *Fixing problems.* Whenever there's a system problem, it is ultimately the system administrator's responsibility to get the system working again.

That's a lot to do, which is why system administrators work to automate as much of the work as possible. They write little programs to handle chores for them. Someone once said that the best system administrators try to put themselves out of work. I'd have to say that good system administrators try to turn their jobs from full-time to part-time.

In this chapter, we'll look at how to create and delete user accounts and groups, how to back up the file system, and how to add a new file system. My examples are based on a small- to mid-size UNIX system without an extensive network.

Most of the system configuration files are kept in the directory /etc. Some of the important ones include:

/etc/passwd   The list of users, their home directories, and shells.

/etc/group   The list of groups to which users can belong.

/etc/shadow   On newer systems, this contains the coded versions of user passwords.

/etc/rc   Commands that run whenever the system starts up. (On some systems, there is more than one rc file or rc directory.)

/etc/inittab   The list of commands (such as **getty**, which controls terminals and starts **login** for each terminal) run by the **init** command.

/etc/hosts   In a networked system, this file lists the computers (hosts) in the network and their network addresses.

/etc/ttys   On BSD-style systems, this file describes the terminals.

Adding a User

Some systems make it very easy for a system administrator to add a new user; they have a command with a name like **useradd** or **adduser**. Other systems require the system administrator to perform all of the tasks manually.

The list of all users is kept in the file /etc/passwd. Each user has a one-line entry, which describes the user's account. Here's an entry from a password file:

```
terry:821s8(SrVP./r:125:20:Terry Cloth:/usr/terry:/bin/csh
```

Each piece of information (or *field*) is separated from the rest by a colon (:). This entry can be broken down into the following parts:

`terry`   The user's login name.

`821s8(SrVP./r`   The encrypted version of the user's password. There are 4,096 different ways to encrypt a password, so it's unlikely that two users will have the same encrypted password even if they have the same password.

`125`   The user's login id number. User numbers are usually greater than 100 (numbers lower than 100 are reserved for administrative accounts). It's best if each user's id number is unique.

`20`   The user's group id number. Most groups have more than one member. Group names and numbers are defined in /etc/group.

`Terry Cloth`   Usually this is the user's name, but it's really just a comment space. It can include any information at all.

`/usr/terry`   The user's home directory.

`/bin/csh`   The user's default shell.

If a user forgets his or her password, the easiest thing for the system administrator to do is to delete the encrypted password. The user then logs in (without being prompted for a password) and uses the **passwd** program to set a new password. Different systems use different tools to edit the password file. On SVR4 systems, the super-user can run **passwd -d** *login* to delete the password for the user *login*. On BSD systems, the super-user can edit the password file with the programs **vipw** or **chpass**.

It's a different story if the system administrator forgets the password to the root account. Many modern systems have ways for the system administrator to regain control, but they're slow and difficult. There are still lots of systems where the only advice one can give about forgetting the root password is, "Don't."

The new user also needs a home directory, so the system administrator must create it. At this point, the directory is owned by the system administrator and the system administrator's group. To give ownership of the directory to the new user, the sys admin then uses the **chown** and **chgrp** commands to change the owner and group ownerships. (The **adduser** and **useradd** commands create the directory and change its ownership automatically.)

Some systems provide utilities system administrators can use to add, delete, and change user information. On System V Release 4 UNIX Systems (or later), these are called **useradd**, **userdel**, and **usermod**.

Removing a User

It's easy to remove a user: simply remove his or her line in /etc/passwd. However, it's difficult to remove a user in a way that won't hurt others. Before removing the line, the system administrator has to consider some other factors.

➤ Does the user have files that others will need?

➤ If so, who gets them?

➤ Will they still be stored in the old home directory, or will they be moved somewhere else?

The answers to these questions determine whether the user's passwd entry is removed or just made inaccessible to that user. (If the super-user deletes the person's encrypted password, the super-user can then change the user's password—locking him or her out of the system.) Usually the passwd entry is made inaccessible, but the system administrator has the alternative of using the **find** command to find all files owned by the user and giving those files to another user.

Two Types of User Accounts

A UNIX system really has two kinds of login accounts. The first kind is a regular user account. You or I login as "johnmc" or "your-name-here" and do our work. The second kind of login account is an administrative account. These are accounts dedicated to one particular task, and the password may be shared by several people. For instance, every Internet site has an administrative account named "postmaster" that handles problems with electronic mail. That's all the account is for. The super-user account is the most privileged of these administrative accounts.

317

Because the super-user is so powerful, the system administrator usually spends as little time as possible logged in as super-user. Normally, he or she is logged in under his or her own name—bob or susan or whatever. This is to prevent accidents; if you think it's a problem when *you* accidentally remove a file, it's hundreds of times worse for the super-user, who can remove *any* file in the system. Most system administrators login as root only to do things that require the super-user privileges.

Some of the administrative accounts don't even belong to people; they just exist because every file has to be owned by some account. The printer account, usually called lpadmin, is like that. It exists because the files special to the printer programs need to be owned by someone.

All of these administrative accounts are given user identification numbers that are under 100. The super-user account is always user id 0, group id 0.

Adding and Deleting a Group

I mentioned groups when I first described the output of **ls -l** back in Chapter 3, "In the Beginning Was the Word: login." Groups provide a means of organizing users with similar purposes. For example, all of a company's accountants and bookkeepers could be in one group, all the programmers could be another group, all the writers could be in another group, and so forth.

Suppose the system administrator wants to give privileges to some assistants without giving them access to the root password. All she has to do is create a group that will own some special files. If the system administrator sets the permissions correctly, these assistants can work on privileged files—but no one else can.

Groups have to be defined before the system administrator can add users to them. To add a new group, the system administrator edits the file /etc/hosts. Each line in the file represents one group. A user can belong to multiple groups. Here's an example entry:

```
manager:*:81:rick,rita,ned
```

Like the passwd file, each piece of information is separated by colons. This entry can be broken down into the following parts:

`manager`   The group's name.

*   The encrypted password for the group.

81   The group's identification number.

`rick,rita,ned`   The login ids of the members of the group. The names are separated by commas.

Some systems provide utilities system administrators can use to add, delete, and change groups. On System V Release 4, these are called **groupadd**, **groupdel**, and **groupmod**.

It's rare that a system administrator would actually have to remove a group, because the need for a group doesn't often go away. However, sometimes if a system is growing or the purpose of a group changes, the system administrator may need to split an old group into two.

Removing a group is like removing a user: deleting the line in the group file is the easy part, but again, the system administrator must also decide what to do with all of the files that currently belong to that group.

Backing Up the File System

One of the most important things the system administrator does is back up files. The files on the system are copied to another medium (usually a tape cassette that looks like a small video cassette) and stored. If something happens to the file system, the old copies can be put back. (Putting them back is *restoring* them.) Although the copies won't be up-to-the-minute versions of the files, users won't lose all of their work, either. Most UNIX systems today provide special tools to make backups easy for the system administrator. The backup tool on SVR4 systems is called **backup**; the backup tool on BSD systems is called **dump**. You can also use standard UNIX tools like **find**.

The system administrator can store all the files on the system; this is called a "full backup." Full backups are the most reliable because all of the files are there. If something terrible happens to the system (the hard disks all blow up or something), a full backup is the easiest to restore.

The system administrator can also choose to store only those files that have changed since the last backup or since the last full backup. This is called an *incremental backup*. **find** has an option that finds all files that have been changed recently. By using **find**, the system administrator can get a list of all the files that have changed and then use the backup utility (traditionally **cpio**, though there are other backup programs now) on those files. (**find** is the system administrator's friend. It has a lot of options that make life easier for system administrators.)

Incremental backups are quicker to do because there are fewer files; most of the files on the system stay the same from day to day. If you have a disaster, however, it can take longer to restore the entire system from incremental backups. You have to restore the last full backup, then the first incremental backup you did after that, then the second incremental backup, and so on until you've caught up to the most recent backup.

Unless the file system is very small (making it easy to do full backups), most system administrators reach some kind of compromise, such as full backups every week and incremental backups every night.

Stopping and Starting the System

A UNIX system isn't like a PC. You don't turn it on when you come in and shut it down every night when you go home. Because many people are using it, a UNIX system is turned on and stays on until it has to be turned off.

A UNIX system can run with multiple users (the normal state) or with only one user, which is called the single-user mode. Only the super-user can use the single-user mode. Some system administration activities (like joining new file systems) have to be done in single-user mode.

Only the super-user can shut down the system. In addition, this task is considered important enough that it can't be done from just any terminal. To stop or start the system, the super-user must be logged in at the *console*, which is the keyboard and screen attached directly to the computer.

The command to stop a UNIX system is **shutdown**. The available options depend on which kind of UNIX you're running. Many systems let you give a time, such as "shut down in 15 minutes." And usually the **shutdown** command broadcasts messages to warn all logged on users of the shutdown and advise them to exit.

Starting a UNIX system is actually not difficult. If it's configured correctly, you don't have to do much more than turn the machine on. The trick is configuring it correctly: You have to decide which programs will be started when and when different file systems are attached (there's not really space to go into it here).

Cleaning Up the File System

The definition of "cleaning up" the file system depends on the system. Some kind of housekeeping program should be set up to regularly get rid of old temporary files.

It's also a good idea to make sure the file system is still intact: that the system really does know where all the bits and pieces of the files on the hard disk are. The program that checks this is called **fsck** (for file system check). It's normally run every time the system starts up, but it may also run at other times.

If **fsck** discovers that there are problems with files (that a piece of a file has been "misplaced"), it notifies the system administrator. The system administrator can then try to fix the problem. Any "fixed" files are put in the directory /lost+found. When a file is fixed like this, there's no guarantee it's fully intact, so the program sends mail to the file's owner to let him or her know it may be bad.

The Least You Need to Know

➤ The system administrator can login to the super-user (or root) account. Like a building manager, the super-user has access to all files, directories, and programs. The super-user is also the only person who can shut down and start up a UNIX system.

➤ The system administrator provides services for users, maintains the UNIX system, installs new equipment and software, and fixes any problems.

➤ To add a new user, the system administrator edits the /etc/passwd file to create an account for that user, and then creates the user's home directory and "gives" it to the user with **chown** and **chgrp**.

➤ To add a new group, the system administrator edits the /etc/group file to add an entry for the group and its members.

➤ When removing a user or group, the system administrator must decide what to do with the files owned by that user or group.

➤ The system administrator makes backups of the files on the system on a regular basis. The administrator may choose to back up all the files (a full backup) or only the files that have changed since the last backup (an incremental backup). The best policy is usually a combination of both.

Chapter 25

Neat Stuff

In This Chapter

➤ Getting jokes

➤ Putting more than one command on a line

➤ Including spaces in command arguments

➤ Repeating commands

➤ Sorting files

➤ Getting dates

By this point in the book, you know everything you need to know to use UNIX. You can create and edit files, print files, send mail, and read news. You know the essentials.

Well, this chapter contains some non-essentials. These programs and tricks are useful enough to be worth knowing (okay, one of them is just for fun), but I can't say they're essential. Tough.

Fortune Cookies

I like funny little sayings. I like jokes. I like quips. I like the command **/usr/games/fortune**. All it does is print a little "fortune cookie" message. Here's one:

```
$ /usr/games/fortune
An Englishman never enjoys himself, except for a noble purpose.
    -- A. P. Herbert
$
```

Because it's a game, this is in the directory /usr/games instead of /usr/bin. If you add /usr/games to your **PATH** environment variable, you can get a fortune just by typing **fortune**. I have **fortune** in my shell startup file so I see one of these messages every time I login. (See Chapter 19, "Environ-Mental Health," for more information about changing your **PATH** environment variable and about adding commands to your startup file.)

Not all of the messages are short like the example above. As a matter of fact, some (like this one) are quite long:

```
$ /usr/games/fortune
Friends, Romans, Hipsters,
Let me clue you in;
I come to put down Caesar, not to groove him.
The square kicks some cats are on stay with them;
The hip bits, like, go down under; so let it lay with
Caesar.  The cool Brutus
Gave you the message: Caesar had big eyes;
If that's the sound, someone's copping a plea,
And, like, old Caesar really set them straight.
Here, copacetic with Brutus and the studs, -- for
Brutus is a real cool cat;
So are they all, all cool cats, --
Come I to make this gig at Caesar's laying down.
$
```

(I don't know where this comes from, but I think it's one of Lord Buckley's recordings.)

fortune has several options. If you only want short messages, use the -s (for short) option. If you only want long messages, use the -l option. Some older versions of **fortune** also have an undocumented -o option, which prints obscene fortune cookie messages.

More Than One Command on a Line

Sometimes you want to be able to give two commands on a line (maybe because you know the commands you're going to give or maybe because it's convenient). Suppose you want to **cd** to a new directory and then **pwd** to show the new directory name. Separate the commands with a semicolon, like this:

```
$ cd ~johnmc; pwd
/home/johnmc
$
```

The semicolon tells UNIX to treat the command as if you had pressed Enter there. (Putting multiple commands on one line isn't the same as running commands in the background; UNIX doesn't act on the second command until the first command finishes.)

If you do want to run one of the commands in the background, put the & character between the command and the semicolon (remember, the semicolon is treated just like Enter). For example, the command to sort and print a file named bigfile is **sort bigfile ¦ lpr**, and the command to return to your home directory is **cd**. If the file is very large, the **sort** command could take awhile, so you want to run it in the background. To put both of these commands on one line, you would use the command **sort bigfile ¦ lpr &; cd**. The command **sort bigfile ¦ lpr** starts in the background, and then you change to your home directory.

If you want to run an entire set of commands in the background, group them with parentheses. I use the following command to create screen captures on a UNIX X-terminal: **(sleep 10; xwd -root > picture.xwd)&**. The command **sleep 10** tells the computer not to do anything for me for 10 seconds (this gives me time to set up the screen I want). The command **xwd -root > picture.xwd** puts the image on-screen into the file **picture.xwd**. And because I'm running it in the background, I actually can set up the picture I want during those 10 seconds. If you didn't use the parentheses, only the command **xwd -root > picture.xwd** would run in the background. With parentheses, the & character applies to all the commands inside the parentheses.

May I Quote You on That?

Sometimes you need to give an argument that contains a space or a tab or an end-of-line character. The most common example of this is in mail message subjects (not many mail messages have a one-word subject).

Normally, the shell interprets every space (or set of spaces) as separating two words. For example, the command line **mailx -sThis is the subject johnmc** is considered to be the following six words:

mailx   -sThis   is

the   subject   johnmc

The **mailx** program thinks that the subject is "This" and that you want to send it to the users "is," "the," "subject," and "johnmc."

When you put something on the command line in single quotation marks (' ') or double quotation marks (" "), the shell treats everything between the quotation marks as one word, whether it contains spaces or not. (You must always remember to use the quotation marks in pairs.) When we put our subject within quotation marks, the command line **mailx -s"This is the subject" johnmc** contains the following three words:

mailx   -sThis is the subject   johnmc

This is called "quoting" the character or phrase.

Quotation mark characters have another use: turning off the special meanings of metacharacters. Suppose you accidentally create the file ;exchange. When you try to delete it (with **rm ;exchange**), you get the usage message for **rm** and a message that says it can't find a program named exchange. Remember, the shell treats the semicolon as if it were Enter. So **rm ;exchange** is interpreted as two commands: **rm** and **exchange**. Put the name ;exchange in quotes, like this: **rm ";exchange"**. The quotes turn off (or hide) the special meaning of ;.

Quotes are useful if you want to turn off special treatment for several characters in a row. If you want to turn off just one character, you can put \ in front of it. The \ also turns off the special meanings of characters. In our example, you could also remove the file with **rm \;exchange**, because the \ character turns off the special meaning of ;.

This use of quoting is handled a little differently depending on which shell you are using. I'm only going to discuss the Korn shell here.

In the Korn shell, single quotation marks ('') are the strongest: they turn off the special meanings for all characters. For example, the command **echo** prints its arguments to the screen. You can use this to see how your shell is interpreting metacharacters. **echo *** gives you a list of all the files in the current directory, because the * is a special character (metacharacter) that the shell interprets as a command to list all files in the directory. (I talked about the * in Chapter 8, "Branching Out: Working with Files and Directories.") However, if you type the command **echo '*'**, you only see the * as output on the screen. The quotation marks turned off the special meaning of *.

Double quotation marks are weaker than singles; they only turn off the special meanings for some characters. Names that start with $ (such as environment variables) and commands in back-quotation marks (') retain their special meaning within double quotation marks. Here's an example of the output you would receive with the use of both single and double quotation marks:

If you want to use the actual quotation mark character in a command, precede it with a backslash (\) to turn off its special meaning:

```
$ echo \'\$HOME
'$HOME
```

```
$ echo $HOME
/home/johnmc
$ echo "$HOME"
/home/johnmc
$ echo '$HOME'
$HOME
```

Those Who Do Not Know History Are Condemned to Retype It

You've got a really long command that has taken you three tries to type right... and you have to run it again! Time to call in a stunt typist? Not at all. Most UNIX shells keep a record of the last few commands you've typed and let you repeat old commands. This record of your commands is called your "history."

Exactly how you access your history depends on which shell you're using. In both the C and Korn shells, the **history** command gives you a history of the commands you've typed. In the C-Shell, you must turn on the history feature with the command **set history=#**. # is the number of old commands you want to store. (The exact number of commands stored in the Korn shell depends on your setup.) Here are my last ten commands, which I got with the **history** command:

```
$ history
178  ls /usr/games
179  cd ~johnmc;pwd
180  man fortune
181  cd alpha
182  nn
183  mailx stephe
184  vi chap25.txt
185  biff n
186  vi chap25.txt
187  history
$
```

To repeat your last command in the Korn shell, use the command **r** and press **Enter**. (To repeat your last command in the C-Shell, use the command **!!** and press **Enter**.)

To repeat an older command, you need to know its number (which you get with the **history** command). In the Korn shell, you can repeat a command (say, command 180—**man fortune** in the example history) by giving the **r** command the command number: **r 180**. (In the C-Shell, you repeat command 180 with **!180**.) Press **Enter** at the end of the command, just as you would normally.

If you want a previously used command but not the very last command you used, you can use the **r** or **!** command with the history number. For instance, if I were to type **r 180** (or **!180** with the C-shell),

UNIX would repeat command 180 from my history (which, in the example above, is **man fortune**).

If you don't want to see the entire history list, you can simply give the first few letters of the command you want to repeat. **r n** (or **!n**) repeats the most recent command that starts with "n." In my example, that would be command 182, **nn**. If necessary, you can give more than one letter to distinguish between commands that start with the same letter or letters. Whereas **r m** (or **!m**) would repeat the command **mailx stephe**, **r man** (or **!man**) would repeat the command **man fortune**. (If there is more than one command starting with m, the program repeats the first command it comes to according to the alphabetical order of the letters in the command.)

Some shells also provide *command line editing*. This is just a way of calling up old command lines and changing them to use again. Just as you have to turn on the history feature in the C-Shell, you have to turn on the command line editing feature in the Korn shell. Normally you turn on the command line editing feature at the beginning of your UNIX session (or you put the command in your .profile file).

The command to turn on this feature in the Korn shell is either **set -o vi** or **set -o emacs**. The **set -o vi** command lets you use **vi** commands to edit old command lines; the **set -o emacs** command lets you use **emacs** commands to edit old command lines. (For an explanation of the **vi** editor, see Chapter 16, "Viva vi!" For an explanation of the **emacs** editor, see Chapter 17, "Circus Emacs-Imus.")

If you're using **vi** editing commands, you must enter edit mode before you can edit command lines; press **Escape** to start editing old command lines. To see earlier commands, press **k** ("move up one line"); you move up through the history list. To see more recent commands, press **j** ("down one line"). The command you're editing appears on the command line. Once you have the command line you want to edit, edit it as if it were a line of text in a file you were editing with **vi**. To run the edited command, press **Enter**.

If you're using **emacs** commands, press **Control-P** ("move up one line") to see an earlier command; each time you press **Control-P**, an older command line appears on your screen. To move down through the history list, seeing more recent commands, press **Control-N**. Once you have the command line you want to edit, edit it as if it were a line in a file you were editing with **emacs**. To run the edited command, press **Enter**.

Sorting Things Out

I've used **sort** as an example in a couple of places because sorting stuff is something computers do well and because **sort** is a useful command. **sort** sorts the lines in files according to your specifications.

Here's a file of names and birthdays, called birthdays:

```
Sandi McMullen May 24
Suzanne Langdon June 27
Louise Koo August 5
Brian Dorion August 8
Brian Embleton January 12
```

Without any other instructions, **sort** sorts the lines alphabetically according to the first character on each line (here, it's the first word):

```
$ sort birthdays
Brian Dorion August 8
Brian Embleton January 12
Louise Koo August 5
Sandi McMullen May 24
Suzanne Langdon June 26
```

When the first words were the same, **sort** checked the next word and correctly put "Brian Dorion" before "Brian Embleton."

For most lists of names, you'd rather sort either by last name or by date. Let's start with last name. **sort** lets you choose which word on the line you want to sort by. (Words are separated by spaces, tabs, and the ends of lines.) To sort by the last name, you'd tell **sort** that you want to sort by the second word on the line. To indicate a particular word, use the argument +*number*, where *number* is the number of the word's position. The catch is, you have to start counting from zero: the first word is +**0**, the second word is +**1**, and so on. Therefore, a sort of the file by last name would look like this:

```
$ sort +1 birthdays
Brian Dorion August 8
Brian Embleton January 12
Louise Koo August 5
Suzanne Langdon June 27
Sandi McMullen May 24
```

sort also has a **-M** option that tells it to treat words as if they're the names of months. To sort this list by month, you need to sort based on the third word. Starting from zero, that's **+2**.

```
$ sort +2 -M birthdays
Brian Embleton January 12
Sandi McMullen May 24
Suzanne Langdon June 27
Louise Koo August 5
Brian Dorion August 8
```

Any line that doesn't have a recognized month in the specified position is put at the end of the list.

To put the output of **sort** in a file, use the -o flag and a file name for the output. The name of the output file can be any name, even the name of the file being sorted. For example, the command **sort -o birthdays +2 -M birthdays** sorts the birthdays file and replaces the old file with the sorted version. Because the output is stored in a file, you won't see the sorted text on-screen.

sort normally sorts in what's called ASCII order, in which all uppercase letters come before any lowercase letters. (In this example, it doesn't matter because all of the words start with capitals.) To tell **sort** to ignore case, use the option **-f**.

Sometimes you want to find the biggest (or smallest) file in the directory. **ls** doesn't have an option for this. You can use **sort** to sort the output of **ls -l** by size. When you do **ls -l**, you see that the size of the file is the fifth word:

```
-rw-rw-r-- 1 johnmc pubs 3072 Sep 29 20:41 system.doc
```

To sort all of the files in the current directory from smallest to largest, use the command **ls -l ¦ sort +4**. To sort from largest to smallest, sort it in reverse order by using the **-r** flag. The following figure shows the directory listing and then shows the same directory sorted by size from largest to smallest.

```
/home/johnmc$ ls -l
total 124
drwxr-xr-x   2 johnmc    r+d             96 Nov 18 16:56 Mail
drwxr-xr-x   2 johnmc    r+d             96 Nov 18 16:57 News
-rw-r--r--   1 johnmc    r+d           1298 Nov 11 18:50 calendar
-rw-------   1 johnmc    r+d            744 Nov 13 19:47 mbox
-rw-rw-r--   1 johnmc    r+d           7288 Nov 13 19:38 phone.numbers
-rw-r-----   1 johnmc    r+d          51599 Nov 12 18:57 screenshot.pcx
/home/johnmc$ ls -l | sort -r +4
-rw-r-----   1 johnmc    r+d          51599 Nov 12 18:57 screenshot.pcx
-rw-rw-r--   1 johnmc    r+d           7288 Nov 13 19:38 phone.numbers
-rw-r--r--   1 johnmc    r+d           1298 Nov 11 18:50 calendar
-rw-------   1 johnmc    r+d            744 Nov 13 19:47 mbox
drwxr-xr-x   2 johnmc    r+d             96 Nov 18 16:57 News
drwxr-xr-x   2 johnmc    r+d             96 Nov 18 16:56 Mail
total 124
/home/johnmc$
```

Use the **sort** command to list your files in order of size.

Calendars and Messages

UNIX provides two commands to keep yourself scheduled, **cal** and **calendar**. **cal** prints the calendar for any year or month you name; **calendar** shows you reminders of things you have to do.

   If you don't specify a month, **cal** prints the entire year you specify. (That usually runs off the screen, so pipe it into **more**.) You can also specify the month either by name or number. The month comes before the year. Here's the calendar for August, 1990:

```
$ cal august 1990
August 1990
Su Mo Tu We Th Fr Sa
          1  2  3  4
 5  6  7  8  9 10 11
12 13 14 15 16 17 18
19 20 21 22 23 24 25
26 27 28 29 30 31
```

The **calendar** program is like a datebook that shows you reminders. If you keep a file named calendar in your home directory, the **calendar** program looks through it and shows you all the entries that are scheduled for today and tomorrow. (If today is Friday or Saturday, tomorrow includes up to Monday.) Each entry in the calendar file can be only one line long. They don't have to be in order. The file must be named calendar so the program can find it.

You have to give **cal** a year, and it has to be the entire year (meaning the century also). If you enter **cal 90**, you get the calendar for the year 90, not 1990.

Here's an example calendar file:

```
friday oct 14 10:30 am annual physical
10/16          6:00 pm dinner with Leslie's folks
10/17 meeting with contractor
Tue October 18       Terry's birthday
```

Here's the output of that command, run on October 16:

```
$ calendar
10/16          6:00 pm dinner with Leslie's folks
10/17 meeting with contractor
```

You can create or add to the calendar file with any of the editors described in Chapters 15, 16, and 17, or you can use the **cat** command and file redirection, as this example shows:

```
$ cat >> ~/calendar
Tue October 18  Terry's birthday^D
```

(Remember, the Control-D at the end tells UNIX that you're finished sending input from the keyboard.) This command returns the day of the week first (if you want it), then the month, and then the day of the month. Capital letters don't matter, and names of days and months can be shortened to three letters. You can also give the month and date in the format 10/27 (the month always comes first).

If you want to run calendar every morning when you login, put the **calendar** command in your .profile startup file. (See Chapter 18, "The Shell Game," for a discussion of startup files.)

The Least You Need to Know

This miscellaneous grab-bag chapter taught you the following tricks:

➤ The program /usr/games/fortune prints a "fortune cookie" message for your amusement.

➤ You can put two commands on one command line by separating them with a semicolon (;). UNIX treats the semicolon as if you had pressed Enter.

➤ The **history** command shows you a numbered list of the commands you've used recently.

➤ In the Korn shell, you can repeat your last command with **r**. You can specify which recent command you're repeating by giving the first few letters of the command (for example, **r ls** repeats the last **ls** command you did) or by specifying the number of the command, which you can find with the **history** command.

➤ The **sort** command sorts lines in a file. You can tell it which word you want it to sort by, whether it should sort in ascending or reverse order, or by month, and what file to put the output in: **sort [-fMr] [-o *output*] [+*number*] file** ....

➤ To see the calendar for any year, use the **cal** command. You must specify the year.

➤ You can create a calendar appointment system with the **calendar** command.

Chapter 26

Common Commands

This chapter contains command summaries for the most important commands discussed in this book. The commands are in alphabetical order by command name.

For an explanation of the conventions used in these command summaries, see Chapter 4, "Your Wish Is My Command Line."

apropos

Displays commands related to a word.

apropos *keyword ...*

man -k *keyword ...*

The **apropos** command finds commands related to *keyword*. See Chapter 5, "Won't You Please Help Me?" for more about **apropos** and searching for commands. The **apropos** command is actually a synonym for the command **man -k**.

Example—To see a list of all the man pages that have to do with manuals:

apropos manual

biff

Turns mail notification on and off.

biff [y|n]

Without any options, **biff** tells you if your mail notification is turned on or off. To turn notification on, use **biff y**. To turn notification off, use **biff n**. See Chapter 22, "Send Me a Letter."

cal

Prints calendar.

cal [[*month*] *year*]

cal prints the calendar for the specified *month* and *year*. See Chapter 25, "Neat Stuff."

Example—To print the calendar for July, 1995:

cal jul 1995

cancel

Cancels print job.

cancel [*jobid* ...] [*printer* ...]

cancel cancels printing jobs that were scheduled with **lp**. Use **lpstat** to see what jobs and printers you have. See Chapter 9, "Printing Is Pressing."

Example—To cancel job 1980034 from the printer named crayon:

cancel 1980034 crayon

cat

Copies file or files to screen.

cat *file* ...

cat copies the file (or files) you name to the screen, without pause. See Chapter 11, "More About Files (Some Useful Tips and Tricks)."

Example—To display the contents of the file .profile:

cat .profile

cd

Changes directory.

cd [*directory*]

cd - (Korn shell only)

If you use the Korn shell, typing **cd** - is a shortcut to go back to the last directory you were in. See Chapter 7, "The Root of the Matter: Files and Directories."

> Example—To change to the /etc directory:
>
> **cd /etc**

chmod

Changes permission mode on file.

chmod [ugoa]{+|-|=}[rwx] *file ...*

The **chmod** command lets you assign permissions to a file or directory. See Chapter 11, "More About Files (Some Useful Tips and Tricks)," for a discussion of **chmod** and modes. See the **chmod**(1) manual page for a description of mode numbers. Also see the **umask**(1) manual page to discover how you can change the default permissions for new files.

> Example—To make the file "private" readable and writable only by its owner:
>
> **chmod go-rw private**

cmp

Compares two files.

cmp *firstfile secondfile*

cmp compares two files of any kind. See Chapter 12, "The Search Is On."

> Example—To compare the files /usr/ucb/more and /usr/5bin/more:
>
> **cmp /usr/ucb/more /usr/5bin/more**

cp

Copies files.

cp [-ir] *originalfile copyfile*

cp [-ir] *first [second ...] destination_directory*

cp makes a copy of a file or a directory. The second version makes copies of *first*, *second*, and so on in the directory *destination_directory*. See Chapter 8, "Branching Out: Working with Files and Directories."

-i   If the copied file is going to replace another file with the same name, this option inquires if you want to go ahead with the copy. Answer **y** to go ahead; any other answer skips that copy. Normally **cp** copies the file even if it overwrites another file (assuming you have permission to do so).

-r   If *original* is a directory, **-r** tells **cp** to copy subdirectories as well. Without **-r**, **cp** only copies files in the directory, not subdirectories.

Example—To make a copy of the file "black" named "white:"

cp black white

Example—To make copies of these files and put them in the directory "colors:"

cp black white red orange yellow colors

diff

Compares two text files.

diff *firstfile secondfile*

diff compares two text files and displays a list of the differences. See Chapter 12, "The Search Is On." Related commands are **cmp**, which tells you if two files differ, and **diffb**, which compares two binary files and shows the differences.

Example—To see the differences between your file ".profile" and the super-user's ".profile:"

diff ~/.profile /usr/root/.profile

dircmp

Compares two directories.

dircmp [-d] *firstdir seconddir*

dircmp compares the contents of two directories. See Chapter 12, "The Search Is On."

-d   Instead of just telling you whether files with the same name differ, the **-d** option tells **dircmp** to run **diff** on the files as well.

Example—To compare the directories /project/old and /project/new:

dircmp /project/old /project/new

ed

Edits file.

ed *[file]*

ed is a line-based text editor. See Chapter 15, "What's My Line (Editor, That Is)?" for some **ed** commands.

Example—To edit the file "memorandum:"

ed memorandum

emacs

Edits file.

emacs *[file ...]*

emacs is a screen-based text editor. See Chapter 17, "Circus Emacs-Imus," for some **emacs** commands.

Example—To edit the files "list" and "summary:"

emacs list summary

339

file

Guesses file's type.

file *[-f listfile] file ...*

The **file** program guesses the type of a *file*—what program the file is intended for—based on its contents. See Chapter 12, "The Search Is On."

-f *listfile* Checks the files listed in the file named *listfile* as well as any named on the command line.

Example— To find out what kind of file /usr/dict/words is:

file /usr/dict/words

find

Finds files.

find *startdir directives*

The **find** program searches a directory tree (starting at the directory named *startdir*) to find files that match certain criteria. See Chapter 12, "The Search Is On."

Directives include:

-exec *cmd* Runs the command **cmd** when a match is found. **cmd** should be quoted.

-mtime *n* True if the file was modified *n* days ago. If you specify +*n*, it checks for files modified more than *n* days ago; -*n* means files modified less than *n* days ago.

-name True if the file's name matches *pattern*. *pattern* can
pattern be a shell wild card expression, but the wild-card characters should be quoted or preceded by a backslash.

-print Prints the file's name.

-user *name* True if the file is owned by *name*.

Example—To find all files in the system owned by user johnmc:

find / -user johnmc -print

Example—To find all files in your home directory that have been modified in the last four days:

find ~ -mtime 4 -o -mtime -4 -print

finger

Shows information about a user.

finger [*loginname*]

finger shows information about users. If you don't supply a *loginname*, **finger** displays information about each user who is currently logged in. See Chapter 18, "The Shell Game." **finger** is not available on all systems. Related commands include **who**(1) and **whois**(1).

Example—For information about the user named "jordan":

finger jordan

fmt

Formats text file.

fmt [-w *width*] [*file ...*]

fmt formats text files, filling and joining short lines and breaking long lines. See Chapter 9, "Printing Is Pressing."

-w *width*   Sets the maximum line length to be *width* characters.

Example—To format the file "letter" to a width of 65 characters:

fmt -w 65 letter

fgrep, grep, egrep

Searches files for text.

grep [-il] [-e] *expression [file ...]*

fgrep *match [file ...]*

egrep [-il] [-e] *expression [file ...]*

These three commands search files for words or phrases (actually regular expressions). See Chapter 12, "The Search Is On."

-e *expression*   *expression* is the text to search for; if you have only one expression, you don't need the **-e** before it. If *expression* contains spaces, it must be quoted.

-i   Ignores case; "i" in the *expression* matches both "I" and "i."

-l   Instead of showing lines that match, only lists the files that contain matches.

Example—To find all files in the current directory containing the word "john" (capitalized or not):

grep -i john *

kill

Kills running program.

kill [*signal*] *process-id*

kill sends a stop *signal* to a running process. You can get the process' identification number (*process-id*) with the **ps** command. See Chapter 10, "When It Goes Wrong."

Signals include:

-1   Hangs-up (the default kill signal).

-9   Terminates (the most severe kill signal).

Example—To kill the process with process id 2001:

kill 2001

ln

Creates a link to a file.

ln [-s] *original newname*

The **ln** command creates *newname* as a link (or new name) for the file *original*. See Chapter 11, "More About Files (Some Useful Tips and Tricks)."

-s   Creates *newname* as a symbolic link rather than a hard link.

Example—To give the file "hints" the second name "secrets:"

ln hints secrets

lp

Sends file to printer.

lp [-d*printer*] [-n*number*] *file* ...

The **lp** command sends a file to your default printer (defined by the environment variable **LPDEST** on a System V system, or the environment variable **PRINTER** on a BSD system). See Chapter 9, "Printing Is Pressing."

-d*printer*   Sends *file* to the printer named *printer*.

-n*number*   Prints *number* copies of *file*.

Example—To print the file "meeting-minutes:"

lp meeting-minutes

lpstat

Shows status of print jobs.

lpstat [-o[*printers*]] [-u[users]]

The **lpstat** command shows you the jobs you have queued for printing on your default printer. See Chapter 9, "Printing Is Pressing."

-o*printers*   Lists jobs for the named *printers*; a list of printer names is joined by commas. If you don't name a *printer*, **lpstat** gives the list for all printers.

-u*users*   Lists the jobs for the named *users*; a list of users is joined by commas. If you don't name any *users*, **lpstat** gives the list of jobs for all users.

Example—To see the list of all print jobs queued for your printer:

lpstat -u

ls

Lists directory contents.

ls [-aFl] [*directory*]

ls lists the contents of a *directory*. See Chapter 7, "The Root of the Matter: Files and Directories."

-a   Lists all files, including those normally hidden.

-F   Indicates the file's *type* after the name: * indicates a program, / indicates a directory, @ indicates a symbolic link, and nothing indicates a normal file.

-l   Uses the long listing for each file.

     Example—To generate a long listing of all files in the current directory, including hidden files:

     ls -al

mailx

Sends and reads electronic mail.

mailx [-s*subject*] *address* ...

mailx [-f *file*]

The **mailx** command sends and displays electronic mail. See Chapter 22, "Send Me a Letter," for a list of commands you can use inside **mailx**.

-f *file*   Reads the mail from a *file* instead of from your usual mailbox file. Use this command to read saved mail.

-s*subject*   Gives the mail message that subject. If subject contains spaces, it must be quoted. If you supply a subject, **mailx** doesn't ask for one.

man

Displays manual page.

man [-s *section*] *command-name*

man [-k] *keyword*

The **man** command displays the part of the online manual describing *command-name*. See Chapter 5, "Won't You Please Help Me?"

-k *keyword*	Searches for man pages related to *keyword*; **man -k** is also available as the command **apropros**.
-s *section*	Restricts the search to the part of the manual numbered *section*. On older versions of **man**, the **-s** isn't necessary; you can just name the *section*.

mkdir

Creates a directory.

mkdir [-p] *directory*

The **mkdir** command creates a directory. See Chapter 7, "The Root of the Matter— Files and Directories."

-p   Creates any parent directories that don't exist. This option is not available on all systems.

Example—To create the directories "fiction" and "notes" in the current directory:

mkdir fiction notes

more

Reads a file.

more *file* ...

The **more** command lets you read one or more files. See Chapter 8, "Branching Out: Working with Files and Directories," for a list of commands you can use inside **more**.

Example—To read the file "grocery.list:"

more grocery.list

mv

Moves or renames a file.

mv [-fi] *oldfile newfile*

345

mv [-fi] *file ... destination_directory*

The first form of **mv** shown here moves (or changes) the file *oldfile* to become *newfile*. The second form moves one or more files into the directory *destination_directory*. See Chapter 8, "Branching Out: Working with Files and Directories."

-f   Forces **mv** to change the file name even if there's already a file by the new name existing in the same directory.

-i   If it is going to replace an existing file with the same name, it interactively asks if you want to move the file. If you use both **-i** and **-f**, **-i** takes effect instead of **-f**.

nn

Reads Usenet news.

nn [*newsgroup ...*]

The **nn** command lets you read Usenet news articles, either from all newsgroups you subscribe to, or just from the *newsgroups* you specify. Other newsreaders are available, including **rn**. See Chapter 23, "Internet Interests."

Example—To read only the articles in rec.humor.funny:

nn rec.humor.funny

passwd

Changes your password.

passwd

The **passwd** program changes your password. See Chapter 3, "In The Beginning Was the Word: login."

pr

Paginates file for printing.

pr [**-o** *offset*] [**-h** *header*] [**-l** *lines*] [*file ...*]

The **pr** command paginates the named *file*, inserting blank lines and a header so page breaks fall in the right pages. See Chapter 9, "Printing Is Pressing."

-h *header*   Uses the text *header* in the header instead of the file's name. If *header* contains spaces, you must quote it.

-l *lines*   Formats the file so each page is *lines* number of lines long. *lines* is a decimal number.

-o *offset*   Offsets the file from the left margin by *offset* number of characters.

ps

Displays process status.

ps [-efl] [-u *user*]

The **ps** command shows you information about the programs (also called processes) that are currently running. The options shown here are for the System V version; the options for BSD systems are completely different. See Chapter 10, "When It Goes Wrong."

-e   Shows information about every process running. Normally **ps** only shows you some of your processes.

-f   Shows the full listing for each process, including the owner's login name.

-l   Shows the long listing for each process, including state of the process and the priority of the process. -l shows the identification number of the owner, but not the owner's login name.

-u *user* Lists only the processes for the named *user*.

pwd

Prints current directory.

pwd

The **pwd** command prints the name of the directory you are currently in. See Chapter 3, "In The Beginning Was the Word: login."

rm

Deletes or removes file or directory.

rm [-if] *file ...*

rm [-irf] *directory ...*

The **rm** command removes files and directories. See Chapter 7, "The Root of the Matter: Files and Directories."

-f   Removes write-protected files without asking.

-i   Interactively asks if you want to delete files; if you give both -i and -f, -i takes effect rather than -f.

-r   Recursively removes directories and their contents. Without this option, **rm** doesn't remove directories, even empty ones.

Example—To interactively remove all files in the current directory:

rm -i *

rmdir

Removes empty directory.

rmdir *directory ...*

The **rmdir** command removes empty directories. See Chapter 7, "The Root of the Matter: Files and Directories."

Example—To remove the directories named temporary and working:

rmdir temporary working

rn

Reads news.

rn [*newsgroups*]

The **rn** command lets you read Usenet news articles, either from all newsgroups you subscribe to, or just from the *newsgroups* you specify. Other newsreaders are available, including **nn**. See Chapter 23, "Internet Interests."

stty

Shows or changes terminal settings.

stty [-a]

stty sane

stty [*settings*]

The **stty** command is used to show and change your terminal settings. See Chapter 10, "When It Goes Wrong."

Example—To see all of your current terminal settings:

stty -a

vi

Edits file.

vi [*file ...*]

vi is a screen editor. See Chapter 16, "Viva vi!" for a summary of **vi** commands.

wc

Displays number of lines, words, and characters in a file.

wc [-clw] *file ...*

The **wc** command counts the number of characters, lines, and words in a file or files. See Chapter 14, "Write Like the Prose."

-c   Counts only the number of characters.

-l   Counts only the number of lines.

-w   Counts only the number of words.

who

Shows who is logged in.

who [am i]

The **who** command shows the users currently logged in; the command **who am i** shows your login name.

Speak Like a Geek: The Complete Archive

absolute path name   A path name that specifies exactly where in the file system a file is. An absolute path name starts with a slash / (at the root directory).

account   Your user relationship with the computer. Having an account just means you're an accredited user, with a user id, privileges, and space on the machine. (Sometimes it's also a monetary account; some schools make students pay for computer usage.)

alias   Another name for a command. If you frequently use one option with a command (such as **ls -F**), you can create an alias for that command. For example, if you make *lf* an alias for **ls -F**, anytime you type **lf**, the system turns it into **ls -F**.

application program   A program you use to accomplish a purpose, such as writing a letter, calculating a spreadsheet, processing words, or killing all the alien space invaders.

argument   An argument is any part of a command line except the command. Just as an adverb modifies the verb of a sentence, an argument can modify the command, or it can represent the thing that the command will act on (like the object of a sentence).

ASCII   One system of encoding letters and characters so a computer can use them. It's not the only way, but it's one of the most common. PCs and most UNIX systems use ASCII.

background process   A command running without direct input from a terminal. By running a command in the background, you can go on to other commands without waiting for the background process to end. When you start an X Windows command, for example, from a terminal window, you usually want it in the background so you can continue to type commands while the X Windows command is running. **Control-C** (the break command) won't stop a background process; you must use the **kill** command.

binary file   A file, such as a program file or a spreadsheet data file, that contains non-printable characters. Many UNIX programs (like **grep**) don't work on binary files; they're meant strictly for text files.

bit-mapped display   A terminal display that can show pictures because the position of every dot on the screen has been calculated. Your television is a bit-mapped display device, and you need a bit-mapped display in order to use a GUI. The screens for almost all personal computers are bit-mapped, but not all terminals are.

buffer   A temporary storage space. For example, each file in **emacs** is stored in a buffer. Likewise, anything you delete in either **emacs** or **vi** goes into a special buffer called the "kill buffer."

bug   An error or mistake in a program. Bugs can be unimportant (a spelling mistake) or serious (the program writes unusable data files). If a bug is really serious, it can cause the program to shut down unexpectedly.

character display   A terminal display that shows only letters. A typewriter is a character display device, and older computer terminals are usually character display devices. Even if X Windows is installed, you cannot use it if you have a character display device.

child process   A process that was started by another process. The term "child" is only relative to the program that created it, which is its parent process. Technically, you can think of every program running on a UNIX system as a child of the command used to start the system.

console   Generally speaking, your console is the keyboard of your terminal. When UNIX people talk about "the" console, however, they mean the keyboard that's attached directly to the computer that's actually running UNIX. Some system administrator tasks have to be done from the console.

cursor   The box or underline that shows where the text you type is inserted. The name is from a Latin word about runners (because it runs ahead of the text), not because you swear at it.

daemon   A program that runs without supervision and that provides services to the users. (The name is from an old religious term meaning "guardian angel.") Daemons are used to automate services on the system. The program that runs requests from **lp** is a daemon.

directory   A file that contains other files and tells you how to find them. A directory "file" contains only the list of file names and numbers where the information about those files can be found. A directory should be named something meaningful: for example, something that relates to the subject of the files it contains.

electronic mail   Messages sent to computer users via computer. To read and send mail messages, you need a mail user program (such as **mailx**). In a mail program, you send mail to a user's address, which is a combination of the user's login name and the computer's name.

environment variable   A piece of information (like your home directory) that is given to all your programs. Many programs check environment variables for some kinds of information. This is how all programs that look in your home directory for startup information know where your home directory is. Using an environment variable instead of a command option enables you to give the same information to all your programs without having to retype it again and again.

file   A bunch of related information stored together. In UNIX, a file can also be a device that can receive or produce a stream of information.

file name completion   The shell's capability to guess what file name you're typing after you've typed the first few letters. Very useful if you use file names like abracadabra and xylophone.

file redirection   Using a file (instead of the screen or the keyboard) for standard input. Output redirection puts a program's output into a file, while input redirection tells a program to take input from a file instead of the keyboard. The symbols for output redirection are > (send output into a file), >> (add output to the end of a file), and 2> (send only error messages into a file). The symbol for input redirection is < (take input from the file).

foreground process   A command that accepts input from the keyboard while running. You run most commands as foreground processes; you can usually stop them with a break signal (**Control-C**).

FSF   The Free Software Foundation was founded by Richard Stallman. Members of the FSF believe that software should be free. However, they don't mean free in the "you don't have to pay me for it" sense, but free in the "I have to give you the source code if you ask for it" sense. They can still charge you for it. (In reality, the FSF only charges for producing the copy, but they don't stop anyone else from charging for it.) And once you have the source code, you can make whatever changes to the program you want—if you're a programmer.

input   The information that goes into a program; literally what you put into it. Unless you indicate otherwise, most UNIX programs expect this to come from the keyboard. (In fact, the keyboard is called standard input, or stdin.) To tell a program that you're finished typing input from the keyboard, press **Control-D**.

Internet   The set of computer networks joined using the TCP/IP protocol. Internet includes a number of government and educational networks (including the National Science Foundation's NSFnet and two of NASA's networks) as well as some commercial and business networks.

job control   The capability to run a job in the background without using any special commands. "In the background" means you can go ahead and give other commands while that job is running. You don't have to wait for a job in the background to finish before you start the next command.

job id number   The number your shell supplies to identify a program running in the background. You can use **%*job-id*** with the **kill** command in the same way you'd use a process id number.

kernel   The part of the operating system that's active in your computer's memory. It's the part that gets files for other programs, checks permissions on files, and starts programs when asked to.

line editor   A line editor is an editor that works on only one line of text at a time. It doesn't show you the line unless you ask it to. (This makes it like editing with your hands in a box so you can't see what you're doing.)

login name   The short name used to identify you and everything you own on the computer. It's like a CB "handle."

man page   A manual section describing one program. It may be more than one page long, but it's still called a man page. If two programs are very closely related, the same man page may describe both of them.

metacharacter   In regular expressions and shell wild cards, a metacharacter is a character that stands for something else. *Meta* means "about" or "of a higher order," so a metacharacter is a character about characters. To turn off the special meaning of a metacharacter, put a \ in front of it. (The \ is a metacharacter that means, "ignore the special meaning of the next character.")

mode   A way of behaving. A program has modes if commands are available only some of the time. Mode-based editors have an *insert* mode (which you use when you type text) and a *command* mode (which you use to give commands, such as to delete or change lines). The same command key can mean something different in each mode.

multitasking   The capability to run more than one program at a time. The computer doesn't actually run more than one program at once; instead, it devotes a bit of time to each job, switching back and forth. (This is kind of like cooking a bunch of dishes to make a meal: you check this one to see how it's going, check the next dish, and so on.)

multiuser   The capability to serve more than one user at a time. Of course, when you do this, you've got to *identify* each user and know what belongs to whom. In UNIX, you have a user id (your login name) and you have a number. You don't need to know your number, just your login name.

news   A collection of messages intended for general readership. An individual Usenet news message is called an "article." See *Usenet news*.

newsgroup   An area of discussion in news. Newsgroups are arranged like file directories, with a dozen or so top-level areas. For instance, **comp** is for computer topics, **rec** for recreational topics, **misc** for miscellaneous topics, and **news** is for topics relating to Usenet news itself. These are subdivided into smaller topics as interest dictates. For example, **rec.arts.books.tolkien** contains articles that discuss the books of J.R.R. Tolkien, and **misc.kids** is for articles and discussions on parenting.

NFS   Network File System. A way of joining file systems on different computers. With NFS, the file system on another computer looks like a directory on your computer. NFS can be slow, but it's widely available. It's even available for DOS, so your PC can get at files on the UNIX machine. (It's rare to find it the other way around, though.) Other similar file systems have names like UFS and RFS.

operating system   A computer program used by other programs to control the computer's hardware.

options   Instructions that change how a command behaves. They're called options because they're, well, optional. UNIX options begin with a dash, like this: -a. Options are sometimes called "flags."

output   The information that comes out of a program. In UNIX programs, this is usually written to the screen, so the screen is called standard output, or stdout.

parent process   The process that starts another process. For instance, your shell is the parent process to every command you run in a UNIX session. A program being run is (appropriately) a child process.

path name   The name of a file or directory. It's like a road map to the file or directory.

pipe   A method for taking the *output* of one command and using it as *input* for another. This works the same as if you saved the output of the first command in a file and then used that file as an argument to the second command—except it's faster. To use a pipe, connect the two commands with a vertical bar symbol (¦). Pipes are meant to work with commands that send their output to the screen.

process   A running program. One of the reasons for giving it a different name is that it's got other stuff attached to it, like who's running it, what the options are, what other files are involved, and what its environment is.

prompt   The character or characters that tell you the computer is ready for another command.

quoting   A way of telling your shell to ignore some special characters in commands, such as spaces.

regular expression   A way to describe a pattern of letters. The simplest pattern is a word, but a regular expression can also include wild card characters (like the ? in the shell, which stands for any single letter). All UNIX programs that search text use regular expressions. If a word or phrase is described by a regular expression, we say it matches the regular expression. And "regular" is just an expression; you'll never find an irregular expression in UNIX.

relative path name   A path name that specifies where a file is in relation to your current directory. An absolute path name never starts with a slash.

root   The word "root" has a lot of meanings in UNIX. root is the login name of the super-user, so the *root password* is the password for the super-user account. The *root console* is the console directly attached to the computer that's actually running UNIX; the super-user must use that console for some tasks. The *root directory* is the directory that holds all the other directories—it's at the root of the file "tree." And last, the root of all evil is the love of money.

screen editor   An editor that shows you a screenful of text at a time, instead of one line at a time. Most word processors and modern editors are screen editors. At one time (the late seventies), there was a fierce debate over which was better, with one side saying that "real" programmers use line editors and the other side saying that "real" programmers like to see what they are editing. Screen editors won. Also called a "display editor."

shell   The program that you use to interact with a computer, including running other programs. The shell program gives you access to the features of the computer system, and is written specially for that operating system. The shell programs for UNIX run programs for you, create pipes, and handle input and output redirection.

shell script   A file containing a set of commands that the shell runs. Like a script, it's a set of instructions. Your shell's startup file is a shell script. A shell script can be as simple as a long command you don't like to retype, or it can be thousands of lines long. Many of a system administrator's special programs are really shell scripts. To run a shell script, either make it executable (give it execute permission) or give the file name as an argument to the shell, like this: **sh *myscript*** or **ksh *myscript*.**

spool directory   A directory used as a storage queue, where files (which are jobs-to-be-done) are stored until they're done. There are spool directories for mail, printing, network news, and certain kinds of file transfers. Spool directories are usually subdirectories in /var/spool or /usr/spool (if you care). The name comes from the fact that in the old days, files to be printed had to be stored on a spool of tape before they could be carried to the printer.

startup file   A file containing commands that are run when a program starts up. Startup files are a way to customize your commands. Because of this, startup files are also called *configuration files*. In UNIX, these commands are in a file that's usually found in your home directory, and their names usually start with a dot and end with "rc" (which stands for "run command"). Startup files for some programs include:

Bourne shell, Korn shell	.profile
C-shell	.chsrc, .login
emacs	.emacs
mailx	.mailrc
News programs	.newsrc
vi, ex	.exrc

super-user   An administrative account for the system administrator, which has the login id root. The super-user account has special privileges: it effectively owns all files and can add, remove, or change any file or directory on the system. The system administrator must be logged in as the super-user to add new programs to the system or to start or shut down the system. On big UNIX systems, more than one person may know the password for the super-user account, which is usually called the root password.

system administrator   The person responsible for maintaining the UNIX system, installing software, fixing problems, and ensuring that the system runs correctly.

terminal   The device used to communicate with the computer. A terminal looks like a PC: there's a screen and a keyboard, and there may even be a mouse. You can use a PC as a terminal if you have a "terminal emulation program" that makes your PC behave as if it were a terminal. With a terminal emulation program, you don't get the full features of your PC because it's trying to behave like a less sophisticated machine.

text file   A file containing only printable characters (that is, text). The opposite of a text file is a *binary file*.

thread   A group of news articles on a particular topic.

Usenet   The "user's network," Usenet is the collection of all computers that share news articles.

Usenet news   A collection of messages intended for general readership. An individual Usenet news message is called an "article."

zombie process   A process that should be dead but isn't. If a parent process doesn't make the proper arrangements before shutting itself down, its children can become zombie processes. In the **ps -ef** listing, zombie processes are identified with a Z status. Some versions of **ps** use the status <defunct> instead of Z.

Index

u

Commands Within Commands

Press	To
	Within **more**
Spacebar	Scroll forward one screen
Enter	Scroll forward one line
q	Quit
/*text*	Search forward for *text*
	Within **vi**
a	Enter text insertion mode, adding text after the cursor
A	Enter text insertion mode, adding text at end of current line
i	Enter text insertion mode, adding text before the cursor
I	Enter text insertion mode, inserting text at beginning of current line
o	Enter text insertion mode, inserting blank line after current line
O	Enter text insertion mode, inserting blank line before current line
Escape	Leave text insertion mode and enter command mode
[*#***]j**	Move cursor down # lines (one without #)
[*#***]k**	Move cursor up # lines (one without #)
[*#***]h**	Move cursor # characters to left
[*#***]l**	Move cursor # characters to right
^ or **0**	Move cursor to beginning of line
$	Move cursor to end of line
[*#***]w**	Move cursor to beginning of #th next word
[*#***]b**	Move cursor back to beginning of #th previous word
[*#***]G**	Move cursor to line # (if you don't supply #, moves to last line in file)
Ctrl-F	Scroll forward one screen
Ctrl-B	Scroll backward one screen
[*#***]dd**	Delete # lines, starting with the current line (one line without #)
[*#***]d***movement*	Delete text from current cursor position to where the *movement* command goes, # times (once without #)
p	Insert last text deleted (for moving text)
P	Insert last text deleted before cursor (for moving text)
/*words*	Search forward in file for *words*
?*words*	Search backward in file for *words*
:s/*old***/***new*	Replace first occurrence of *old* on this line with *new*
:s/*old***/***new***/g**	Replace all occurrences of *old* with *new*
:%s/*old***/***new*	Replace first occurrence of *old* on each line with *new*
:%s/*old***/***new***/g**	Replace all occurrences of *old* with *new*
:w *file*	Save file as *file*
ZZ	Save file and quit
:q!	Quit without saving file
	Within **emacs**
Ctrl-X Ctrl-C	Quit **emacs**
Ctrl-H or **Backspace**	Get help
Ctrl-N	Move cursor down one line
Ctrl-P	Move cursor up one line
Ctrl-A	Move cursor to beginning of line
Ctrl-E	Move cursor to end of line
Escape-<	Move cursor to beginning of file
Escape->	Move cursor to end of file
Ctrl-X Ctrl-S	Save file
Ctrl-X Ctrl-F	Load new file for editing
Ctrl-X Ctrl-B	Show list of buffers
Ctrl-X *filename***Enter**	Switch to buffer *filename*
Ctrl-X K	Kill current buffer
Ctrl-S *text***Enter**	Search forward for text
Ctrl-R *text***Enter**	Search backward for text
Ctrl-X 2	Split current window in two
Ctrl-X 1	Make current window the only one
Ctrl-X 0	In X Windows **emacs**, remove all other frames
Ctrl-X 50	In X Windows **emacs**, remove current frame
Escape-% *old***Enter** *new***Enter**	Start search forward and replace current instance of *old*
Space or **y**	Replace current text
Delete or **n**	Skip current replacement
!	Replace all occurrences of *old* text in file with *new*

The Complete Idiot's Reference Card

About Commands and Files

Understanding Usage Statements

You get usage statements with the -? option. Within those statements, you'll see the following symbols:

[ ]	Something optional
¦	A choice: one or the other, but not both
...	More than one allowed

Structure of a Command

command-name [*-option* ...] [*argument* ...]

File and Path Names

You might see the following special characters at the beginning of a path or file name:

/ at the start indicates an *absolute path name*; otherwise it's in your current directory.
./ stands for the *current directory*.
../ stands for the directory containing the current directory.
~/ stands for your *home directory*.
~*name* stands for the home directory of *user name*.

You might see the following special characters anywhere in a path or file name:

? stands for any one character
[*abc*] stands for any one of the characters in square brackets
* stands for any number of characters

Useful Commands

Use This Command	To
cd [*directory*]	Change to new directory
cd	Go to home directory
cp [-i] *file ... directory*	Copy a file to a directory
-i	Inquire before replacing an existing file
cp [-i] *file copyname*	Copy one file
-i	Inquire before replacing an existing file
man [-s *n*] *command* ...	Get help on a command
-s *section*	Look only in part *n* of online manual
ls [-aFl] *directory* ...	List contents of a directory
-a	Show all files, including hidden ones
-F	Show file types (/ is a directory, * is a program)
-l	Show long file listing
mkdir *directory*	Make a directory
mv *oldname newname*	Move (or rename) one file
mv *file ... directory*	Move a file to a directory
lp *file* ...	Print a file
rm [-ifr] *file* ...	Remove a file
-i	Inquire before removing file
-f	Remove files without inquiring (force)
-r	Remove directories and contents
rmdir *directory* ...	Remove an empty directory
grep [-i] *text* [*file* ...]	Search files for text
-i	Ignore differences between upper- and lowercase letters
pwd	Show current directory

tear here

alpha
books

The UFO Encyclopedia

by **MARGARET SACHS**

A PERIGEE BOOK

to Nicholas Vreeland

Acknowledgments

THE WRITING OF A BOOK of this nature cannot be done without the help of many people. I am deeply grateful to Alex Rebar and Sylvia Hom, who helped me with my research; my photo consultant, Hilde Kron, who was invaluable; Glenn Cowley for his guidance; my editor, Diane Reverand, for her encouragement; Harry Lebelson for reading and commenting on the manuscript; Mark Hurst for his editorial suggestions; and my husband, Bill, for his patience and assistance.

I would also like to extend special thanks to my friend Ernest Jahn, who coauthored my previous book, *Celestial Passengers*.

I also wish to thank J. Richard Allison, Rose Marie Amico, Peter Aubrey-Smith, William Boyes, Al Chop, Trevor James Constable, Leon Davidson, John DeHerrera, Pat Gallagher, Beverly Gray, Gabriel Green, David Haisell, Leslie Hugunin, Philip Klass, Norman Lamb, Alvin Lawson, Bill LeValle, Jim Lorenzen, Giovanni and Piero Mantero, Jim Moseley, Laura Mundo, Francine Newman, Robert Newman, Kevin Olden, M.D., Kathy Parks, Michael Parry, Dennis Pilichis, Art Podell, Jenny Randles, David Rees, Carla Rueckert, Luis Schönherr, Issy Shabtay, Marcia Smith, R. Leo Sprinkle, Maggie Starr, Brad Steiger, Jun-Ichi Takanashi, Colman VonKeviczky, Glen Welker, Lindy Whitehurst, Mr. X and Patricia Zimmerman.

Special acknowledgment is made to the Aerial Phenomena Research Organization, the Association des Amis de Marc Thirouin, the Centro Internazionale Ricerche e Studi sugli UFO, the Comitato Nazionale Independente per lo Studio dei Fenomeni Aerei Anomali, the Interplanetary Space Travel Research Association, the Manchester Aerial Phenomena Investigation Team, the Modern Space Flight Association, *The National Enquirer*, the National Investigations Committee on Aerial Phenomena, the Novosti Press Agency, the Page Research Library, Project SUM, Sun Classic Pictures, the UFO Information Network and the *UFO Space Newsclipping Journal*.

Library of Congress Cataloging in Publication Data

Sachs, Margaret.
  The UFO encyclopedia.
  Bibliography: p.
  1. Unidentified flying objects—Dictionaries.
I. Title.
TL789.S16   001.9'42'03   79-27450
ISBN: 0-399-12365-2
SBN: 399-50454-0 Pbk.

Designed by Bernard Schleifer

PRINTED IN THE UNITED STATES OF AMERICA

Perigee Books
are published by
G.P. Putnam's Sons
200 Madison Avenue
New York, New York 10016

First Perigee Printing, 1980